Fraud and Corruption in Public Services

Fraud and Corruption in Public Services

A Guide to Risk and Prevention

PETER JONES

LONDON AND NEW YORK

First published 2004 by Gower Publishing

2 Park Square, Milton Park, Abingdon, Oxon OX14 4RN
711 Third Avenue, New York, NY 10017, USA

Routledge is an imprint of the Taylor & Francis Group, an informa business

First issued in paperback 2017

British Library Cataloguing in Publication Data
Jones, Peter
Fraud and corruption in public services: a guide to risk and prevention
1. Public utilities – Corrupt practices 2. Civil service – Corrupt practices 3. Fraud 4. Fraud – Prevention 5. Fraud investigation
I. Title
364.1'323

ISBN 978-0-566-08566-6 (hbk)
ISBN 978-1-138-24969-1 (pbk)

Library of Congress Control Number: 2003114401

Typeset in 9 point Stone Serif by IML Typographers, Birkenhead, Merseyside

Contents

List of Figures

List of Tables

Using this Book

This book is primarily intended for practising managers, accountants, auditors, compliance officers and others who need to combat fraud and corruption or at least encourage awareness and action in their peers and subordinates. Those responsible for political leadership in the public services will also be keen at times to encourage such awareness.

The chapters have been selected to cover certain vital areas of activity and key issues. Practical aids are available such as appendices, listings and grids and these are intended to focus attention on vulnerable, high risk and key control points. It is, however, important to appreciate that no two organizations are the same and such practical aids are not intended to be exhaustive.

In each organization the advice and techniques used in this book must be tailored to suit the particular situations and circumstances. While this is often so in practical works on any business or managerial topic it is even more so in dealing with fraud and corruption, as these are far less predictable in origin and nature than most innocent business and management. Public services are highly diverse in their organizational motivations, structures and regulatory requirements and all this means that each body must adapt the guidance here to the changing risks faced. One size most definitely does not fit all.

The special role of audit

Throughout the public services sector there are well established and widespread expectations that auditors will play a key role in combating fraud and corruption. This book re ects such expectations and draws widely upon the role and techniques of public services auditing. This counter-fraud role of public service auditors may at first seem rather intrusive compared to that of auditors in commercial organizations. Companies have a long history of managers, and in smaller organizations owners, being directly expected to counter fraud and corruption without as much help from auditors. But in the public services sector it has long been appreciated that appointed officials and elected politicians, with access to extensive public funds, need to be further reinforced by a directly acting and independent third party, that is, auditors. It is interesting to note that from time to time and in recent years in particular, auditors in the private sector are called upon to undertake a more proactive counter-fraud role not unlike that expected in the public services.

This vital and still developing role for audit in countering fraud can present a problem for anyone not familiar with auditing. Added to this is the need from time to time to adopt counter-fraud approaches based essentially on auditing techniques. For these reasons some attention has been given to explaining the role and approach of auditors in Chapter 3.

CHAPTER 1

Characteristics of Fraud and Corruption

Introduction

This chapter covers a variety of basic knowledge that sets the background for combating fraud and corruption in the public services. It explains what is meant by fraud and corruption, terms that are easily open to misinterpretation. Straightforward descriptions of the basic conditions that give rise to fraud and corruption are given and the special requirements of the public services are emphasized.

The bulk of this chapter deals with legal and professional requirements and the basic regulatory framework that applies to most public bodies. Key aspects of regulatory control are considered in detail. The chapter emphasizes the importance of achieving a regulatory framework relevant to day-to-day operational considerations. Sound, practical operational standards and regulations are vital controls in helping to prevent fraud and corruption becoming established in the workplace. For those charged with investigating fraud, recent regulations have also introduced precise documentary requirements above and beyond those which managers or fraud investigators needed to follow in the past.

The chapter finishes with a detailed case study outlining the effects of a poor regulatory structure and inadequate reporting and regulatory control on one key part of an organization. The general conclusions which are drawn can be widely applied.

Basic conditions surrounding fraud and corruption

We will consider some detailed definitions later in this chapter but for now it is worth noting that fraud, in common with some other criminal acts, is deliberate (as distinct from innocent error), it involves deception and it leads to loss for the victim.

Given the deliberate and damaging nature of fraud and corruption these can, and usually will, occur when two basic conditions exist:

Intent

There must be intent in the mind of the perpetrator. Intent may arise from a great variety of causes and whether these originate from within the person or from the person's environment makes no practical difference in most situations.

Opportunity

There must be opportunity to perpetrate a corrupt or fraudulent act. An opportunity may be created after being planned and contrived at great length, or it may arise from a chance taken in a passing moment.

Intent

Intent is given relatively limited attention throughout this book. This is because intent is more the specialist realm of the criminologist and criminal psychologist than the auditor, accountant or manager. However, behind intentions lie motivations, which can, if recognized in time, indicate the likelihood of fraud and perhaps prevent it occurring.

Table 1.1 Motivations towards fraud and corruption

Personal nancial problems
Particularly indebtedness, family and gambling-related problems. This category is often very difficult to recognize. Circumstances that are completely beyond the tolerance of one person may seem quite a minor problem to another.

A corporate ethos tolerant of corruption
The 'everyone-else-is-doing-it' syndrome. This may only pervade isolated parts of the corporation, at least at first. It is often very difficult to correct if some individuals feel that their own low standards are normal and acceptable. Corrective action and reinforcement of sound corporate ethics must be taken, firmly, from the top down.

Peer pressure
Closely linked to the previous category, but even individuals who recognize what everyone is doing is wrong may be under too much pressure from others to do anything about it.

Disgruntlement and malice
All organizations will have underdogs, rivalries and cooperation problems. These many and varied causes of disaffection can get out of hand and people who feel they have been wronged may try to get even. In this category there are a wide variety of under-rewarded pay and perks motivations, particularly if these have persisted for a long time.

Ego
Beating the system by perpetrating a fraud can represent a challenge particularly, or so it seems, in respect of computer-related fraud, as discussed in Chapter 5.

Ideological
These include various political, interest group and even religious factors, ranging from general 'anti-commercial' motivations to feelings against particular products or trading relationships. Fraud and corruption may not arise directly from such motivations but may be tolerated or even encouraged by those seeking a negative impact upon the organization. Also in this category (and possibly partly under 'Ego') can be placed 'Robin Hood' motivations of fraud to redistribute wealth from rich to poor, usually including the perpetrator.

Motivations can be extremely complex and because of this they are usually easier to recognize with hindsight than before the event.

Various general human weaknesses are not listed in Table 1.1. Greed, for example, is not listed because it is something that is all-pervading and most people will usually be greedy to some extent. The same might be said of being error-prone, lazy or forgetful. Such general human weaknesses will of course exacerbate the specific and identifiable motivations listed in Table 1.1 but are usually common throughout the workforce. Managers and colleagues may be able to spot an excessively greedy or lazy person and this may lead to action to counter or curb such failings. But the exceptional, additional motivations, that relate to particular circumstances and operate over and above general human weaknesses pose a more direct threat of fraud and corruption; when faced with these an employee not otherwise likely to commit fraud may lapse. When particular and additional motivations or potential motivations become recognizable they can provide a useful warning signal, thus they are worth considering in broad outline.

Table 1.1 outlines some of the more commonly mentioned additional motivations. Each one is a genuine cause of concern whether or not it becomes the cause of intent to perpetrate fraud or corruption. Most auditors and senior managers would take notice of these motivations and try, informally at least, to bring them to the attention of other senior managers, or trained counselling staff. Often the manager or auditor will be able to discuss his or her concerns directly with the officers affected. If this is done in time, managers may be able to 'cure' these adverse motivating factors. This is, after all, no more than sound management practice.

These motivations or causes of intent could be subdivided and reclassified to seemingly unlimited extents. Beyond what we have said the matter of intent becomes a complex psychological and moral issue outside the scope of this work.

Opportunity

Opportunity, unlike intent, is very much the concern of this book. In particular many of the techniques outlined and cases discussed seek to enable the auditor and more often the manager to identify the risks and minimize opportunity for fraud and corruption.

Opportunities can arise from almost any conditions. Long-term stability can lead to complacency – 'Joe always uses the same route to the bank   the same computer password   the same firm of contractors   and so on.' Change can also lead to opportunities, often arising from confusion – 'No one told us who was actually responsible for the bank reconciliation of the new accounts   what exemption would apply to religious orders under the new benefit rules   and so on.' Changes in personnel, changes in location, account codes, indeed almost any change of a manual or computerized nature can present opportunities that previously were absent. The regulations, system controls, relationships, attitudes and awareness needed to minimize these opportunities are explained in this book.

Corruption is usually less tangible than fraud. It is a state of mind or ethos that can spread among the individuals that make up an organization. Corruption can lead to fraud which is but one of the effects caused by corruption. From an audit viewpoint corruption is often more complex than fraud.

Evidence

The conditions surrounding fraud can be complex but in most cases recorded evidence of a fraud exists. For the fraud to remain undetected evidence must be hidden directly by concealment, or indirectly by falsifying records and even the appearance of physical artefacts. For example:

- accounts may contain false entries or be left uncompleted;

reconciliations may be 'faked';
records may remain unchecked or contain false entries;
inferior items may be substituted for genuine articles; and
crucial documents may 'go missing'.

And so on.

Evidence, and how it has been concealed and falsified, will form much of the discussion in later case studies. The recurring question that must be addressed is whether managers can make the evidence of actions and the effects they cause available and 'visible'. For the auditor availability ensures an 'audit trail' and for the manager it ensures responsibility and accountability for the work undertaken.

Such a trail of responsibility shown by written authorizations, well-defined duties, allocation of performance targets, computer passwords or other means, usually enhances quality of output and service. Poor quality is often, but not always, indicative of lax control which may in turn provide opportunity for fraud.

The greater complexity surrounding corruption arises because whereas an effective fraudster may conceal evidence, corruption can occur without generating evidence in the first place. This makes detection during routine audit almost impossible.

Recruitment, promotion, redundancy (or remission there from) are oft-cited activities where favouritism and prejudice can play a determining part. Beyond these lie the generally more serious examples involving the awarding of major contracts. Favouritism often goes hand in hand with bribery, also largely unrecorded, though favouritism may arise from family or social connections in which the pecuniary interest is often difficult to ascertain.

The extent of fraud and corruption

The quantifiable extent of fraud is sometimes estimated using surveys that refer to types of fraud (for example, computer fraud) or to geographical areas (for example, the USA, UK, the city of London). Examples include the Audit Commission survey of computer fraud, which is done approximately every three years and the Treasury's annual Fraud Report for Government departments (see the Bibliography). Occasionally fraud crime statistics are published on a national or sector basis. Recent figures put public sector reported fraud at £100 million excluding benefit fraud. Estimates of UK-wide fraud costs are often in the billions. The Serious Fraud Office reported estimates running at £5 billion per annum in the late 1990s and the Home Office estimates run at around double that amount in the early 2000s. Headline-grabbing totals appear in the press from time to time such as 'Auditors battle with £14 million health fraud', or 'Bill for fraud hits £76 million', or 'Banks top of fraud league' and in 2003 a survey by the accountants KPMG indicated that the value of fraud cases actually heard in UK Crown Courts was £717 million. Although public services fraud is thought to be lower in absolute terms than fraud in the private sector, National Audit Office (NAO) estimates in a 2003 report were of benefit frauds at around £2 billion with another £1 billion being paid in error, notwithstanding improvements in tackling the problem. The truth is though that few, if any, of such statistics are reliable. Some figures are very rough estimates extrapolated from reported losses plus associated investigation, costs, others relate to proved cases of convicted fraudsters. Even well respected surveys such as those done by the

Audit Commission are limited both in the extent of response and in the estimates and summary statistics provided. For example, in the 2001 survey the average value of detected IT frauds was £36 000, though it is well known that over the years some IT frauds have run into millions – many go undetected and even some of the detected ones are not reported for fear of serious damage to commercial reputation. Most importantly, whatever the frauds that come to light, uncovered and often unsuspected types of fraud cannot be taken into account.

In contrast to known or estimated fraud, no one has yet made a realistic attempt to quantify the extent of corruption by reference to value or frequency of occurrence. The most that can be assumed is that the known cases of fraud form but part of the total illegal or unjust actions of corrupt individuals. In the public sector one of the most significant aspects of this problem is its close connection to value for money. Public money can be diverted for personal gain or used for corrupt or very suspect purposes, without public awareness and control, often on a gradual, incremental basis, and with few if any grounds for directly prosecuting particular individuals. Sometimes such matters eventually come to light but they often remain hidden. Unlike the private sector there may be no obvious drop in profitability, no angry individuals clamouring to know what has happened to their money, or no proprietors facing bankruptcy. Eventually of course wanton disregard of public interest and prudence may filter through to higher taxation, but by then the issue is part of a much wider political debate and individual cases are obscured. Sometimes individual cases result in a public scandal that sparks off popular cries of fraud with demands (often ignored) for resignations and public enquiries. Suspect activities often involve major contracts, alleged, bribes, 'backhanders'. Such public scandal often goes hand in hand with badly controlled expenditure programmes running into tens if not hundreds of millions. Some such cases that have come to light have been selected for discussion in Appendix 14.

Favouritism is one of the main manifestations of such public corruption, which often goes unrecorded, even at times unnoticed in the public services. This is a just cause of concern, though without the overriding profit motive for a public body, or any acknowledgement of problem-ownership by named individuals, favouritism is difficult to combat. This problem is particularly widespread in some developing countries of the Third World where it lies behind the devastation of whole economies, but even in developed nations it comes to light often enough and is of sufficient magnitude to undermine public confidence.

On balance it is probably not worth paying a great deal of attention to specific surveys or estimates that give precise-sounding figures. The point is that based on past events and knowing what has come to light, fraud and corruption are growing in both the public and private sectors and are bound to have a serious impact on managers and politicians for the foreseeable future.

Corruption and the funding of public bodies

Corruption in a public services body may not be seen as such in the private sector. Who could call a father corrupt for favouring the employment of, or awarding of contracts to, his son or daughter in the context of a family business? Such behaviour is generally an acceptable custom in society. The critical difference is one of ownership.

The owner, or major shareholder with a controlling interest, is acting on his or her own behalf and in his or her own interests. The public servant is acting on behalf of the taxpayers or their elected representatives. Most large public quoted corporations, plcs, are analogous to the public services in this respect; share capital is often diffused among thousands of individuals and other organizations and sometimes ultimate ownership is difficult to disentangle among complex intercompany holdings, though the analogy begins to break down when possible liability is considered, as shareholders are not liable for more than share value, whereas taxpayers may have to foot the whole bill for fraudulent or corrupt public officials. But in any situation, public or private sector, an employee is generally held to act corruptly when putting personal gain before public or corporate interests in his or her professional decision-making capacity.

This commonly-held professional ethic can, it would seem, be remarkably difficult to remember in the heady atmosphere surrounding major financial decisions. Some of the cases illustrated later in this book revolve around this problem.

Funders of commercial enterprises have the option of avoiding or withdrawing their funding from an enterprise they consider to be run corruptly; funders of public bodies, that is, taxpayers, do not have such an option. In these circumstances it is hardly surprising that the law recognizes the particular responsibilities of public servants to be seen to be above suspicion of corruption, as we shall discuss below.

The law

Many people are surprised to find that no effective definition of fraud can be gleaned from English law. Fraud is more of a generic term. It is used to describe any significant and deliberate misrepresentation of financial affairs for the benefit of the perpetrator, or others for whom the perpetrator is acting, possibly without their knowledge. For practical purposes almost any definition of fraud and corruption is likely to be inadequate, or far too long for convenient recall. The act of intentional deception by the perpetrator distinguishes fraud from common error but obtaining proof of intention is usually one of the most difficult aspects of a fraud investigation.

Not only are we faced with the lack of a legal definition of fraud, though corruption is better defined, but not all criminal law that could relate to fraud is recorded in statute. In 1965 the Law Commission was set up and it has attempted to codify much of the common law, particularly that relating to criminal law, and many of the statutes in the fraud section of Appendix 1 arise from this work. Nevertheless this level of codification is complex and means that unless an auditor is to specialize in regulatory audit or 'audit law', legal advice will almost certainly be required at the first signs of potential criminal prosecution.

Corruption causes particular concern in public bodies. The prevention of corruption, or indeed any suspicion of corruption, is generally a matter of great political significance whatever may or may not be proved in a court of law. History is not short of examples of politicians being forced to resign amid allegations of fraud or corruption.

Local government law in particular requires members and officers to declare any interest in dealings with companies and other third parties. This is often a crucial requirement in preventing corruption during public–private partnerships and capital works contracts (see also Chapter 4). In general, if a public servant can be shown to have accepted or to have agreed to accept any significant gift or inducement, he or she is almost certain to be considered guilty of an offence. Such action, in serious cases, can lead to imprisonment as well as a fine and even relatively modest inducements may lead to serious disciplinary action. In fact public services employees may have to assume they will be considered guilty unless they can prove their innocence:

> *Any money, gift or consideration [given to or received by a public servant] shall be deemed to have been paid or received corruptly unless the contrary is proved.*
> See the Prevention of Corruption Act 1916, Section 2 which is reproduced in Appendix 1.

The Prevention of Corruption Acts are, at the time of writing, expected to be replaced by a new Act which is at the draft Bill stage – the draft Corruption Bill.

The law relating to forgery is in some ways even stricter than that relating to fraud. Forgery may be committed even though the 'forged' items have not been used and, perhaps, no intention to use them for financial gain can be proved. Thus the act of reproducing, say, a licence may be an offence in circumstances where it cannot be proved when, or indeed how, its use was intended.

Over the past decade legislation has been enacted to deal specifically with the startling increase in computer-related crime. The Computer Misuse Act 1990 is the most directly relevant of the three such acts listed in Appendix 1 and these will be discussed in more detail in Chapter 5.

Since 2000 we have needed to take account of 'human rights' legislation and this is considered in more detail later in this chapter.

Professional accounting guidelines

Consider the following:

> The Chartered Institute of Public Finance and Accountancy (CIPFA) have at times defined fraud as: 'Those intentional distortions of financial statements or other records which are carried out to conceal the misappropriation of assets or otherwise for gain'. Fraud is always intentional and dishonest and the CIPFA's definition does at least seem to convey this message.
> The following is an essentially external auditors' definition. The Auditing Practices Board (APB), states: 'fraud comprises both the use of deception to obtain an unjust or illegal financial advantage and intentional misrepresentations affecting the financial statements ' – from SAS110 Fraud and Error.
> The Audit Commission's Code of Audit Practice (2000) defines fraud as 'The intentional distortion of financial statements and accounting records and/or the misappropriation of assets involving deception'.

The APB's auditing guidelines are meant to be followed by all qualified members of the Consultative Committe of Accountancy Bodies (CCAB) but the one quoted above may not have been drafted with the public services clearly in mind. The auditor is being asked not merely to consider any illegality but also any injustice, a much wider term, in the above definition. What, after all, is an 'unjust' financial advantage?

The APB's definition seems to imply that 'unjust' and 'illegal' will coincide. Exceptions might occur at the margin where the law is unclear but, unless the amounts are material in relation to a company's accounts, legality and justice will usually be taken as synonymous. But for the public services auditor 'unjust' can have far wider implications of public interest.

Questions of justice open up areas of political debate that are the realm of the elected politician rather than the auditor or the manager. But whatever political decisions are made, detailed regulations and day-to-day judgements still have to be made by public officials. Although it must be expected that no bribes are accepted to bend the rules, a public servant may well have a great deal of discretion to act 'justly', or not. Benefit assessments, property valuations, grants for worthy local causes and other discretionary expenditure all require an element of interpretation and judgement. A wide variety of statistics and financial figures must be presented to political decision-makers, often on behalf of organizations or individuals who have a degree of vested interest in the outcome. Senior management is generally expected to ensure that such figures are not misrepresentations. Detailed and complex regulations must be drafted to apply, sometimes nationally, sometimes locally, in a wide variety of circumstances. Individual cases and claims must be examined in the light of these regulations. Decisions to allow, amend, impose a penalty, prosecute, and so on, must be made. The APB's term 'justice' and the Audit Commission's term 'misrepresentations' are, in such circumstances, subject to political sensitivity rather than being merely a matter of what the law will allow.

At least though, we can see that the definitions quoted above imply that fraud must be:

deliberate;
involve deception, and
lead to loss for the victim.

Internal regulations

Well-framed internal regulations usually play a passive yet vital role in preventing, or at least substantially reducing, fraud and corruption. Badly framed internal regulations can be worse than useless, possibly encouraging a widespread attitude of contempt for honesty and consistency in dealings throughout the organization.

Regulations that guard against fraud and corruption are generally included in laid-down financial procedures, though general management regulations (particularly in respect of recruitment, promotion, discipline and relationships with outside bodies) may also be relevant. Internal regulations come under a wide variety of headings: 'financial regulations' and 'standing orders' are used in many local and health authorities; 'Government Accounting' is a widely used set of accounting regulations applying to the government and civil service (the latest version is available over the Internet). These high level regulations are often supplemented by additional, lower level, departmental or trading unit's own instructions. Whatever they are called, certain key features are generally applicable to regulations designed to guard against fraud and corruption. For convenience these have been classified under the headings of:

content;
responsibility;
unforeseen events;

style and presentation;
regulations required under higher authority;
arbitration and enforcement;
relevance and implementation.

CONTENT

Scope and relevance are vital in ensuring that the contents are useful. All areas of financial and related procedures of a regular ongoing nature must be included. For example:

cash collection procedures
banking arrangements
budgetary controls and financial planning
stocktaking and stores accounting
insurance arrangements
ordering and procurement procedures
payment procedures including sundry creditors
investments and lending controls
borrowing controls
setting and collection of fees and charges
payment of allowances for subsistence, and so on
salaries and wages payments
bonus, commission and overtime payments
estates management accounting
audit arrangements, internal and external
bookkeeping and recording
accounting arrangements – financial and management
security of value stocks
inventory preparation
virement
loans fund operations
appointment of consultants
contract letting arrangements
pensions and superannuation
debt raising, write-off and cancellation
year-ending accounting arrangements
grant accounting and recording
revenue (tax, charge, and so on) variation approvals
financial appraisal procedures
anticompetitive practices.

Such lists will, of course, vary greatly between bodies according to the nature of their work. Most, for example, will have regulations governing banking, bookkeeping, financial accounting and audit. Virement is more appropriate to central and local government, and this is discussed in Chapter 9. Many bodies will not be sufficiently large to warrant a loans fund. Grant accounting regulations may pertain to 'grant-in-aid' monies used to fund a central government function or grants given by local authorities to fund a local charity or other voluntary body. The important point, when framing the regulations, is that they are kept up to date and relevant with all ongoing areas of financial significance covered.

RESPONSIBILITY

Responsibilities must be clearly set out. Phrases such as 'subject to general agreement', or 'in accordance with accepted practice' should be avoided. Responsibilities should be clearly allocated to individual line managers. If this is not possible, responsibilities should relate to definite departmental functions which are easily and unambiguously recognized as the responsibility of a director, departmental head, or, if considered to be politically or otherwise sensitive, to committees of elected members or the Board.

UNFORESEEN EVENTS

Wherever possible, contingency should be made for unforeseen events, especially events that make it impossible for a regulation to be followed without con icting with other higher regulations or acting directly counter to the interests of the organization. Provisions should be made for a timely written explanation, to be reported by named officers, to the appropriate minister, board, elected members or similar level, setting out the reasons for the regulation(s) being waived.

As part of good risk management, contingency planning should involve appropriate risk models and the use of risk-based audit. Chapter 3 examines this in greater detail.

STYLE AND PRESENTATION

The regulations should be clearly numbered, cross-referenced to each other and to policy statements and kept as short as possible. They should, if at all possible, be written in a house style that has become familiar to employees and is commonly used throughout the organization in reports, memoranda and so on. The contents should be summarized at the start and each section should be headed up in a clear and precise manner.

REGULATIONS REQUIRED UNDER HIGHER AUTHORITY

Whenever internal regulations are made under a statutory or other requirement, this should be noted and a suitable reference included. For example, Data Protection regulations made under the Data Protection Act 1998 (see Chapter 5) or 'whistle-blowing' regulations made under the Public Interest Disclosure Act 1998.

ARBITRATION AND ENFORCEMENT

The consequences of non-compliance, whether deliberate or accidental, should be made clear. No one should be left in doubt about disciplinary actions, appeals, dismissals, or the possibility of prosecution. But, beyond a personal level, complex regulations and agreements relating to service requirements should allow for arbitration over internal disputes or with any outside third parties such as contractors. Any agreed authority for arbitration of disputes arising from con icting interpretations of the regulations should be made clear. On an internal basis this might typically be undertaken at Director or CEO level. External disputes with say, contractors or suppliers, are usually best catered for by arbitration clauses naming agreed arbitrators.

RELEVANCE AND IMPLEMENTATION

Regulations, particularly financial regulations, should be kept regularly under review by those responsible for their drafting and/or enforcement. Usually this involves senior financial managers and auditors. Updating should be undertaken so that relevance to operational circumstances and system changes is maintained. All those likely to be affected by changes should be kept fully involved or at least informed in writing, quoting the precise amendments made. Staff receiving new or updated regulations should, as a control, confirm receipt and implementation by say, signing and returning a list of the contents/paragraph numbers.

'Desk' instructions and other specialized regulations

These instructions refer to particular areas or activities of the public body at an operational level, rather than to the body as a whole, and many of the above points apply here too. Desk instructions are commonly overlooked in works on fraud and corruption. At best these are given relatively short shrift in internal reviews of organization-wide instructions. Two likely reasons for this lack of consideration are, first, that such instructions can be of immense diversity even within any one organization and second, that they are sometimes drafted by relatively junior management or supervisory staff. These circumstances may create a general impression that desk instructions do not really matter very much. On the contrary, when it comes to matters of fraud and corruption nothing could be further from the truth.

Senior managers cannot usually be expected to give high priority to reviewing desk instructions during day-to-day operations, when their minds are concentrated on meeting targets, clearing a backlog of work, planning new projects, or on similar pressures. Unfortunately desk instructions tend to get the urgent attention they usually need only 'after the horse has bolted': perhaps after blank cheques that were not locked safely away were stolen and cleared through the organization's account.

Important internal controls (see Chapter 3) are often written into desk instructions, such as requirements for cheques to be countersigned or duties to be performed by separate officers who are specifically mentioned. Sometimes poor, or completely absent, desk instructions can indicate areas of serious system weaknesses.

Auditors should generally ask to see and should review desk instructions during each major audit assignment. If none are available or can't be found easily, this should be noted. The latter stages of an audit visit are often a suitable time to raise the issue of poor desk instructions. The auditor will have gained greater insight into the current system towards the end of the audit and can make more useful suggestions for expanding, contracting, or otherwise improving the desk instructions.

The points relating to internal regulations for the whole organization should also be applied to desk instructions such as operational manuals, workshop rules, and so on. Even though the auditor cannot be expected to be familiar with every page of an organization's desk instructions he or she should review their general relevance to the operational procedures and to any key events, transactions and so on. The managers should ensure that arrangements for updating and review are adequate and that all staff likely to need to refer to desk instructions have copies. This latter point is particularly important where staff are relatively inexperienced and may need to deal with unfamiliar circumstances.

Managing and controlling investigations

Although the main thrust of this book is combating fraud in a preventative sense, experience shows it is impossible to eliminate fraud and corruption and that one of the main deterrents is effective investigation. Sadly, and although prevention is much preferred to cure, an experienced auditor will rarely avoid investigation work altogether. Because of this some attention must be given to the key aspects of the control and regulation of such work. Well performed investigation can encourage a culture of preventing fraud from recurring.

RESPONSIBILITIES FOR INVESTIGATION AND PREVENTION

A persistent debate, sometimes strident, more usually rumbling along, has dogged relationships between auditors and managers. This debate revolves around the precise roles and duties of each party in relation to fraud and corruption, and particularly who should take responsibility for investigation, at least until matters are handed over to the police, and even about who should have prevented the fraud in the first place.

Current legal and professional precedents leave little doubt that management bears the main responsibility for ensuring that reasonable measures are taken to prevent fraud and corruption (see the sections on corporate governance in Chapter 2). It is usually to management that occurrences or suspicions of malpractice are first reported. Yet sometimes the auditor may be approached by parties who know, or suspect, that management is implicated in a malpractice.

In any event it is common practice for managers to request assistance and advice from auditors upon suspicion or discovery of fraud. In some circumstances managers prefer to involve auditors in investigations to make it plain to all concerned that these are being conducted by an independent third party without, initially at least, involving the police and risking possible criminal proceedings.

Many cases of fraud involve a complicated trail of transactions and laundering that line managers and police find difficult to unravel. Most auditors are also accountants and are more likely to be able to deal with such situations.

There is little doubt that, despite their ultimate responsibility, managers' efforts in respect of investigation generally benefit from the involvement of auditors. This is hardly surprising; apart from what has already been said, auditors direct much of their time and effort towards recommending improvements in internal controls that directly or indirectly guard against fraud and corruption.

It is perhaps because of this very concern with internal controls that an element of confusion arises. A manager may feel, perhaps with some justification, that an auditor who failed to point out serious inadequacies in internal controls in the manager's system should bear some of the blame when these inadequacies enable malpractice. Increasingly auditors are being expected to offer some form of formal 'assurance' about the reliability of internal controls. Traditionally, internal auditors employed in the organization have provided reports about internal control on a system by system basis, though nowadays this work is typically planned using some form of risk analysis. Since the rise of corporate governance (see p.35), external auditors have also been under pressure to offer formal assurance on the effectiveness of internal control.

Nevertheless the final responsibility must lie with managers unless the auditor has given specific assurance regarding particular controls or the absence of error or fraud. The analogy is sometimes drawn with the MOT testing of a motor car. If, say, a car is found to have a bald tyre immediately after passing its MOT test, the garage is clearly at fault. If the tyre is found to be bald 1000 miles or 10 weeks later, the garage is probably in the clear. The auditor must be careful to document all the work he or she undertakes and especially all the tests performed. If the auditor checks a sample of items he or she reasonably believes to be representative of the rest, say, a sample of orders, checking that these have been agreed to invoices and payments are correctly authorized, within budget and not *ultra vires*, and draws conclusions consistent with this evidence, he or she cannot readily be held responsible for internal control failure, errors or fraud relating to one particular unchecked order.

Unless a fraud in particular can be shown to relate directly to matters on which the auditor has checked, or expressed specific views in a clear manner, it is unlikely that the manager can rely on an audit to provide an excuse for not preventing a fraud. Of course many other factors such as collusion between an employee and a claimant may have negated any reasonable steps the manager could have taken.

CONTROL AND REGULATION OF INVESTIGATIONS

Towards the end of the last century a rather controversial piece of legislation, the Human Rights Act 1998, was passed by Parliament in Britain, though it did not actually become law until October 2000. The Act was often seen, rightly or not, by many as an attempt to codify and control rights along the continental tradition as opposed to the British and English-speaking world's tendency to accept people's rights unless the law denied them. Lord McCluskie, a Scottish Judge, was quoted in *The Times* (1.10.00) as predicting 'a field day for crackpots, a pain in the neck for judges and legislators and a goldmine for lawyers'.

Article 8 of the Act specifies the right to respect for private and family life. It was widely felt that this article in particular would enable legal action to be taken against investigatory bodies; clearly the police, customs, and the security services but also against less obvious targets such as investigators into welfare benefit and insurance frauds. The Regulation of Investigatory Powers Act 2000 (RIPA) was described by the Government as a measure to balance individual human rights with the need to continue effective investigation. It was in effect designed to give the backing of legal sanction to what would otherwise be challengeable investigatory practices and regulate and formalize in a defensible fashion the way investigations were undertaken. It is only fair to point out that investigations have a long history of formal regulation. Many of the provisions of RIPA were already addressed through the Police and Criminal Evidence Act 1984 and the codes of practice of various investigatory agencies both in the UK and abroad.

One of the main impacts of RIPA on the public services is likely to be upon the work of less well-known investigators including a wide range of internal auditors, benefit inspectors, immigration officials, financial services managers, forensic accountants and others. Statutory Instrument 2417 of 2000 sets out those public officials able to authorize surveillance and intelligence gathering under s27–s30 of RIPA. Detailed consideration of RIPA is beyond the scope of this chapter but anyone who needs a basic overview of the requirements should refer to Appendix 2. Readers are advised that the Home Office web site contains the latest statutory provisions and consultation papers for those interested in updating this information.

SURVEILLANCE

Overt surveillance, for example CCTV cameras in the high street, so long as it is not directed at the privacy of particular individuals or into private property, is likely to fall outside the scope of RIPA. But where covert surveillance is required the Act distinguishes two broad categories, 'directed' and 'intrusive' (see Appendix 2) both of which should be authorized by persons falling within the classifications of SI 2417, which may include for example various directors, heads of internal audit, security chiefs, senior managers, and so on. Interestingly, it seems that even in the UK the RIPA-recommended procedures and suggested documentation are not compulsory for public bodies. But it is very strongly recommended both here and in the Home Office Code of Practice that these are followed, not least to avoid subsequent challenge under the legislation in force in many countries, such as the Human Rights Act.

Both directed and intrusive surveillance need to be justified and fully recorded so that the investigating managers and operatives can be held accountable. This was always good practice but under RIPA detailed standards and even suggested forms are laid down. Appendix 2 sets out some of the key procedures but readers are advised to obtain and follow the Home Office guidance in detail.

GENERAL (NON-SURVEILLANCE) INVESTIGATIONS

Surveillance of fraud suspects is likely but by no means inevitable. Much routine fraud investigation is centred on the workplace and dominated by documentary and computer-based records. Face-to-face interviews are often the investigators' main source of evidence, leading on perhaps to a disciplinary hearing or much less frequently to criminal proceedings. The latter outcome will usually involve handing over the investigation to the police at an earlier stage. Even though the level of recording and control implied by RIPA may not be essential for non-surveillance situations it does point the way to good investigation management.

Often the initial suspicion of fraud and corruption is unfounded. Yet certain working environments are more conducive to fraud. Combating fraud and corruption, as we mentioned on page 3, involves preventing the opportunity to perpetrate fraud. In an environment full of such opportunities fraud may be absent – but not usually for long. Familiarity with fraud cases often reveals common factors which, while not exhaustive by any means, are useful in warning both managers and fraud investigators that they may be in a fraud-prone situation.

Some of the more common corporate level signs are listed and discussed in Appendix 3 along with key stages and procedures in a non-surveillance investigation.

INTERVIEWS

Interviews are an integral part of many fraud investigations. In most situations, particularly when suspicions begin to appear well founded or a fraud has been openly declared, interviews should be conducted by the police, customs officers and others specifically trained to do so. The method of gathering evidence from interviews requires particular care, otherwise efforts may be wasted in terms of any successful prosecution. Even if a prosecution is not envisaged evidence must be gathered objectively, systematically, and in a well-documented manner. In many cases the employing organizations may decide to take disciplinary action and disciplinary tribunals often require the same high standards from any investigation. This is usually consistent with good audit practice and reinforces the points made above regarding the need for audit involvement.

At times events may overtake the auditor's or manager's practical ability to call in the police. A routine audit may reveal the possibility of fraud which requires investigation before, say, funds are due to be transferred abroad or the prime suspect is due to take a holiday. Sometimes a routine interview regarding some apparently innocent errors elicit unexpectedly an admission of wrongdoing. In any event it is unlikely that management or auditors would call in an outside agency before any in-house work had been undertaken to establish the initial facts. These can be sensitive times for all concerned and Appendix 3 under 'What if you cannot involve the police or need to interview urgently?' sets out some of the more important points of which to be aware.

The points set out are, it must be stressed, no substitute whatsoever for adequate training and awareness of important details such as the Police and Criminal Evidence Act 1984, RIPA, and the other legislation and guidance.

Summary

This chapter has outlined important legal and professional interpretations of fraud and corruption. Although precise definition of fraud is difficult its general nature should be apparent and specific instances will be clarified further as this book progresses, particularly in the case studies. The basic environment surrounding fraud and corruption has been outlined in terms of the two prime conditions of intent and opportunity.

A regulatory hierarchy has been outlined. This hierarchy is one of descending authority and precedence, but not necessarily of descending relevance and 'usefulness' in preventing fraud and corruption, as shown in Figure 1.1.

Responsibilities for investigation and interviews are subject to some debate. But in all circumstances a degree of control and accountability is required. Since the beginning of this century investigation in this country has often required compliance with RIPA. Where suspects need to be interviewed under caution and there is the likelihood of arrest the police should normally be invited to take over from managers, auditors, compliance staff and others not usually involved in prosecuting criminal cases. But in any investigation – and most do not involve the police or lead to criminal cases but rather to disciplinary and dismissal proceedings – the standard of management is generally rising. Although different agencies and different standards are in operation there is a definite movement in the UK, USA, Canada, Australia and parts of Europe towards more control and accountability where:

each case is managed and controlled impartially, outside national or local politics,
ad-hoc, unauthorized fraud investigations are disappearing as each needs to be clearly justified,
investigations and decision points need to be recorded and open to scrutiny.

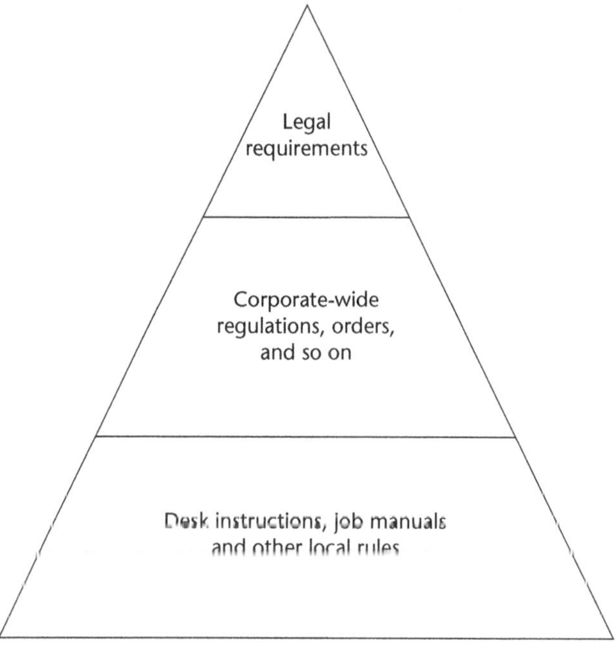

Figure 1.1 Regulatory hierarchy

CASE STUDY 1.1

TOXINS RESEARCH AND STORAGE CENTRE (TRSC)

This, the first case study, illustrates how lax regulations encourage poor internal control in terms of both procedures and organizational structure. It also outlines a situation where poor control procedures are probably worse than none. An auditor and manager deal with the urgent need to improve both standing orders and desk instructions.

BACKGROUND

TRSC is a small outstation of a major government ministry employing 29 scientific and 15 security, administrative and manual staff. They carry out vital military research involving chemical agents. The high-security facilities make TRSC a suitable temporary depository for storing dangerous substances, sometimes on behalf of civil authorities such as police or customs officers.

TRSC forms part of the cyclical audit strategy of the ministry's internal audit. Total expenditure was considered to be relatively low in relation to similar cyclical responsibilities, currently £700 500 per annum and income, from recharging for storage, was generally only around £15 000–£16 000 per annum No significant financial risk factors were known to exist and TRSC was classified for audit purposes as a low materiality, low risk establishment, to be visited approximately every three years.

CASE STUDY 1.1 *continued*

SUMMARY OF EVENTS

The audit proceeded smoothly until a serious fraud was uncovered. Income, it appeared, should have far exceeded that recorded in the books. The main sequence of events was as follows.

During the audit several comments were made to the auditor to the effect that extra storage space was urgently required. The administration manager, who doubled as finance officer for the site, stressed that they were having to turn away shipments from civil authorities worth approximately £500 per month in storage charges. A senior scientific officer hinted that someone, that is, the auditor, should undertake a value for money (VFM) investigation into the financial returns that could be gained from 'investing' in an adjacent site of waste land owned by a local farmer.

The auditor was puzzled. He had at no time budgeted for VFM work (and in any case he had heard that the local farmer was the father of the senior scientific officer whose judgements in the matter might not be completely unbiased). More importantly his experience of similar sites indicated that, for the number of deliveries, income was low. Also, he was not aware of any similar problem at two other research stations he had visited recently, both with storage facilities of about the same capacity.

A relatively brief analytical review of income confirmed his worst fears. Containers were sometimes hired from outside companies, sometimes they were those specially constructed by the ministry. The capacity of the yard was 4500 m^2. Containers were not stacked on top of each other due to the hazardous nature of some contents.

The manager's personal impression was that the yard rarely had more than 200 m^2 of space unused. A brief review of the past month's records of deliveries and containers in stock confirmed this. The auditor, to err on the prudent side, allowed in his estimate for 500 m^2 of unused capacity.

Storage charges had been set at £1.00 per m^2 per week for the past year.

It was immediately clear that if only, say, 4000 m^2 of space capacity was used up, for the entire year income would amount to $4000 \times £1.00 \times 52 = £208\,000$. This was so far in excess of actual income that even allowing for slumps in demand, suspicion of serious misstatements, if not false accounting and fraud, was warranted. Further investigation led eventually to the dismissal of the manager in charge of stores and his conviction, together with the employees of outside hauliers, on criminal charges involving theft, forgery and false accounting.

The basic weaknesses were:

1. Lack of any reasonable separation of duties due to concentration of responsibilities in the hands of the single stores manager; and
2. A complete absence of any checking by more senior or independent officers.

The stores manager's position in the organization's hierarchy is shown in Figure 1.2.

Nominally the stores manager, although relatively low down in the hierarchy, reported directly to the very much more senior administration and finance manager. In practice this link was difficult to maintain as the administration and finance manager had officers far more senior than the stores manager demanding his attention. Also, in practice, the finance and administration and finance side of the organization placed few demands upon stores; the scientific side were the effective stores users. This meant that an 'unofficial' reporting link had arisen from the stores manager to one of the higher scientific officers (HSO) who acted on behalf of the scientific side to avoid the cumbersome

CASE STUDY 1.1 *continued*

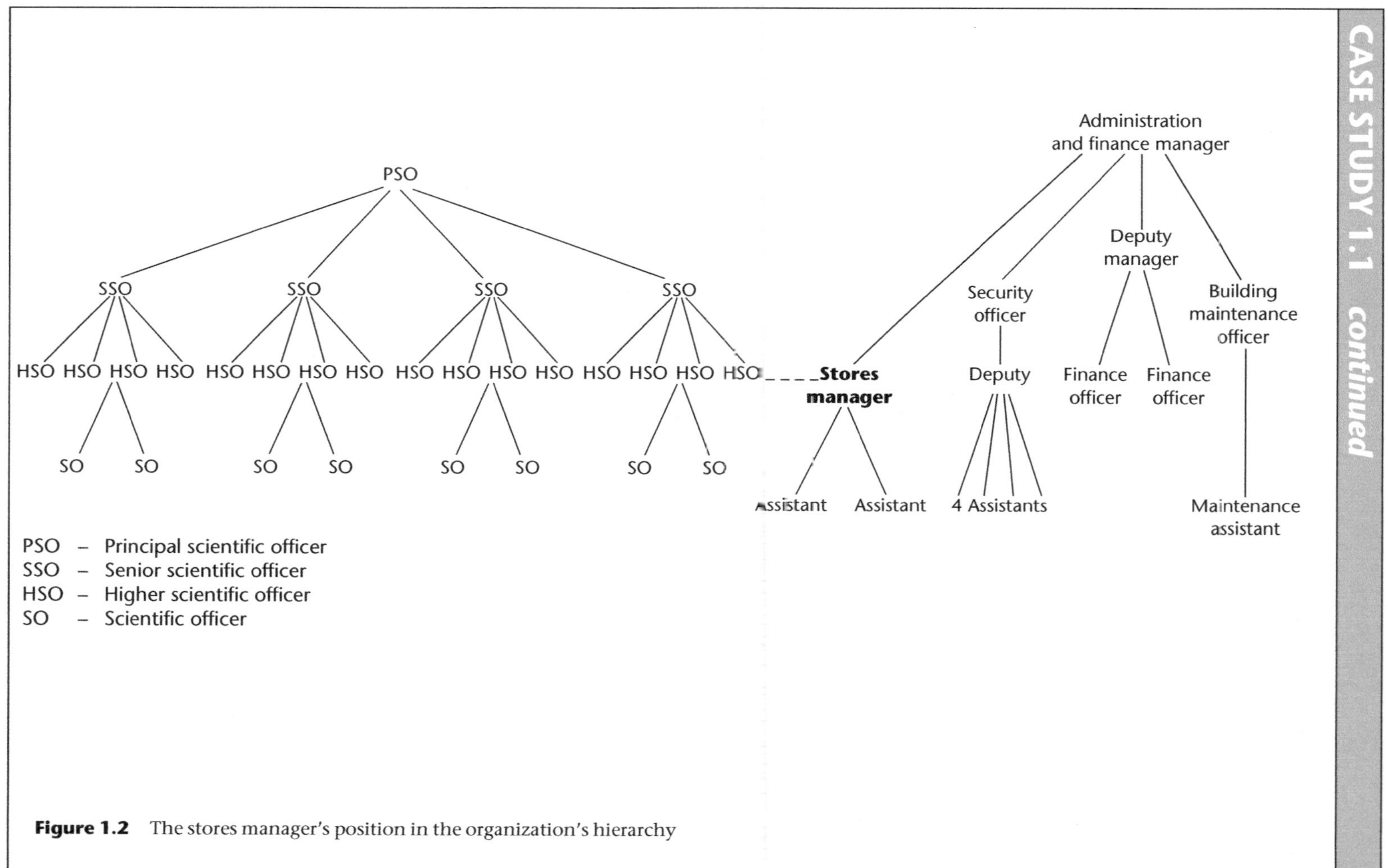

PSO – Principal scientific officer
SSO – Senior scientific officer
HSO – Higher scientific officer
SO – Scientific officer

Figure 1.2 The stores manager's position in the organization's hierarchy

CASE STUDY 1.1 *continued*

procedure of making requests up one side of the hierarchy via the principal scientific officer and then down the other side via the administration and finance manager. These arrangements meant that the organization structure enabled the stores manager to operate virtually unsupervised as a free agent within the organization. The stores manager made sure that occasional requests from scientific staff were routed along with administration requests, well documented and properly authorized by the administration and finance manager. This gave the superficial impression of sound control to any outsider or anyone who had to stand-in for him while he took leave.

All deliveries of containers (and any other consumables such as laboratory or office equipment) were authorized and controlled by the stores manager, usually on the basis of verbal requests from the HSO. Returns of containers and any other movements in and out of the yard were also controlled by the stores manager.

No trading accounts were prepared for TRSC and so the value of stock was of little significance from a financial accounting viewpoint. Stock checks were rarely carried out and those that were undertaken were the sole responsibility of the stores manager rather than an independent officer. A previous auditor had mentioned the poor quality of the annual stock check record and stores records generally. However, management was not inclined to treat the matter seriously as these records had, it was thought, little financial or operational significance in terms of performance. The deputy administration and finance officer had said at the time of the visit, 'I don't think anyone will be inclined to steal the stuff we have in stock – I'm more worried about the possibility of a terrorist bomb attack'.

The stores manager had realized several years ago that the yard was rarely used beyond 50 per cent of its capacity. He also knew that storage of dangerous chemicals, particularly from industrial waste products, was an expensive business. Initially he had offered his 'services' to small hard-pressed firms with expensive waste to store or dispose of at TRSC. TRSC had special high-security disposal arrangements, the stores manager had access to the necessary documentation and could arrange for authorization for disposal either by himself or by the unsuspecting HSO with whom he liaised. The presence of extra containers caused no suspicion, in particular because before long they appeared to come from the same firms on a regular basis. In fact the stores manager usually arranged for the fraudulent deliveries to be let in through the gate by personally notifying the security officer on duty.

CORRECTIVE REGULATORY ACTION

The administration and finance manager and the auditor reviewed the internal regulations of TRSC together with current operational practices and agreed on the changes given in Figure 1.3 (pp. 20–21).

The manager and auditor also agreed that in future the day-to-day line of reporting should be from the stores manager to a senior scientific officer (SSO). Although all stores-related financial procedures and records would still be the ultimate responsibility of the administration and finance manager, operational matters such as day-to-day deliveries, issues and movements were determined by the needs of the scientists. Also such matters as stores opening and closing times and the physical storage arrangements were determined largely by scientific officers' needs. Thus, finance officers would need to be satisfied that the checking, costing and recording of items were being undertaken to their requirements while the actual daily stores operation would meet the requirements of the scientific officers.

CASE STUDY 1.1 *continued*

Revised regulation	**Original regulation**
Regulation 4.2 Deliveries of goods, equipment, parcels (non-Post Of ce) etc.	*Regulation 4.2 Deliveries of goods, equipment, parcels, (non-Post Of ce) etc.*
4.2.1	4.2.1
All deliveries must be agreed to pre-arranged notification by one of the following officers prior to entry on site. PSO – A. B. JOHNSON SSO – C. D. SMITH SSO – E. F. BROWN SSO – G. H. BLACK HEO – I. J. JONES Administration and finance manager: K. L. Jones Deputy manager: M. N. Smith	All deliveries must be agreed with an appropriate officer prior to entry on site.
4.2.2	
In the case of any query A. B. Johnson or K. L. Jones must agree all inbound deliveries.	
Financial Regulation 1.6. Stocktaking records	Internal regulations did not provide for stocktaking records.
1.6.1 The stores manager shall be responsible for the care, custody and recording of all stores items held in the main store room or the adjacent yard. 1.6.2. All stock records shall be in a form approved by the administration and finance manager – K. L. Jones. 1.6.3 All stock movements (goods received, issues and returns) shall be initialled by the stores manager or the assistant on duty in the space provided on the relevant form. 1.6.4 Issues will only be made on receipt of an official requisition authorized by an officer at HSO level or above. 1.6.5 All write-offs of obsolescent or damaged stocks must be approved in writing by the administration and finance manager.	On searching the existing regulations the manager noticed that the only references to stores records was in Regulation 1.4.3, under 'year end accounting' which stated that 'the officer in charge of stores shall tabulate all stores of value as at 31 March of each year.'

Figure 1.3 Revised and original regulations of TRSC

CASE STUDY 1.1 *concluded*

Financial Regulation 1.7. *Stock checking procedures.* 1.7.1 An annual check of all stock shall take place during a convenient weekend as close as possible to the financial year end. This work is to be undertaken by officers delegated by the PSO and the administration and finance manager. During this stock check the stores shall be closed but the stores manager will be on hand to answer any queries. 1.7.2 During the annual stock check the stores manager and his assistants shall not undertake any official duties other than to answer queries as allowed under 1.7.1. 1.7.3 The on-going independent checking of stock shall be arranged in addition to measures at 1.7.1 at the discretion of the PSO. 1.7.4 All stock checking procedures shall be recorded and evidenced by the initials of the officers taking part on records approved by the administration and finance manager.	*Financial Regulation 1.7.* *Stock checking procedures.* 1.7.1 An annual stock check will be undertaken as at 31 March each year. The stores manager may, if he considers it necessary, close down normal stores operations during the period of the stock check.

Figure 1.3 Revised and original regulations of TRSC – *concluded*

Separation of duties between requisitioning and ordering movements (scientists); custody (stores officers); and checking/recording (finance officers in conjunction with scientists) would be a significant improvement. These measures, including supervision by the SSO, should ensure no repetition of unauthorized 'independent services' being provided. The improved stock checking and recording requirements should also ensure that risk of any pilfering (though thought unlikely) is reduced to an absolute minimum.

In all probability internal regulations of such poor quality as those of TRSC would need substantial revision. At first sight officers will often question the apparent increase in complexity arising from such circumstances, but it is often far less than first impressions indicate. As a general rule revised regulations should not impose extra duties on officers unless, as in the case of TRSC stock checks, these have been agreed as being required to meet management (rather than audit) requirements.

Concluding points

Although no manager, security officer, compliance specialist or auditor or anyone else can be continuously aware of what good or evil motivations may be in people's minds, or how these may arise from their environment, he or she should not assume that good intentions will *always* exist. Well-drafted and implemented internal regulations, like other internal control features discussed later in this book, should minimize temptations and allow both managers and those they manage to be reasonably assured of an acceptable environment and honest working practices.

A regulatory framework should, ideally, be detailed, exible, show as clearly as possible where responsibilities lie and at the same time be unobtrusive. In this way people will adhere to acceptable regulations almost by second nature, rather than by effort.

CHAPTER

2 The Public Sector

Introduction

This short chapter has been written to portray the public services in a wider context than will be possible during the detailed financial and administrative arrangements considered later.

No apologies are made for questioning the very existence of a public services sector, or for digressing from the practical theme of this book into wider historical and public finance issues. We live in an age when the size and extent of public services has come under increasing scrutiny from politicians and voters whose queries many readers will, as public servants, be duty bound to consider.

In this chapter broad historical developments are brie y outlined and basic questions concerning the rationale of the public services are considered, followed by insights from economists and others into the nature of public services finance. This useful, if basic, background is intended for managers, accountants, auditors and others who need to understand the special nature of public services bodies compared to most other organizations, which in turn affects the nature of public services fraud and corruption.

The public service sector – its special nature

Civilized societies have always displayed public services. By public services we usually mean all communally provided goods and services that are paid for by taxation or other revenues raised by law. In a democracy 'raised by law' means revenues raised by common consent, or at least acquiescence, but in any society this revenue-raising function of government is, if necessary, backed up by force or threat of force. An RAF aircraft and a National Health Service (NHS) funded hospital, for example, are part of the public services. In contrast a private airline or an unsubsidized private health clinic are not part of the public services, neither is a non-profit-making voluntary charity. Although there will always be small areas of overlap such as NHS private beds, three broad distinctions can be drawn on the basis of 'enforceability' of funding. First there is a legally enforced public services sector, second a market-driven private sector and third, voluntary clubs, charities, and so on.

In the previous chapter we noted that the law regarding corruption and the funding of public bodies makes the requirements for public servants stricter than the general requirements of the Theft Acts. The element of force, or threat of force, that lies behind taxation and the fact that public servants are always dealing with other people's money gives additional weight to the view that public servants have extra requirements to be seen to be honest and fair. Public servants may even at times be assumed guilty unless they can prove their innocence. The arguments in favour of this state of affairs run something like the following.

A 'master' may choose freely to trust his or her 'servant' in the private sector world of normal trade and business, whether these servants are the employees of a small private company or the directors acting on behalf of the shareholders of a large plc. But that choice is not available to the taxpayers cum electors and public servants cannot simply assume they will be trusted with the funds in their control. They must always be accountable. If, for whatever reason, they cannot account for any losses then the public have a right to assume the worst. In local government this might lead to councillors or officers being surcharged. These arguments go some way to help explain the extra red tape sometimes associated with governments.

An historical view

Historians would be hard pressed to define accurately the first examples of public services; their origins lie in the origins of civilization itself. Ancient public works are well researched by archaeologists – there are even examples of public audits during the building of the pyramids. Public works were often defence or crop related, such as fortifications and irrigation schemes, and at the same time they usually owed much to religious organization. Grain stores needed supervision and, no doubt, some method of controlling issues and calling in new stocks. The defensive walls and architectural achievements from the ancient and famous walls of Jericho to the many excellent Roman roads required public organization, foresight, technical skills and, no doubt, enforced taxation.

The many writings on early civilization and particularly the growth of cities, such as Lewis Mumford's famous work *The City in History*, generally point out the importance of early societies' ability to produce sufficient surpluses. The surpluses of food and wealth were used to support priests, soldiers, craftsmen and others. These surpluses made early societies attractive targets, hence the overriding importance of military works.

The unsung forerunners of today's civil administrators, engineers and accountants have, over thousands of years, supported public services that made possible the famous achievements of generals, monarchs and empires. Throughout their long history public officials have, with varying degrees of success, been held to account for their actions by their masters, whoever these were at the time.

Despite such a long historical tradition, it is possible for us to ignore most of the development of public bodies until relatively recent times and still attempt to understand the emergence of the modern public services in Great Britain and other similar developed western countries. We can do this largely because the agricultural and industrial revolutions and the associated growth of western-style democracy has, over the past two centuries or so, completely changed the nature of the public services sector. Public administrations created to serve monarchic and autocratic societies, based upon overtly military and religious power, have generally been replaced by, or evolved into, bodies created to implement the policies of political parties. A sceptic might add that some of the adaptations have not been wholly successful. But change on such a gigantic scale is seldom without its failures.

The Industrial Revolution first evolved in Britain, and the main developments took place over the period from the eighteenth century onward. Without going into great detail, three broad trends are worth noting from the viewpoint of the development of public services:

1 an increasing regulatory role of the state;
2 an increasing level of direct provision, especially welfare; and
3 the effects of large-scale wars.

The earliest trend was the increase in administrative and judicial apparatus required to cope with the effects of industry and the related social changes. This trend may be seen as an increase in the regulatory and to a lesser extent the enabling role of the state, both of which are described in more detail later in this chapter. For now we may note that poverty was a major factor inspiring this regulatory expansion, for example the Poor Law Acts, from 1536 right through to the Poor Law Amendment Act of 1834. These acts attempted to deal with the problems accompanying the great social upheavals such as overcrowding and famine caused by, or coinciding with, the Agricultural and later the Industrial Revolution. The Poor Law Acts were followed by the Old Age Pension Act 1908 and the National Insurance Act 1911. Public sector regulatory expansion set the scene and encouraged the expansion of the Welfare State, indicative of the second broad trend. The Welfare State has often usurped the role formerly given to religious and private charities. Charities were totally incapable of dealing with the effects of population growth, urbanization and the disappearance of vast tracts of common land. In many ways local boards for health, education, sweated trades and so on and later local authorities filled the demand for social regulation and relief of poverty that the church and the aristocracy could not manage to meet. Welfare in its broadest sense of, say, basic health and education needs, became seen as a right rather than as a reward for service or loyalty. The distinction so often mentioned in the earliest years of the Industrial Revolution between the deserving and undeserving poor became increasingly blurred.

The original regulatory and enabling role became increasingly one of direct provision and state intervention. The rise of the Labour Party and British socialism generally did much to encourage the expansion of the Welfare State with the public services seen as a direct provider of welfare goods and services.

This directly providing role may be reducing, collapsing some would say, under the last decades of Conservative and New Labour policies including privatization and the greater role for private sector involvement in former state monopoly services. Still a substantial core of public sector goods and services such as social housing and care of the very disadvantaged in society seem bound to remain as such. This is discussed later in the chapter when we consider brie y the views of some public services economists.

The third basic trend is often described as 'war prompted' expenditure. Whatever the magnitude of expanding regulatory and welfare-related expenditure, large-scale wars appear to have boosted this trend. After each boost the public expenditure level, though falling back a little, has remained higher than before. This trend is also considered further when we discuss the views of economists.

Before we tackle an economic view and proceed to the practical issues that are the main purpose of this book, further questions concerning the broad nature and development of the modern public services must be considered – questions which address some basic moral and political issues from which can be gained a wider appreciation of the practical causes of public services fraud and corruption.

Some basic questions

JUSTIFICATION

Perhaps the most important question is this: is a public services sector inevitable? This very basic question is of fundamental importance. Although, as we have seen, history seems to support a positive answer, the question should not, on account of this, be sidestepped. In fact an honest official may be concerned with this question not simply to understand the nature of the public services but to justify his or her employment in its cause.

If it were possible to have as economically productive and varied a society with no public services sector then taxpayers who would, if given the choice, choose not to use the goods or services provided by the public services sector could argue that they were being institutionally robbed. If, however, a public services sector is inevitable then such a choice is meaningless for all practical purposes. Those who would choose not to consume any public goods and services might argue that the world was unfair to them, but they could not justly point the finger of blame at the public services sector or its servants. The public services, they would be told, exist because the 'world' is the way it is and has been, historically speaking, since the earliest civilizations. To avoid public services one would first have to change the world, that is, human nature.

If public services are inevitable then public servants can be, to varying degrees, merely honest or dishonest; competent or incompetent. The question best asked by the usually hard-pressed taxpayer is not 'Am I being robbed?' (that is, forced to pay for nothing or at best for something I could realistically avoid given the choice) but rather, 'Is what is provided, provided lawfully and justly and is it good value for money?' The answer to this question depends, ultimately, on subjective values such as moral attitudes, conventions of justice and political values. Despite the subjectivity of this answer it is generally possible to make basic assumptions that are acceptable to most people in most situations. From these assumptions it is possible to undertake quite precise checks and measurements. If this was not the case any attempt to combat fraud and corruption would be doomed to failure from the start.

If a public services sector is inevitable, what is the basic role of the public services? For most practical purposes public services provision tends to take place due to three, slightly overlapping, roles. These roles have been mentioned brie y when we considered the three basic historical trends earlier in the chapter. They are the following.

A regulatory role

This represents the very minimal function of the public services: regulations are legion in any modern society, from regulation of the airwaves at a national level to regulation of local rights of way. Regulations have a varied role in public safety and control and in public expression at least they purport to have an enabling role as we discuss below. But at the same time regulations define the basic identity of a state whether this includes a formal constitution or not: subjects swear allegiance to the ruler, obey the law of the land, use such and such legal tender, drive on the right hand side, and so on. These while of course providing for greater control come eventually, or are aimed, to give a sense of common community, whether they have arisen out of arbitrary dictate or popular expression. New rulers, revolutions and new states spend much effort on reforming or composing regulations not just out of specific policy needs but often to encourage wider acceptance of the new authority. New management can often be seen to be a microcosm of the new state in this respect – change designed to bring a sense of identity and acceptance of the new order.

An enabling role

The ultimate purpose of most regulations can be seen to be an enabling one – even if this is simply to confer a sense of legitimacy. Parking restrictions, unpopular though they nearly always are, enable traffic to ow and road safety to be maintained. But often the enabling role demands a more active role by the public services than simply setting regulations and by-laws – compulsory purchase of land for roads for example, or, more fundamentally, the maintenance of law and order to enable most ordinary life to function unhindered.

Direct provision of goods and services

The enabling role merges, often imperceptibly, into the direct provision of goods and services. Some public services underpin the very concept of the state and have historically been associated with it: defence and law enforcement are traditional examples. Others have had at most an intermittent history, until the vast increase in the welfare state considered earlier, low cost social housing, health and education, for example. Much direct provision is not provision of pure public goods and services, a concept discussed below, rather it is a changing portfolio of services driven by varying political policies. Privatization, compulsory competitive tendering, the Private Finance Initiative, various public/private sector partnership arrangements and the general rise in private sector involvement in public services have, in recent years, eaten into the directly providing role of the public services.

Some services, it must be admitted, are difficult to categorize. Street lighting, for example, is a directly provided public good but few people 'consume' street lighting for its own sake, rather it enables them to walk safely about their towns and cities for work or pleasure.

Despite the involvement of private finance and some grey areas, the progression from regulatory to direct provision follows a general pattern of increasing administrative and technical complexity in the public bodies set up to undertake the tasks involved. From laying down, say, ef uent emission standards to constructing a network of top secret radar defence stations the involvement of the public services becomes increasingly direct, controlling, complex and generally costly.

PUBLIC GOODS

We mentioned above the term 'pure public goods'. Are some goods and services inherently better in some way when provided by the communal, tax funded, actions of public services? This would seem to be implied if a public services sector is indeed inevitable. Economists often refer to 'public goods' meaning goods (and services) that the free market fails to provide, at least to a standard considered socially acceptable. The free market may provide defence in the form of mercenaries but most modern societies do not rely on mercenaries for defence.

How, then, can we define a 'public good'? Usually it is one that most people say they want but for which no one individual can be readily persuaded to pay. The street lighting and armed forces mentioned above are examples. The market 'fails' as the goods and services cannot be divided up into privately consumable parts and the state or local community has to raise taxes and provide the good or service directly as a monopoly, or subsidize/sanction its provision through a chosen private contractor. Although the giant state producer monopolies, the nationalized industries and large public corporations of the last century have largely been privatized in the UK, a trend which has spread to many other countries, these were not public goods in this sense but simply examples of public control of 'naturally occurring' private enterprises, taken over in pursuit of a particular political and economic policy such as the aim of controlling the commanding heights of the economy. Many public goods are still provided in the form of a national or local monopoly or near monopoly, funded or heavily subsidized via taxation. This is often still the case even if the service is delivered by private contractors who have bid for a periodic or geographical franchise. Some examples together with suggested distinguishing characteristics are outlined in Figure 2.1.

The last characteristics of Figure 2.1 (columns 3 and 4) are particularly important for this book. For example, the many government inspectors of health, schools, safety, pollution, and so on, must be paid by an independent and largely incorruptible body (even if its employees are not all incorruptible). Consider, say, a private health inspectorate that found one of its major 'clients' provided food from disease infected kitchens. Could it afford to lose its client (and its income) by closing the client down, or causing it to go into bankruptcy by disseminating adverse publicity? Even if an inspectorate were to act in secret, what would happen if the client did not do as ordered? A serious con ict of interest clearly exists. The judiciary is a similar case in point; if judges, like barristers, could be 'employed' by the wealthy how could their verdict be seen to be impartial?

Not only does some level of public services activity appear inevitable but some goods and services appear more suited to public provision than others. Public bodies have proved capable of adapting to accommodate the drastic upheavals in work practices, politics, population distributions, trade and technology that accompany a shift from pre-industrial to developed society. Often, as we shall discuss, there has been more than a mere reactive accommodation by the public services sector.

THE GROWTH OF PUBLIC EXPENDITURE

One very important question still remains: why have the public services of the western developed nations expanded so dramatically since around the middle of the twentieth century?

Mostly, when economists talk about the public services they talk in terms of expenditure figures. They encounter many difficulties in defining and measuring public expenditure. Transfers between central and local government or subsidies and grants to other bodies should not be double counted. The expenditure of various departmental trading funds can be difficult to class, and complex questions are raised by trading at arm's length by various semi-autonomous bodies.

Although these problems are interesting they are incidental to the main issues. Variation in methods of measurement may be politically controversial but rarely operates on an historical scale. The causes of growth of expenditure since around 1900 appear to lie more with the changes taking place in the economy and in the size, characteristics and expectations of the population.

Public expenditure is often measured as a proportion of gross national product (GNP). GNP is the national output including the costs of capital consumption or replacement and the value of overseas output. Statistics of this magnitude are invariably subject to inaccuracies, but virtually all published sources show a marked increase in public expenditure around the late 1940s and into the 1950s to around 40 per cent of GNP and to nearer 50 per cent for much of the late 1970s, falling back to around 40 per cent by the late 1980s. This compares to generally less than 30 per cent in the interwar years and less than 20 per cent throughout the 1800s and early 1900s. In fact public expenditure is historically estimated at around 8 per cent to 12 per cent of GNP from 1890 to 1910.

Over the past century or more the growth in social services is particularly noticeable, as is that of environmental/economic infrastructure. The dominance of central government in terms of expenditure has been significantly challenged by the rise of local government.

Characteristic / Public good	1 Once the goods have been provided the exclusion of individual consumers is impossible or not worth the cost	2 Commonly accepted philanthropic values exist	3 Risk of corruption is very high under free market provision	4 General need to control monopoly powers
Defence	✓		✓	✓
Roads (excluding tolls)	✓	✓		
Streetlights	✓			
Means-tested benefit		✓	✓	
Police force	✓		✓	✓
Fire service	✓	✓		
Health, etc. inspectors	✓		✓	
Road traffic safety campaign	✓	✓		
Judges			✓	✓
Police			✓	

Figure 2.1 Examples of public goods and their characteristic rationale

Central government was the larger during the nineteenth century but the two were virtually neck and neck by 1910; by the early 1980s central government once again held the main share, around 70 per cent, including some areas that had formerly been the responsibility of local government.

A nineteenth-century German economist, Wagner, propounded what has been called a 'law of increasing state activity' – that government expenditure must increase at a *faster* rate than economic output while countries are undergoing an industrial revolution. This law was based upon empirical observations of the countries of western Europe during the Industrial Revolution. Wagner's observations pointed to the increasing complexity of economic and social activity such as the increasing division of labour and social friction caused by the stark contrasts of industrial life. Society needed more policing and a more complex legal framework to maintain order (the regulatory role). Large amounts of capital investment in infrastructure, health care and education were demanded by employers and workers (the enabling and providing roles). The free market could not rise to the occasion and meet the new demands for what were largely public goods and so the nature and scale of the modern public services emerged.

Some economists, particularly W.W. Rostow, outline a basic model of development stages which help explain the, historically speaking, relative suddenness of economic growth and thereby offer an insight into the expansion of the public services. Rostow outlined how a traditional society tends to modernize with increasing trade and industrialization until it reaches a critical mass which enables it to take off into sustained growth and eventually reach a stage of economic maturity. These economists' insights into the rise of the Industrial Revolution and post-Industrial Revolution society (in Europe and North America at least) fit rather neatly into historical events discussed earlier.

Other economists, notably A.T. Peacock and I. Wiseman in Britain, offered further insights also based largely on empirical observation. The in uence of wars in increasing public expenditure and apparently then allowing it to remain at only slightly reduced levels in the following peacetime was noted. The Boer War and, to more noticeable extents, the First and Second World Wars show this effect quite starkly.

In peacetime large increases in taxation, certainly if greater than increases in wealth, are unlikely to be acceptable to voters. But in wartime the increased tax burden is accepted for reasons of national survival. After hostilities are over, the new obligations of the state tend to persist and any reduction in taxation can be questioned by supporters of various programmes. Wars, it is also argued, tend to focus the government's and voter's attention on social needs that were not so seriously considered during peacetime. Evacuation of children from the cities during the Second World War is said to have highlighted cases of malnutrition and hitherto largely hidden poverty. Wars are often accompanied by expectations of a 'land fit for heroes' to be built afterwards.

Welfare theorists such as Pigou and Dalton have pointed out that the natural or logical outcome of free choice is for voters to demand a level of public expenditure such that the net benefit from the last or 'marginal' pound of taxation would equal the marginal cost to the taxpayers. Ideally, such theorists maintain, the marginal utility of each type of government expenditure should be the same. Governments should divide their spending such that the net utility of an extra pound spent on, say, roads was the same as that spent on, say, hospitals.

J.M. Keynes and other economists expounded ideas which, grossly simplified, were taken by post-war politicians to justify large-scale attempts at managing the national economy. Terms such as 'demand management' and 'pump priming' became fashionable. Government was seen as a controller of the economic machine. Demand, the economists' common soup of man's desires, could, it was said, be stimulated by public spending to offset the effect of an economic slump. Political will allowing, demand could also be dampened down during economic booms should in ation get out of control.

Both demand management and ideas of the welfare theorists may seem impractical and idealistic to an ordinary manager. How, after all, can one reliably measure such subjective concepts as utility or national demand? Is it even reasonable, when the meaning of such measures may change, to plot historical trends?

Nevertheless welfare economics and demand management help us understand the ideas that lay behind what might be called the welfare confidence of the 1950s, 1960s and early 1970s. The Beveridge Report of 1942 (Cmnd 6404 – *Report on Social Insurance and Allied Services*) set the tone for confident welfare measures.

This report recommended free medical services, unemployment insurance, retirement pensions, child allowances, funeral allowances and generally inspired the National Assistance Act 1948. The so-called 'cradle to grave' Welfare State, which the aforementioned act ushered in, was perhaps the most obvious manifestation of a growing feeling of welfare confidence. The country and our allies had won the greatest and most terrible war in history. Britain still had an empire. The government was powerful and in control, in a 'Keynesian' way, of the economy. Government experts – economists, social scientists, and managers – could, or should, be able to solve any problems, starting with poverty.

By the late 1970s in the UK and the US the so-called monetarists (who emphasized the importance of controlling the supply of money in circulation, basically as a measure of lowering in ation and interest rates) were gaining the upper hand over the Keynesians. Welfare confidence in terms of the increasing role of the public services as a direct provider gave way in the face of 'stag ation' – rising in ation combined with rising unemployment and economic stagnation.

We have already referred in passing to some of the major shifts in economic policy and events of the 1980s and early 1990s that began under the Conservative governments of Margaret Thatcher, for example privatization and the increasing in uence of monetary policy. So pervasive have Thatcherite policies become in this century, that even some harsh critics of such policies have been heard to say that 'we're all Thatcherites now!' Our concern is with public services fraud and corruption, and one of the oft-mentioned tenets of Thatcherism has been the 'rolling back of the boundaries of the state'. Given the continuation of broadly Thatcherite policies – privatization programmes, the outsourcing of many local government services originally via compulsory and later voluntary competitive tendering (CCT and VCT), and the spreading use of the private finance initative (PFI) and various private and public services partnership arrangements – it is perhaps remarkable that the proportion of GDP used by tax-funded, public services remained stable at about 40 per cent for most of this time.

Although large privatizations have taken place, reducing the drain on taxation from this direction, at the same time the size and funding of the public services overall has meant a relatively small reduction in total. It is as if the public services have expanded to take up the 'slack' despite some temporary reductions in taxation. Compared to some other western countries UK taxation levels are at a roughly comparable level although lower than some EU nations. It seems as if the growth of public expenditure has reached a stage where, unlike the wide uctuations of earlier centuries, it is nowadays politically difficult to reduce it below a roughly comparable level with other developed western nations.

PRIVATIZATION AND THE PUBLIC SERVICE ETHOS

Despite the relative stability of public expenditure levels we have seen an important shift in emphasis over the last few generations from the privatization of what were originally commercial organizations, starting in the 1980s, to the increasing commercialization of formerly public services bodies. At times it has almost seemed as if successive governments have been scouring the public services to find new and more controversial candidates for privatization or private sector funding. Arguments in favour of private sector efficiency and lowering the burden on taxpayers have been behind much of the privatization and sources of private finance – 'it's not how it is financed but how well a service is delivered'. This has implications for the public ethos that underpins much of the effort to combat fraud and corruption in public services work. This ethos is not bound to be unique to the public services (similar values are expounded for large corporations as we shall see later under corporate governance, p.35) but it is arguably more vital, complex and intrusive even for small public services bodies. Nor is public service ethos solely concerned with providing any particular standard of service, rather it is about the way in which the service is provided; the arrangements involving checks and balances that are often not readily apparent to those unfamiliar with public services. The earlier and largely successful privatizations unburdened taxpayers of the poorly performing state-funded industries – telecommunications, steel, coal, shipbuilding, car manufacturing and even a state-owned brewery – largely former commercial organizations with a history of operating in the private sector and a private sector commercial ethos. Many had been the subject of various levels of political control which sometimes attempted to encourage or at least pay lip service to commercial, profit-seeking values. Such industries were not providers of pure public goods but simply profit-oriented commercial companies that had been nationalized originally to achieve socialist policies revolving around the control of the means of production. Their ethos had never been greatly in uenced by public service values or management procedures aimed at ensuring public openness, impartiality, and accountability to the public or at least to elected representatives. For example, in principal it is generally acceptable that private entrepreneurs be free to run their businesses, awarding contracts on the basis of personal values determined by their own perceived interests – but this is the very opposite of public service values. The public servant should always seek to act and be seen to act in the interests of the wider community and should avoid any hint of acting in his or her own interest. This is after all at the heart of the Prevention of Corruption Acts mentioned in the previous chapter. The massive previously nationalized industries showed little resemblance to the public good provision of many originally public service bodies that have since been effectively privatized such as local parks maintenance, prisons, social housing, and so on, few if any of which have a history of a commercial profit-seeking ethos. Although there is no surgical separation between privatization of former nationalized industries and public corporations that lend themselves to commercial values and the commercialization of long-standing public services bodies providing essentially public goods, a trend is evident. This has led to a dangerous increase in risk of fraud and corruption or at least private exploitation of public good provision. Many of the public goods fall naturally into monopoly or near monopoly provision, that is why they are public goods in the first place, and commercialization of former public bodies has often retained this monopoly element, which in a commercial situation is very open to exploitation. Even though public bodies may be one of many, such as local authorities, or may retain an outward public service appearance while becoming more commercialized such as colleges, such bodies still often need the controls and ethos of a monopoly public good provider to avoid increasing risk of fraud and corruption. Often one of the main risks is that management in the newly commercialized public body will ape the private sector without taking on board the rigours of full commercial competition; or that simple lack of experience will render managers vulnerable to corrupt practices. Thus officials and former public servants will be expected simply to make a profit but without much chance of being called to account either by the market in terms of facing bankruptcy or angry shareholders or by political control through say, local government committees. Like all individuals there is a high likelihood they will act in their own interest and often it has been realized too late that individuals and systems have fleeced the taxpayer and millions have been pocketed or wasted. There have been many such examples in recent years, usually of systems for spending public money being subjected to private sector commercial ethos but still expected to function in the public interest. Perhaps one of the most widely publicized examples was the scheme for Individual Learning Accounts run by the Department for Education and Skills from 1997 to 2001 using private sector contractors. A lack of basic controls or appreciation of the temptations faced by individuals and companies to act in their own interest led to spending of £273 million against a budget of £199 million and reports by the NAO and others that the department did not know how many accounts were opened and how much money went to unscrupulous companies. In 1992 £67 million of taxpayers' money was under investigation and it was reported that a quarter of registered learners had not undertaken courses. A similar example came to light when Training and Enterprise Councils (TECs) were reported to have made £14.6 million overpayments in 1996/97 of which £6 million was fraud related to training provision. There have been well documented cases of fraud relating to management buy-outs and relationships between public officials and private sector contractors. In the infamous 'West Wilts' scandal of the 1990s moneys were paid unlawfully and former public servants from chief executive and directors down to middle managers were charged with using public funds improperly and fraudulently, while setting up a commercial operation to outsource on the county council's computer function. The so called 'fat cats' debate of the 1990s applied not just to the well publicized accounts of directors of private companies who were able to award themselves unreasonable remuneration, but in the public services to directors and senior managers who obtained the trappings of corporate success, the top flight remuneration packages, luxury cars and corporate expense accounts.

To some extent policymakers have recognized the risks of monopoly or near monopoly provision and the lack of competition, particularly for the privatized industries, by setting up industry regulators' bodies such as Office of the Rail Regulator, Ofwat for the water industry, Oftel for the telecommunications industry and so on. These bodies generally deal with the very large industry-scale issues such as pricing and consumer protection; although they encourage competition they are not usually equipped to intervene in the operational day-to-day arrangements that underpin the fight against fraud and corruption. Industry-wide regulators do not of course encompass much of the public services such as central and local government and many smaller public services bodies.

The risk for the public services in continuing privatization in one form or another is not that the private sector does not work to provide greater efficiencies – the large scale privatizations in particular were generally an economic success. Rather it is that managers fail to appreciate the difference between the private sector ethos, that fits the privatization of naturally commercial enterprises for which a natural free market exists, and the need to maintain a public service ethos in the provision of public goods for which no or very little natural free market exists (or for which an artificial market must be created as with the internal market in the pre-1996 NHS). Otherwise we will see more and more examples of fraud and corruption as individuals and organizations in the public services ape the private sector with little control and accountability. There are already outward signs of this as bodies dependent on tax-funded grants and subsidies seek to distance themselves from the public services in the interests of a more business-like image. Often quite small public services bodies seek to avoid being recognized as such, although their efforts lead less to the rolling back of the boundaries of the state than the boundaries of terminology. Thus in a plethora of quangos, DSOs, agencies, associations, and companies directors have replaced chief officers, treasurers have become financial directors and limited companies that are dependent on tax funding to provide a public good such as social housing to the very disadvantaged have been set up. Many public services bodies contain marketing managers whose main role is basically to organize the receipt of public services funding, while some public services bodies pay large sums for commercial advisors and consultants. Such cosmetic changes are not of themselves a direct cause of fraud or corruption, and they may even encourage a more business-like management approach. But while these changes encourage a private enterprise and often more efficient mindset they also encourage less openly accountable procedures and standards while at the same time the managers involved are often relatively free from the entrepreneurial risk of financial bankruptcy: a combination of factors that is likely to increase the risk of fraud. Money from taxpayers cannot be used as if it had been won in the face of fierce commercial pressures by dint of entrepreneurial acumen rather than political largesse, without increasing the risk of fraud and corruption or at least serious waste.

To counter such risks the basic public service ethos must be maintained. In particular the following measures, while by no means an exhaustive list, have long proved useful:

All income expenditure must be clearly and openly accounted for and in fine detail.

Accounts must be subject to public audit, mainly by the NAO or the Audit Commission or their equivalents and in most cases with provision for ongoing internal audit.

Public access to query items in the accounts or bring matters to the attention of auditors.

Performance must be judged independently, by for example committees of elected politicians, independently appointed boards, ministers, and so on – the lack of effective competition requires this.

Clear separations between awarding contracts and any other connection with the contractors must be maintained with all public servants and politicians required to declare any con ict of interest, excluding them from related debates and decisions.

A general requirement to conform to the best practices of corporate governance in a specific public services context (see pp. 35–7).

The immediate response of some managers to such measures is to say this is simply more red tape, but this is the cost of public accountability where a genuine free market mechanism is absent or weak. The alternative cost is more fraud, corruption and waste and a gradual loss of the public service ethos.

Such basic questions sometimes seem remote from day-to-day management but they are useful in helping to understand the broad span of what has occurred, at least in western industrial democracies, and as a backdrop against which the public services manager might take his or her decisions. The manager will be likely to appreciate his or her role more fully if it can be seen in its wider context. But beyond this the author does not propose to go. An appreciation of public services origins, nature and the rationale of their existence is useful and necessary but far less than sufficient for good fraud prevention, and good management decision-making.

The rise of corporate governance

The economic and political shifts of the last decades of the twentieth century have been accompanied by a relatively quiet revolution in the strategic control and accountability of large organizations. Corporate governance has had a particularly strong impact in the UK and the USA, initially at least inspired by the need to deal with corporate disasters that have undermined confidence in the stock markets. Although we are concerned with the public services it is to the private sector that we must first turn to understand the origins of corporate governance.

During the late 1980s and early 1990s a series of financial scandals rocked the City and even began to threaten wider public confidence in industry and commerce. Well known names such as The Mirror Group, Bank of Credit and Commerce International, Barrings and Polly Peck were brought down. These were by no means the first, nor were they to be the last or even the most serious of such scandals. But they came at the start of an economic recession (often a catalyst in revealing frauds as falling profits and balance sheet values uncover hidden losses) and at a time when intense media attention focused on the 'fat cats' of industry – directors who voted themselves large remuneration packages as their firms performed poorly, including directors of privatized utilities.

CADBURY

In the private sector the London Stock Exchange and the UK accounting profession sponsored the formation of the Committee to report on the financial aspects of corporate governance, chaired by Sir Adrian Cadbury. It published a major report in 1992, *The Cadbury Report* which incorporated a code of best practice.

Among the major points of the Cadbury report were the following:

The identification of three basic principles of corporate governance:

- Openness
- Integrity
- Accountability.

It applied to boards of all stock exchange listed companies.

The auditors of the companies should review the board's compliance with the code.

The boards of listed companies should establish committees to deal with remuneration and with audit.

The board should be clearly responsible for adequate accounting records and financial statements.

> The board should report upon the extent to which the corporate body has effective financial controls.

It was this last point in particular that led to further guidance being required.

A working group was set up under the auspices of the Auditing Practices Board to recommend guidance on the nature of financial controls and the form in which directors should report. It suggested various approaches, but the essence was that they should give some reasonable assurance to shareholders that the corporation has satisfactory financial control arrangements.

GREENBURY

The Greenbury Committee was set up to look into the details of the remuneration of directors, and in 1995 it published a code of practice recommending how the remuneration committees should determine reasonable rewards for directors and disclose the policy and the packages awarded.

HAMPEL

In 1998 a further report under Sir Robert Hampel offered a 'combined code' of best practice taking the relevant parts of earlier codes and reports. This combined code has been very influential in the corporate governance of business in the UK. It placed particular emphasis on the audit and control of business and the need for openness and accountability. The code stresses the importance of the audit committee of the board and that they should receive reports from auditors and review the extent of audit and non-audit work. It requires that the directors should review, at least annually, the effectiveness of internal financial, operational and compliance control. This has had a major impact on the strengthening of control environments and control procedures in corporations. Accountability has been enhanced by requiring non-executive directors to sit on the audit committees and encouraging a formal internal audit function within corporations, whose audit duties include the review and testing of the internal controls throughout the organization.

TURNBULL

In 1999 a working party chaired by Nigel Turnbull published detailed guidance on the role of directors and internal control, requiring for example that internal control should be embedded in the organization of companies and capable of reporting quickly. Turnbull emphasized the need for corporate risk assessments. The stock exchange requirements now require compliance both with the combined code and Turnbull guidance.

HIGGS

In 2003 the Chairman of the committee on corporate governance published a report largely about the role of directors and non-executive directors (NEDs). After financial scandals such Enron and Worldcom in the US there was a perceived need for bolstering the independence of NEDs and keeping them well informed.

SMITH

In 2003 the Chairman of the recently enhanced Financial Reporting Council, Sir Robert Smith, issued specific guidance on how audit committees should follow the combined code. Again, this was thought to be timely after the public scandals in the US and the involvement and subsequent demise of Arthur Andersen, one of the world's largest accounting firms. Among the many lessons from this tragedy is the need for auditors and audit committees to be above suspicion and act to the highest standards. The outcome of both Smith and Higgs reviews was a new, revised 'combined code', effective from November 2003.

Public services reaction to corporate governance

The influence of Cadbury, Hampel and so on upon the public services was at first muted compared to its influence upon the private sector; the corporate governance issues were seen as a private rather than public services development. The Audit Commission generally encouraged and supported local authorities to adopt Cadbury-style measures but often encountered a lack of enthusiasm for the process.

NOLAN

In 1994 John Major's government set up a Committee on Standards in Public Life under Lord Nolan. Although this development mirrored the impetus given to corporate governance in the private sector, it owed more to the widespread media reports of sleaze in government and the damage caused to political reputations. Nolan's first report in 1995 marked a turning point in the public services.

Nolan was clearly in sympathy with corporate governance and especially the three principles mentioned in the last section – openness, integrity and accountability. He identified seven key principles of conduct for public services managers and others:

1 Selflessness
2 Integrity
3 Objectivity
4 Accountability
5 Openness
6 Honesty
7 Leadership.

The Committee on Standards in Public Life has continued to produce reports into major aspects of public services. Various guidance has been issued by the Committee and other major oversight or professional bodies such as the Audit Commission and CIPFA (see the Bibliography):

Concluding points

We have considered very briefly some legal, moral, historical, economic and governance insights into public services. The lack of choice underlying taxation imposes a special duty on public servants and fraud and corruption take on a special significance in the public services.

There is a long and constantly changing history of public services bodies. But in a modern western society the public services sector, however defined, seems bound to account for a sizeable proportion of GNP. This means that there will always be considerable public interest in the standards of public accountability and any suspicion of fraud and corruption will need to be positively refuted.

Although continuing public services appears inevitable, safeguards and internal controls sufficient to ensure full accountability, fairness and honest behaviour have to be deliberately sought and maintained. The remaining chapters of this book aim to show the reader how to seek out and maintain such practices and behaviour without encouraging the amount of red tape to increase beyond reason.

The rise of Thatcherism and the privatization and private sector involvement in public services from the 1980s onwards has done much to alter the structure and appearance of the public services. Nonetheless the underpinning rationale and public service ethos remains as important as ever and is coming under increasing strain with regard to its ability to resist corrupting in uences.

One of the developments that has gained widespread support in both the public and private sectors to counter fraud and corruption is the rise of corporate governance, but while this may offer a useful framework to reduce the risks of these threats recent history shows that the underlying arrangements and controls to counter fraud and corruption can still be ineffective.

CASE STUDIES

This chapter has contained some implications for fraud and corruption but it is a chapter that considers the macro view of public services. Rather than select one or two particular cases, the reader is referred to Appendix 14 for details of a wide range of real life cases and the way these relate to the public services in general.

CHAPTER 3

Using Risk and Systems-based Auditing

Introduction

This is an appropriate point in the book to consider fraud and corruption from the point of view of auditing. This single chapter is not adequate space to explain in great detail the nature of auditing and the many skills and working practices needed. But auditing is often bound up with preventing fraud and corruption, particularly in the minds of lay people and politicians. In some respects this is unfortunate as most audit work is relatively routine and not particularly concerned with fraud. Yet it is generally true that good audit work, like good management and sound operations in general, will help to deter fraud and make life difficult for fraudsters. In this chapter we will brie y consider some of the main developments in auditing, then the main stages of a systems-based audit, before suggesting ways in which all this can be adapted or refined to be particularly useful in combating fraud. Readers who are auditors or already understand auditing may find this chapter covers familiar territory. Even so it is often helpful to stand back from that with which one is familiar and consider its wider implications.

Background and developments

Until the 1960s and 1970s audit was largely a matter of 'vouching', that is, checking a large number of transactions to evaluate the accuracy, validity and disclosure of the figures in the financial accounts. Much of this type of work is still relevant but it developed in a pre-computerized world of smaller and simpler organizations. In the public services there has also been a long history of checking that the intentions behind 'voted' moneys are followed, that is, that the sums have been used for legal and intended purposes. In the public services, although this was often called a 'probity' approach, it was essentially vouching.

Most modern commentators point out that the basic approach and methodology of audit has changed radically over the past half a century or so. The increasing size and complexity referred to earlier has made vouching alone inadequate. It is difficult to single out a date when 'systems-based auditing' or the 'systems-based approach' (often simply called SBA in either case) became more popular than traditional vouching. There has been more of a gradual changeover than a revolution – an evolutionary development that many of today's auditors, including the author, have witnessed. The development of SBA to take account of risk, sampling and other refinements is still continuing and some talk of a post-SBA audit. Certainly SBA was widespread by the 1980s and commonplace by the 1990s.

It was perhaps inevitable that faced with the impossibility of simply being able to vouch or test sufficient numbers of transactions to come to a reliable conclusion about the figures churned out by systems, auditors would come to test and rely more and more upon the operation of internal controls. The basic idea is that internal controls in a system are arrangements, procedures and events designed to give assurance that the system will work as well as intended preventing any deviation, error or fraud. So, if the internal controls are working reliably one can vouch far fewer transactions. As we shall see later on, in the wider sense an internal control can be anything that guards against a risk.

SBA has been widely adopted not just because of the increasing size, complexity and computerization of systems but also because it highlights the strengths and weaknesses of a system for the benefit of management and audit in general. This is particularly important for internal auditors.

For the benefit of anyone not familiar with audit it should be explained that audit has two broad professional standpoints, external and internal. External auditors including the National Audit Office, the Audit Commission and some large private audit firms are appointed from outside the organization to express a professional view on the published accounts of a public services body: are these 'true and fair' or a 'proper presentation' of the financial affairs? The accounts of public services bodies vary widely but the main focus of the external auditors work is on what has happened in the past financial year and how fairly and reliably it has been reported to the public. This is why the amount of vouching and other testing is important in terms of the practical resource requirements of the audit. This is basically the same as external audit in the private sector, though in the public services external auditors also have some other public duties related to value for money and public accountability. Internal auditors on the other hand are usually employed directly by the body at a senior level, or work inside the body under contract, or are part of a consortium of similar bodies such as NHS trusts. Their main focus is SBA as an end in itself, or part of a wider management-agreed remit covering a range of possible audit objectives, including of course the prevention of fraud and corruption.

In summary then, although the traditional vouching/probity approach may still be required, SBA offers certain definite advantages:

1 It can highlight 'risky' areas of weak control that often go unsuspected in a traditional approach.
2 It can offer a more structured and efficient approach to planning and carrying out the audit. In particular SBA can reduce the overall level of audit testing and point to areas where vouching should be concentrated.
3 It can offer systematic audit evidence on the totality of a system (rather than being limited to its individual parts). Of course, the evidence may indicate that the system is unreliable, in which case further detailed testing will still be required if an opinion on the accuracy of the system output, for example, a final balance sheet figure, is required.

Modern audit works devote considerable attention to the systems-based approach to audit and it is not our intention to reiterate this in detail; see the Bibliography for some useful references. However, it is useful in terms of combating fraud to understand the impact of risk modelling and the basic approach to SBA. We will therefore devote a little attention to the recent developments in risk and risk modelling before we go on to outline the main stages in a typical SBA.

Risk and risk models

We have been using this term as if risk was so well understood nothing more need be said. But what do we really mean by risk? Defining risk in general and trying to identify particular risks is a rather 'risky' task in itself: we are apt to suffer from preconceptions and bias. Sometimes we ignore risks that later seem with the benefit of hindsight to have been glaringly obvious, sometimes we include others that later seem laughable. Many risk-experts draw up risk models and risk modelling has become something of a goldmine for consultants and an attraction for academic researchers in recent years. There are usually very many possible factors one could include in a risk model. In many situations there is a tendency to simply list as many risks as possible. Various 'brain storming' events, 'SWOT' analyses (strengths, weaknesses, opportunities, threats), risk self-assessment exercises and so forth may be involved, and are sometimes very useful. At times such efforts can be rather dispiriting as more and more apparent risks are suggested and need to be factored into ever-lengthening and complex, algebraic formula-based, models. Perhaps this approach can suffer from asking the wrong basic question: instead of asking 'risk *of* what?' we should be asking 'risk *to* what?'

Although we can often learn a lot from the past, risk models can suffer from a backward-looking historic perspective. Risk is about the future, and in our terms future threats to corporate objectives. Essentially an open-minded, lateral thinking, imaginative approach is called for, one that sees the past as one among many trains of thought and in the context of the future. This is often difficult, and complex models might not be the best solution.

LIMITATIONS OF RISK MODELLING

Perhaps it is because the development of risk modelling has been heavily in uenced by financial risk models that the complex formula-based approach has been so popular. These have often been aimed at investors or insurers who are usually heavily in uenced by past events and trained and experienced in quantative and financial data analysis. In recent years as more operational risk models have developed these have addressed some of the limitations just mentioned, though usually still based on long formulae. These often have their origins in a systems-based approach but analyse the threats to different systems in terms of the relative impact and likelihood of various negative events. A typical example of this genre, contained in an IIA paper:

$$20(x/n).[(4f+3g+5h+4j)/80].[(3k+4l+5m)/60]$$

including several sub formula required four sides of A4 to describe it (see the Bibliography). No doubt audit and consultancy readers will have seen similar models that can be very useful for existing situations and types of operational risk already foreseen in the mind of the modeller, and the components of the formula can be quantified or at least clearly predicted. But the mind and actions of a fraudster are notoriously unpredictable, even when dealing with obvious targets of fraud and corruption such as diverting cash and bribes to officials.

THE IR.CR.DR MODEL

External audit risk models offer a simpler and more adaptable approach that may help. The most popular is the 'IR.CR.DR' model where the total amount of audit risk (AR) is calculated in terms of percentages of inherent risk (IR), control risk (CR) and detection risk (DR).

Thus $AR = IR \times CR \times DR$

> Where IR is the risk of errors occurring in the first place given the nature of the financial system;
> CR is the risk of the financial controls not preventing or correcting such errors; and
> DR is the risk of the auditor's tests not uncovering any errors that manage to get past the controls.

For example, if the IR was judged at 90 per cent, that is, a high inherent risk of error or fraud occurring in a system, the CR was estimated at say 10 per cent, that is, controls good enough to prevent or detect all but 10 per cent of the errors or frauds that occurred, and DR was judged to be 50 per cent, that is, a 50 per cent chance of the audit tests uncovering the errors or frauds that had occurred but escaped the controls, then the overall AR would be 90 per cent × 10 per cent × 50 per cent, that is, 4.5 per cent. The auditor can do little about the IR and CR, but can adjust the level of DR to obtain the required overall AR by increasing or decreasing the level of audit testing.

While this model is able to include many causes of errors and fraud and offer a simple and exible approach, it is essentially aimed at the risk of the external auditor coming to the wrong conclusion from available evidence, not at predicting or preventing fraud and corruption. As a model the IR.CR.DR approach is still formula based, the values used will be subjective assessments and, arguably, it does little to encourage imaginative and exible thinking about the future.

However, this external audit approach can be adapted and more easily made compatible to risk managers if they think in terms of a wide range of countermeasures for controls, and in terms of 'remaining' risk (RR) instead of detection risk. This remaining risk can be seen in both terms of probability and impact. One usually assumes that the probability of inherent risk is high, particularly in most financial systems, though this may not always be so in non-financial systems, and that the impact would at least be material to the organization's financial accounts – if there was no likelihood of any material impact then why bother to model the risk? The final level of risk reduces both in probability and impact after the effectiveness of countermeasures is taken into account, leaving a remaining or residual risk in terms of impact and probability. In practice, in most systems any inherent level, or acts, of fraud are likely to be material and serious countermeasures failure would leave a significant remaining risk in terms of impact. In which case the key question is, basically, what is the probability of any level of remaining risk?

This IR × CR × DR approach is still subjective. How can one place quantifiable percentages or other numerical values on rather speculative chances of fraudulent or other threatening events happening? Even if one assumes for the sake of prudence that a high score should be attached to IR, 100 per cent perhaps, the measurement of countermeasure risk in terms of the likelihood of their failure is still as much a matter of personal experience as professional testing, and as in most systems the testing will be on a sample basis the parameters of which will have been subjectively determined it is only fair to stress that this approach will, at best, be a rough and ready tool.

MAINTENANCE AND DEVELOPMENT RISKS

One of the drawbacks of operational and audit risk models in particular is that they tend to deal better with maintenance than development scenarios. In maintenance situations the system (for example, payroll, stock control and so on) is already up and running, its objectives are generally understood and the aim is to avoid it failing. Thus controls are built into the system to keep it on track and counter any errors or deliberate fraud. In developmental scenarios where systems are being developed (though there may of course be a system to develop systems) the development's objectives may still be evolving. The risks of error or fraud are generally thought to be more difficult to predict and control in a development scenario where tried and tested controls may not exist or will tend to be complex processes, rather than specific relatively simple procedures as is usual in maintenance systems. The volatility and haziness of developmental risks make for greater vulnerability and most people would tend to view the risks of fraud and corruption as greater in developmental situations.

Yet developmental risks usually get most of the attention from top managers and project development teams staffed by high-paid experts. In most organizations mainenance systems are managed by people charged with ensuring the routine is followed: the work is vital but unlikely to attract the more creative and highly skilled. Even when maintenance-type managers spot risks they often lack the authority to act directly and will need to report to a higher level. Often this is a recipe for indecision leading to more serious risk or control failure. In short, developmental risks usually attract top level attention while maintenance ones are brushed aside to accumulate until things go seriously wrong.

THE SIMPLE ORC RELATIONSHIP

It is against this background of the limitations of complex risk models and the need to accommodate both developmental and maintenance-type risks that many managers have sought an improved approach to risk. One of the approaches gaining ground is to focus effort upon the basic objectives-risks-controls (or countermeasures) (ORC) relationship. This is not a revolutionary new approach but simply the formalization or systematic use of the three key components that have always underpinned good risk management. This approach links both risks and controls to corporate objectives in a non-formulaic, exible and imagination-encouraging way. (See references in the Bibliography.)

Here it is vital to clearly identify, at an organization-wide level, the corporate objectives and then, on a system by system basis, each system's objectives. It becomes natural and productive to view new developments and routine systems in terms of their impact upon such objectives. This makes it easier to predict and define the risks in terms of anything that poses a threat to these objectives. One is only limited by one's imagination, not by the need to quantify or (however useful at times) to continue along the same line of thinking as in the past. This in turn makes it easier to sort out the key controls in any situation from among the often complex and voluminous systems descriptions, plans and other information about who does what, which information ows where and so on. This is because just as a risk is any threat to an objective so a control is anything that counters such a threat. This could be a procedure or an arrangement such as an authorization, particularly in a maintenance system, or an event or a process such as regular agreement at meetings, particularly in a developmental situation. Appendix 5, Objective and controls grids, lists some typical objectives, risks and controls. If, in practice, one is uncertain about the importance of different procedures, arrangements and so on, then one can ask, are these vital key controls in a system, or simply routine administrative arrangements or events? If they guard against a key risk then they will be a key control, if not then they are not. By placing the control in Figure 3.1 and relating it to a risk, and hence to an objective one can sort out the vital from the less vital. This is particularly important during times of downsizing, outsourcing, reorganization and upheaval, nowadays quite common phenomena among public services.

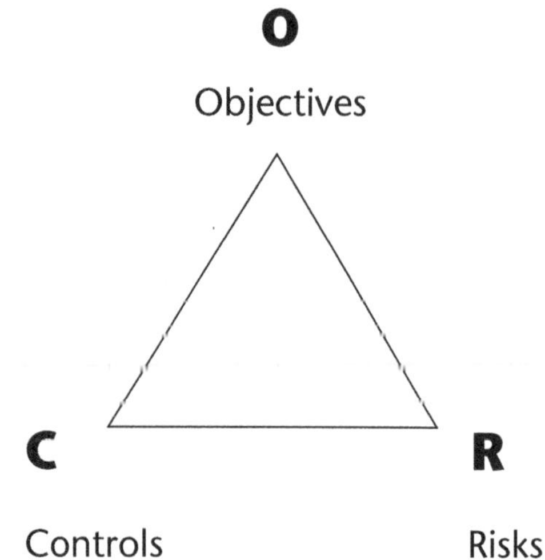

Figure 3.1 The simple ORC relationship

In this way rather than following lists of controls so typical of audit work, for example or commissioning an expensive risk analysis, building up a permanent awareness of the ORC relationship among senior managers can help them assess risk themselves. They more than anyone else are probably aware that so-called controls in a textbook sense will not work in the situations they face and are best placed to create new controls to meet their specific needs. This is particularly so when new objectives are set. New objectives will usually leave people facing new risks and needing new controls – a confusing situation well suited to perpetrating and hiding fraud.

The ORC relationship is vital when understanding SBA in any new or unfamiliar system, where risks and controls are often not obvious and relying on published lists can often lead to missing out some vital control or failing to recognize how experienced line managers have learnt to cope with unusual situations.

ASSURANCE

Many auditors and their clients would add another component to the ORC relationship outlined above – assurance. The main purpose of the auditor's work in testing the controls is to offer assurance to the clients both that the controls were actually operating as intended and by implication that these controls can be relied upon to give assurance that the system output, usually accounting balances, can be relied upon. The simple model above becomes more a relationship at the heart of auditing and similar professional opinion-forming work such as that of consultants, compliance managers and the like: the ORCA relationship (see Figure 3.2).

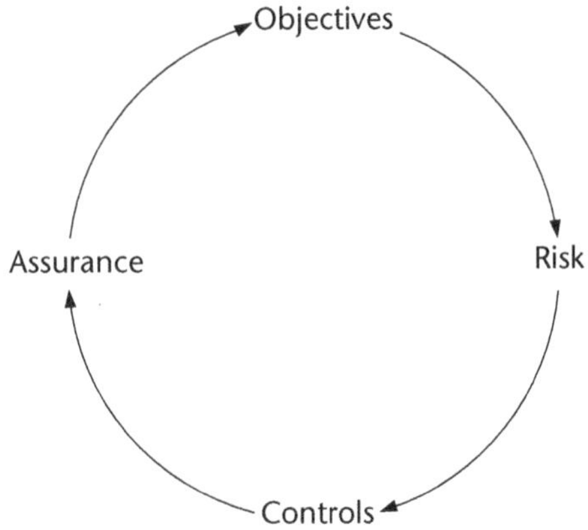

Figure 3.2 The ORCA relationship

A summary of the systems-based approach to audit

For the benefit of the manager or any other professional who is unfamiliar with a systems-based audit, we present below a brief overview. This is split into eight broad stages that, taken on their own, may tend to give too narrow and rigid an impression of the course of a typical audit. This simplification is unfortunate but, short of including several lengthy chapters devoted entirely to systems-based audit, it will have to suffice. Even this short summary should, it is hoped, be sufficient for the non-specialist reader to appreciate the important role of systems-based audits in helping to prevent fraud and corruption. More importantly, it will help you when dealing with auditors in any context but particularly in ways to prevent fraud and corruption, and give you a useful insight into the SBA approach. This approach is behind many of the ideas and suggestions later in this book and is one that has been used a great deal over the years to help make systems secure and able to counter the risk of fraud.

A widely used definition of a system, expounded by the APB, sees a system as a series of interrelated procedures composed of processes and controls designed to operate together to achieve a planned objective. This is very much in line with the ORCA relationship discussed above. SBA essentially seeks to give assurance about the effective design and operation of a system in meeting its objectives. Although this implies a risk-based approach to help identify threats to the objectives, in many well established financial systems the risks are so common between different organizations and well appreciated by accountants, financial managers and others that there is a tendency to take these for granted. This can lead one to make a mental link directly between objectives and controls, or even to take both the objectives and the risks for granted and just consider the controls. The danger is of course that familiarity will breed contempt and important risks are overlooked or underestimated in a particular system. With the benefits of hindsight many accountants and others would later admit that this problem often explains why fraudsters have been able to go undetected.

The key issue is therefore how much reliance can be placed upon the system's internal controls. This is vitally important both by the managers and internal auditors who want assurance that things will go well in future and by the external auditors who want assurance that things have gone well in the relatively recent past (they can then minimize the level of costly, detailed substantive testing and still give a true and fair view report). Figure 3.3 gives an overview of the stages involved, each of which we will then expand upon a little further. At first sight this tabular format gives the impression of a series of separate stages in strict sequential order. In practice of course things overlap a little and work may be proceeding on more than one stage at a time.

1 Initial clarification of the system and its objectives
2 Detailed documentation
3 Identification of apparent internal controls and any obvious weaknesses
4 Compliance and substantive test programmes drawn up
5 Compliance tests undertaken and conclusions drawn
6 Substantive tests undertaken and conclusions drawn
7 Overall conclusions and professional opinions reported
8 Assurance (or otherwise) offered to Audit Committee/Directors

Figure 3.3 Stages of a systems-based audit

Let's look brie y at summaries of what happens at each stage before we pick out some of the items for a little more detailed discussion.

1 Initial clarification of the system and its objectives
  - The auditor must have a clear understanding of the nature and extent of the system. How shall we define this system? What are the boundaries between this and other systems? He or she must examine its role within the organization.
  - Clarification of the system objectives and thereby the objectives that determine the risks and controls. In an 'upward direction' these objectives should be in harmony with and support any high level corporate objectives. In a 'downward direction' the objectives of individual internal controls that will be later identified should be in harmony with and support these system objectives.
  - Clarification of basic audit objectives and approach. Part of the audit planning process.

2 Detailed documentation
  - Recording or updating records of the system covering in particular its structure, the tasks of key staff, procedures and document ows. Techniques vary but during this stage the auditor will usually compile detailed systems notes, owcharts, copies of systems manuals, undertake interviews and perform 'walk-through' tests where transactions are

followed through the system to confirm what he or she has been told. By this stage too the auditor should have formed a clear view of the inherent risk in the system.

3 Identification of apparent internal controls and any obvious weaknesses
   - This stage should take account of the risks identified earlier and seek to identify controls that (in theory) counter such risks.
   - A clear assessment of the likely ability of the designed controls to counter the risks should be recorded. Any significant lack of controls should be reported to management and corrective action agreed.

4 Compliance and substantive test programmes should be drawn up
   - Compliance testing involves the auditor seeking evidence that the controls have been operated in the intended manner. This may for example be evidence that something was authorized or performed in accordance with specific regulations, or checked and reconciled. It does not seek to verify the detailed quantities and values of transactions or other events, just that they were controlled and protected from risk during their passage through the system.
   - Substantive testing is usually either 'direct' checking of the accuracy, completeness, disclosure and validity of individual transaction values or other events (usually taking a sample), or 'analytical review' of the broad trends and relationships between macro level figures such as account balances at the year end. The programmes for each type of test would usually state the appropriate objectives, explain how the tests should be undertaken in terms of particular documentary evidence to be examined, any observations, recomputations and recalculations, measurements, physical verifications and so forth. The programmes would usually record who undertook each test and be cross-referenced to any supporting documentation, statements, detailed working papers and so on.
   - In practice the substantive testing will often be delayed until some or all of the compliance testing results have been evaluated in case the controls are poorer than expected and additional substantive testing is therefore needed – see point 5 below.

5 Compliance tests should be undertaken and conclusions drawn
   - The results and conclusions of compliance testing should be used to update the initial assessment of internal controls – see point 3 above – and form a view on the level of control risk.
   - These conclusions will also help the auditor to agree the level of substantive testing required: in general the more reliable the operation of the controls the lower the level of substantive testing required. As substantive testing is usually the most time consuming and expensive part of the audit, keeping it to an optimal level has important resource implications.

6 Substantive tests should be undertaken and conclusions drawn
   - These tests will often form the bulk of direct evidence and should be sufficient to ensure the level of detection risk is kept as low as required.
   - Clearly there will be a large element of professional experience and judgement behind the auditor's decisions on how much substantive testing to undertake whatever risk model (or none) is used.

  - The results of substantive testing should be reviewed and conclusions about the likelihood that the system has/will continue to output figures reliably should be drawn.

7 Overall conclusions and professional opinions should be reported
  - The compliance and substantive test conclusions will form an important part, usually the most important part, but not the whole, of the evidence available to the auditor. The test results may need to be viewed for example in relation to work done by management, quality control inspections, benchmarking exercises that compare performance to similar organizations, value for money audits, fraud investigations, management reports and submissions and so on.
  - For an external auditor the work carried out on each system will be need to be assessed in its totality and in the light of recent events and other judgements before an opinion can be drawn about the truth and fairness and proper presentation of the published accounts.
  - For an internal auditor the work carried out on each system together with the other audit work just mentioned will usually form the basis of comprehensive reporting to an audit committee on the overall adequacy of controls and counter-fraud measures throughout the organization.

8 Overall assurance offered to Audit Committee/Directors
  - In some organizations this is simply a matter of representing the reports from point 7 to the directors responsible for the area audited and pointing out how much reliance and assurance can be placed upon the controls in this area. For other organizations this stage is a much more complex one involving the collation and further analysis of the results system by system, risk by risk across the entire organization so that the Audit Committee or at least the Financial Director can assess the assurance that can be placed on the statement made about the adequacy of controls throughout the organization. But this stage will not be considered in detail in this book, as it is essentially a more specialized aspect for senior and experienced audit work.

For those readers who feel comfortable with a more diagrammatic approach, Figure 3.4 sets out a ow diagram of the main stages and the likely documentation involved.

Let's now look in detail at selected aspects of conventional SBA.

RECORDING THE SYSTEM

To do this the auditor will need to be clear what he means by the 'system'. He will need to set boundaries, which may be quite arbitrary at times, to separate procedures that are related and designed to achieve a planned objective from those that are not. This is often not as difficult as it sounds. The audited organization usually has management-defined systems which correspond well to systems from an audit viewpoint. Purchases, debtors, creditors and payrolls are large main systems that usually form key parts of the financial structure of an organization. These and some others are given as examples below:

Purchases
Stock control

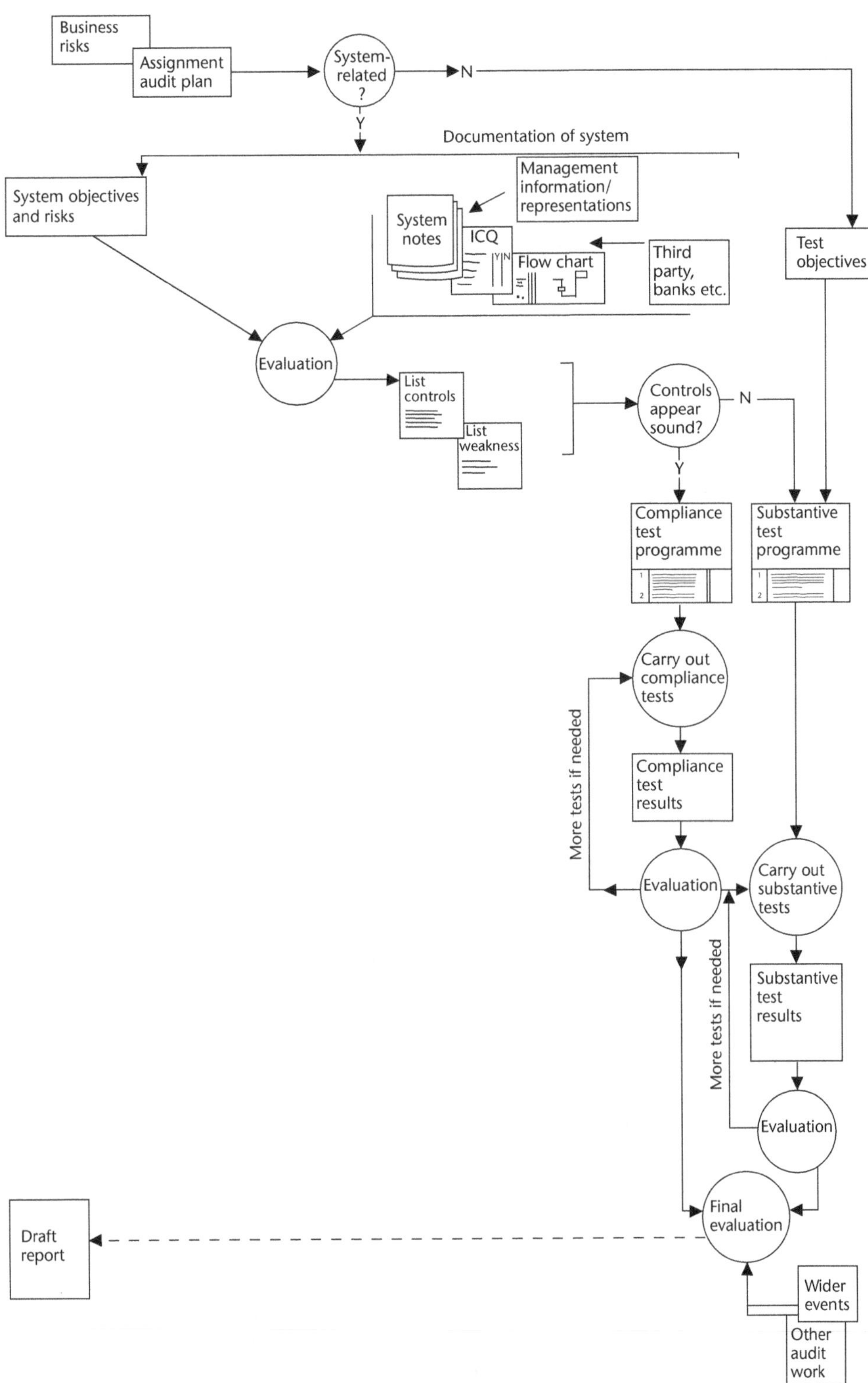

Figure 3.4 The ow of an audit

Creditors' payments
Debtors (sundry)
Payrolls
Capital expenditure
Loans
Investments
Cash collection
Fixed assets accounting
Means-tested benefits (housing benefits, social security, and so on)
General bookkeeping and accounts
Grant (income/expenditure)
Tax/income (revenue collection).

Most auditors record the system using a variety of working papers, including diagrammatically ' ow charting' the procedures and compiling system notes. (Detailed examples of ow charting are given in various texts, see the Bibliography.) Completing an internal control questionnaire (ICQ) – a series of questions and answers designed to document the important control procedures – is also useful. At times simply copying and amending management's own procedural instructions, work manuals, and so on, may be sufficient. Often what merits attention as a large main system in one organization may be of little consequence in another. The main source of income for many public services bodies is from exchequer grants and the main cause of expenditure can be salaries and wages. Other bodies have a mixture of fees, grants, and taxes and may move funds about in complicated ways. The auditor must decide which systems merit attention and the precise cut-off (if any) between, say, purchases and creditors' payments – two systems that often overlap.

Whenever a systems-based audit is undertaken, subsystems tend to become apparent. Debtors may arise from several billing sources; fees may be charged by different, sometimes relatively isolated, parts of the same organization. Stocks may be controlled from more than one storehouse or depot. Again, the auditor must define, using professional judgement and bearing in mind his own and management's objectives, the extent of the system or subsystem under audit.

UNDERTAKING AN INITIAL EVALUATION OF THE SYSTEM

Initial evaluation involves defining the system control objectives and isolating those procedures or relationships within the system that constitute controls from those that do not. These very important aspects usually make up most of the effort involved in any initial evaluation and are explained in detail later in this chapter. For the moment we shall consider some overview aspects of the initial evaluation that can easily be overlooked when the auditor is under pressure.

Overview aspects

Initial evaluation should consider the overall suitability and adequacy of the system to fulfil its basic role or objectives. Such a basic role is sometimes forgotten amongst the detail of procedures. For example, the auditor should check that creditors' payments are not merely a poorly organized adjunct of various devolved purchasing arrangements but are undertaken, usually centrally, in an organized and controlled environment. The auditor should consider too the financial information produced by the system and whether or not such a system is suitable for its intended output. Another example might be fixed assets which may be shown as 'depreciated' or simply retained at cost but supplemented by 'capital discharged' in the main accounting system. Is the system he or she is considering able, at least in principle, to comply with the statutory requirements and any internal regulatory provisions laid down? If such wider questions as these are not given attention before the bulk of the work is undertaken much effort may be wasted. Opportunities to see the wood despite the trees can easily be missed.

Detailed evaluation

Once such overview aspects have been considered the auditor sets about defining the control objectives and identifying the key internal controls (from among all the procedures he has recorded) that help satisfy those control objectives. There are some examples in Table 3.1. If the non-specialist reader has difficulties in appreciating their full significance, the examples may be reconsidered after control objectives and key controls have been discussed later on in this chapter.

Note that these examples can present only a fraction of the possible internal controls. For a great many systems control objectives and descriptions of controls will have to be tailor-made to suit the individual audit assignment. Identification of controls requires experience and judgement and usually looks easier than it actually is!

Table 3.1 Examples of control objectives and key controls to meet those objectives (neither the listed objectives nor the possible controls are meant to be exhaustive)

System	*Control objective*	*Possible key control*
Sundry debtors	(1) All debts due are raised. (2) All debts raised are correctly calculated and coded to the correct amounts. (3) All debts raised are recovered or otherwise actioned as follows: (a) payments received; (b) debt cancelled/credit note issued; and (c) debt written off. (4) All debts are recovered or otherwise actioned in reasonable time.	(1) Value of invoices raised is monitored continuously against debt generating activity. (1) Spot checks are carried out by management on all fee charging activities. (1) and (2) Outstanding debtors are 'circularized' by auditors. (2) Only officially checked and authorized invoices are used to collect debts. (3) Invoices are pre-numbered and payment is instructed to be made only to the organization's account. (1) to (4) A separation of duties exists between debt generating activity/ debt accounting and management (including credit control)/ bank reconciliation.

Table 3.1 – *continued*

System	*Control objective*	*Possible key control*
		(3) and (4) Debtors control accounts and aging report are actioned by senior management. (2) and (4) All write-offs and cancellations are authorized by a senior manager without direct responsibility for the sundry debtors function. (3) and (4) All write-offs over a minimum value are reported to a committee of political members/appointees.
Sundry creditors	(1) Only bills made out to and due by the organization are paid. (2) All bills paid are for goods and services satisfactorily received or performed. (3) All goods and services received were genuinely requested by the organization. (4) All payments made are correctly calculated (including coding to correct account, taking into account any credit notes and discounts allowed).	In most sundry creditors systems some kind of payment authorization either accompanies all invoices to be paid or might even be stamped on the invoice. This usually performs a key control function and should include recognizable signatures certifying that: (3) the invoices has been matched to the appropriate order(s); (2) goods/services have been checked and found satisfactory; (4) the calculation are correct. (1) to (4) A senior officer should sign to authorize payments, checking (1) and that responsible officials have agreed (2), (3) and (4). (2) Delivery advice notes are signed by storeman and a copy retained. (It may not be possible for a storeman to check all items delivered before the consignor's vehicle leaves the premises. If the storeman is forced to check the delivery sometime after it has taken place he should immediately annotate any discrepancy on the advice note and *not* sign any payment authorization until the supplier or consignor has agreed to the discrepancy.)

Table 3.1 – *continued*

System	*Control objective*	*Possible key control*
		(1) All invoices are stamped 'paid' after payment. This helps avoid deliberate or accidental duplicate payment.
Salaries system	(1) Salaries costs are incurred only for authorized employees. (2) All starters, leavers, promotion and similar major changes are correctly and promptly actioned. (3) All salaries costs are correctly calculated and coded.	(1) to (3) A separation of duties exists between the authorization of recruitment, promotion and similar changes – usually done by a personnel branch – and payroll input/accounting – usually the responsibility of an accounts branch. (1) and (2) A reconciliation of authorized staff in post from personnel records to payroll is undertaken by independent officers, e.g. internal audit on an *ad hoc* basis. (2) and (3) A payroll supervisor checks and initials all major payroll entries, e.g. on starting, promotion, leaving or upon changes in pay rates, allowances, etc. (3) Minor changes, e.g. address or bank code, are initialled by the officer updating the payroll.
Rent collection	(1) Rent debits are raised for all properties. (2) All rents are correctly calculated and charged (including any arrears/adjustments/allowances). (3) All rents are collected. (4) All collections are brought fully to account.	(1) The total rent roll is reconciled periodically to rent debtors figure and to the property 'terrier'. (1) Purchases and sales of properties are notified to the housing rent accountant upon exchange of contracts, or on completion if new builds. (1) and (3) All new lets are notified to a housing rents accountant upon receipt of signed leasing agreements.

Table 3.1 – *concluded*

System	*Control objective*	*Possible key control*
		(2) All rent reviews are authorized and notified to collectors and rent accountant.
		(3) and (4) All rent payments are receipted on official rent account cards.
		(3) and (4) All rent collections including overs/unders are balanced against collection sheets and signed by the collector.
		(4) All collections are banked by office cashier after agreement and signature on bank paying-in slip.
		(1) to (4) A separation of duties exists between collections (collectors), rent accounting (accountant), banking (cashier) and, if possible, bank reconciliation (accountant).

UNDERTAKING COMPLIANCE AND SUBSTANTIVE TESTING

It is all very well for the auditor to identify internal controls but the most important question is: were the controls actually put into operation and maintained effectively throughout the period in question? To decide the answer to this the auditor must undertake compliance testing. *Compliance testing*, basically, seeks to check that control procedures which have been identified are in practice actually operated, and then to record the evidence of this operation for further audit work and evaluation. Evidence could be, for example, that:

1 authorizations were signed by the appropriate manager;
2 reconciliations balanced correctly;
3 a separation of duties was observed;
4 official pre-numbered receipts were given; and
5 management checks were fully recorded.

A classification of broad types of internal control is given in Table 3.2.

Table 3.2 – A traditional classification of internal controls

Physical: such as strongroom combinations helping to control access to documents, control of keys limiting access to specific individuals.

Accounting: such as financial reconciliations and some non-financial reconciliations, for example the bank reconciliation and reconciliation of say, personnel records to a head count of the payroll: many accounting checks and balances such as arithmetic checks on orders and invoices, cross checks from one source of information to another for example, application forms to credit details, or contract details to payment instructions. The reconciliation of computerized input to output or simple run-to-run totals are often useful as internal controls. It is important to appreciate that in the broad context in which we are using 'accounting' it can apply to financial and non-financial control. Accounting controls in non-money terms are well established in many bodies – many types of stock checks or the way in which work is administered such as cross checks between marketing and production information.

Authorization: these controls highlight a trail of responsibility, usually involving the approval of transactions or other transfers. For example, certification of contractual obligations and purchase orders. or payment invoices. Authorizations together with the ability to agree totals transferred between different records make up the traditional 'audit trail' or 'responsibility trail' concepts essential for anyone questioning the design of a system.

Accounting and authorization controls are particularly likely to be combined in one control operation or duty, such as agreeing an application form to supporting information and then certifying the application for further action.

NB: Computerized evidence of authorization and accounting controls
Although authorizations, reconciliations and similar, are traditionally evidenced in writing, computerized evidence can be equally sound provided it can not subsequently be changed or tampered with in any way. For example, as soon as the authorization is keyed in the person whose password is being used to access the computer might have their initials or log-on code displayed in a 'tamperproof' field, perhaps also automatically generating a paper record for security filing. Often strict password and access/change controls can ensure sound internal control over computerized authorizations. The critical point is to ensure the identity of the officer responsible can not be 'fudged' or deleted and that the relevant record is retained for any statutory period.

Structural: such as clear structure of responsibilities and formal delegated powers determining who can undertake particular duties critical to controlling and decision-making.

Supervisory: these might be classified as structural too, except that supervisory has less permanent overtones. It usually refers to day-to-day arrangements for control via checking and overseeing work of junior staff. For example, supervision of the opening of incoming mail often acts as a control to ensure the completeness of cash and other recorded items.

Separation of duties: primarily to avoid concentrating excessive control responsibility into a single post or narrow function. For example, separate staff are typically responsible for purchasing, custody and recording the transactions relating to incoming goods. The invoice, other documents, or computer records showing a trail of responsibility for authorization of payment might bear evidence of separation between:

the decision to purchase (line management/budget holder);
the placing of an order (buyer/purchasing clerks);
the initial receipt/checking of goods (stores); and
the payment of suppliers (accounts).

Table 3.2 - *concluded*

In practice the line managers may sometimes receive goods direct and usually receive services directly: some goods may be sent direct to a branch or remote site rather than a central stores. Stores personnel may routinely order sundry office supplies and similar fast-moving supplies, referring to line managers only when a change in the 'reorder level' is thought necessary. Size of operation may also restrict separating duties. However, the final decision of how much control to place in a single officer or function is a critical decision for senior managers. Few circumstances justify concentrating all purchasing, custody and payment functions within a single person or office.

Although the separation of duties relating to transactions is particularly important, this must not overshadow the control value of other, sometimes less obvious, separations. For example:

separate responsibility for recruiting and payment of staff;
separation between the computer programming/software development and operations (this is increasingly achieved by buying-in application software); and
separation between earning, and authorizing payment of bonuses or allowances.

It is possible to carry on subdividing organizational controls but they become increasingly difficult to classify into categories that do not overlap and still retain some meaningful distinction. We will draw the line after one more broad category.

Managerial (administrative): these are very diverse. Control can be effected by for example, regular updating of instructions, budget monitoring, some personnel functions particularly formal recruitment procedures. This category is a 'catch all' one likely to overlap with the others above.

If the auditor seeks assurance that the system actually managed to produce accurate and reliable figures or other output, substantive testing is an essential supplement to compliance testing. *Substantive testing* seeks to substantiate the accuracy, validity and completeness of assets, liabilities and transactions that occurred. In almost all audit assignments an element of substantive testing will be undertaken. After all, a system with inadequate control might still have performed well. Sometimes, in contrast, a system with very good controls that operated correctly and effectively for the whole audited period may have missed some unforeseen event. No system is perfectly designed. The amount of substantive testing will usually be determined by the results of compliance testing and the level of assurance the auditor wishes to offer the audited client.

The terms 'control' and 'test' objectives are sometimes found confusing. In fact they are virtually the same. It is important for the auditor to ensure that the control objectives that should have been satisfied by internal controls are still satisfied for each transaction tested substantively. When substantively testing the transactions the term test objectives is often preferred. For example, a control objective in a purchasing system may be that 'all purchases are genuinely required for the organization'. The auditor would usually check that controls exist to ensure all purchases are authorized by a senior officer and that any unusual items are likely to be questioned, perhaps by ensuring a separation of duties is maintained between:

1 custody of the purchased goods;
2 authorization of purchases by a senior officer; and
3 bookkeeping and recording by an accounts section.

If the auditor found, perhaps during compliance testing, that such controls were not operating in the purchases system, he or she would normally (after reporting the fact to management) proceed to undertake some level of substantive testing. The total level of testing would probably be greater than would have been envisaged at the start of the audit. For each purchase transaction the auditor would (among other things) still check it was genuinely required, that is, valid, and therefore satisfied the objective outlined above. In this case the term test objective is commonly used rather than control objective.

REVIEW

Although not separated out as a separate stage in Figure 3.3, review is vital to audit work, both to provide a second more experienced opinion on the work done by more junior staff and to ensure the desired quality of work is maintained. An auditor after all will be delving into the work of others and usually will have less experience or knowledge about their specific working environment and its problems. Review usually involves at least two distinct stages:

First there is one or more 'interim' reviews during the work in progress, often at the early stages to ensure the audit is properly planned and likely to succeed within the time and resources available, and during key points such as when compliance test results are available.

Second there will be a 'final' review by senior audit managers/partners and so on, to ensure that all previous reviews have been through and the final draft report is to their liking.

All the audit evidence should be reviewed from initial documentation through compliance testing to substantive testing. Audit and control objectives should be reconsidered in the light of the auditor's developing knowledge of the system. Any statements by management, replies from circulars or other enquiries sent to debtors and banks, any audit papers from other auditors, any analytical review work (a specialized form of substantive testing) and any other relevant evidence should be considered. Given the importance of carrying out reviews it is usual practice for the reviewer to sign each document reviewed so that there is a clear trail for quality control purposes. The importance of well presented and easy to follow working papers and files soon becomes apparent to anyone new to audit.

OPINION FORMING AND REPORTING

The auditor may well have been forming opinions throughout the audit and these should be annotated as interim conclusions or points for attention at the final review. The final overall opinion may be expressed brie y in a clear external audit certificate or it may be expressed at great length in a major internal audit report. In between these extremes lie various management letters, shorter audit reports, 'reports in the public interest' and so on.

The foregoing stages are, not surprisingly, a gross over-simplification. A systems-based audit may be an end in itself or form part of a wider audit with several systems-based assignments. Some audit work does not fall neatly and easily into the systems-based approach. The boundaries of the auditor's responsibilities are always changing and currently they are expanding into a wider consultancy-type role. Nevertheless this brief outline is essential for an understanding of the basic approach adopted by auditors.

An adapted counter-fraud systems-based approach to audit

For the rest of this chapter we seek to provide an adaptation of the basic systems-based approach designed to emphasize the aspects that will best guard against fraud and corruption. Much of what has already been said will be looked at afresh and from a more selective point of view.

In practice internal and external auditors, particularly in the public services, work to a wide range of audit objectives designed to suit individual clients and assignments. For external auditors most work is aimed at forming a view of the published year end accounts. It is important to stress that for more general audit objectives, particularly attestation audits, value for money audits and broad-based systems audits, this adapted approach would almost certainly be a less than an adequate basis on which to form any professional opinions. The general auditor is far more concerned with 'innocent' errors (often repeated on a large scale), inaccurate or misleading disclosures of accounting information, waste and efficiency, or simply inadequate bookkeeping and management reporting. These wide-ranging concerns will rarely be satisfied simply by ensuring everything possible is being done to prevent fraud and corruption.

We must therefore be selective when dealing with fraud and corruption, though it still helps to start with the basic ORC relationship discussed on pages 43–4.

Using the ORC relationship

Typical examples of high-level audit objectives are summarized in Table 3.3.

Table 3.3 Examples of high-level audit objectives for different types of audit

Systems-based audit
To report upon the reliability of the internal controls operating in the system and the accuracy, completeness and validity of the financial information produced.
To appraise the system, identifying and testing the controls (and weaknesses) most likely to guard against (or exacerbate) risks to the system objectives.
Attestation (for example, external audit opinion) audit
To form an opinion and report on the financial statements (balance sheet, revenue account, and so on) in accordance with statutory and professional requirements (for example, truth and fairness opinion).
To form an opinion and report on the accuracy of a contractor's final account (for example, for local government capital works).
Value for money audit
To report upon the economy, efficiency and effectiveness of public bodies' operations.

The foregoing high-level objectives have been chosen to exemplify the different types of audit undertaken. They are all variants on a theme – forming professional opinions and expressing them in a report to the appropriate level of management. Clearly such high-level objectives could be framed in terms of say, computer audit, fraud investigation and so on and worded to suit particular situations.

The term probity audit is sometimes used to describe the detailed vouching of individual transactions or investigation of an auditor's suspicions of irregularity. Probity audit is generally subsumed under detailed substantive testing.

Using the ORC relationship mentioned earlier, we need to identify and single out the risks and controls that relate to fraud and corruption for special attention. This needs some predictive thought. Clearly, some risks and controls relating to say, cash collection, stock control, payment processing and such like will relate directly to counter-fraud objectives. Many such risks and controls will relate to maintenance-type systems. Other risks and controls will relate to routine management objectives which do not appear to have counter-fraud implications – those relating to say, workload allocations, management of the electoral register system, health and safety systems, and so on. However, fraud and corruption can arise from such a variety of motivations and in so many unexpected ways that one should be wary of writing off any controls as being permanently irrelevant. Rather, having identified, as far as one can, the main risks of fraud in any particular system or organization, it is vital to ensure that controls, often routine in nature, are highlighted for attention. This may be simply a matter of making sure these are singled out for attention during routine audits or collected and collated for separate attention as part of say, a counter-fraud review. (See Table 3.4.)

Table 3.4 Stages of an adapted counter-fraud SBA

1 The high level objectives of audits need to be broken down into sub-objectives and any relating to prevention of fraud and corruption clearly identified for separate attention.

2 Risks (developmental and maintenance) need to be clarified in relation to these objectives.

3 Existing controls and countermeasures relating to these risks need to be singled out for testing (compliance testing).

4 Any apparent lack of controls (that is, weaknesses), need to be the subject of suggested additional controls.

5 Substantive testing needs to be undertaken to see if these weaknesses have led to any occurrence of fraud and/or error.

6 If appropriate in larger or risk prone bodies, a specific organization-wide counter-fraud review along the above lines needs to be undertaken on a system objective by objective basis.

A more detailed look at counter-fraud SBA

In practice it is usually stages 3 to 5 of Table 3.4 that need most time and attention whether as part of a pre-planned audit strategy or on an *ad hoc* basis. Work broadly covering stage 6 is becoming increasingly popular among auditors, particularly since the rise in importance of corporate governance. Let us look at this work in a little more detail.

During a major audit assignment such as the attestation audit of a large set of financial accounts, or during two or three similar internal audit SBA assignments, numerous internal controls will be considered and usually a great deal of testing will be done. The fraud and corruption audit objectives will not, initially, be the primary objectives of the auditor. Later on, if the auditor becomes concerned with fraud and corruption he may well need to plough his way back through a great many working papers and reports.

Much of this effort can be avoided, or at least shortened significantly, by introducing two standard techniques to help work through the stages in Table 3.4: first the compilation of a 'key control questionnaire' at the start of each audit to help with stages 1 to 3; and second the compilation of a fraud and corruption checklist at the end of the audit when all the controls and weaknesses have been fully assessed.

KEY CONTROL QUESTIONS (KCQs)

The auditor's method is, basically, to stand back from the fine detail of the system and in the light of the audit objectives (see Table 3.3), to ask what are the key risks?

The manager can adopt the same approach, though he is more directly concerned with the management objectives of the system: what can go so seriously wrong that the whole or a large part of the purpose of the system is negated? This is why KCQs are sometimes referred to as 'nightmare scenarios'.

Financial systems rarely have more than a few main purposes. Normally these involve the payment of expenses or receipts of income, or both. The guarding of valuable assets including the prevention of disclosure of confidential information, the maximization of benefits (for example, investments) or minimization of losses are other examples. This is why the number of KCQs is usually only three or four, perhaps six at most. The method is best explained in detail by examples.

Example 1 of a KCQ. This is a straightforward sundry creditors' system, the basic objective of which is simply *to pay genuine creditors the correct amount, on time.* Within this basic objective is subsumed concern for proper authorization, trade discounts, the cash ow position of the organization and any other appropriate management objectives.

Can only properly invoiced bills be paid? The general rule is: No invoice, no payment. The invoice must be proper to the organization, not, say, an employee's gas bill, and it must have gone through an acceptable set of authorizing procedures, including checking the calculation of the invoice and agreement, when appropriate, to supporting orders and other documents.

Are only goods and services that have been satisfactorily received or performed paid for? This, again, assumes a reasonable payment authorizing procedure in which some senior officer takes responsibility for certifying satisfaction with the goods or services.

Can only goods or services that were genuinely required by the organization be received or performed? It is not unusual to observe sound controls over payment once, say, work has been done; but was it really necessary, and if so who authorized it? Similarly were all goods, even if they were received in perfect condition, actually ordered by an authorized officer who is confident they will be used in the near future? In recent years the number of 'false billing' agencies has increased. A service such as inclusion in a trade or international directory is usually selected by such agencies as one for which responsibility within an organization is often not immediately apparent. The assumption, often correct, is that one officer will think another has requested the service and no one will expect to be in possession of evidence of the service before making payment.

Is the organization billed for all goods and services properly received? At first the auditor or manager may be tempted to ignore this question. ('If our suppliers forget to bill us – tough! All the more for us!') But there are two serious concerns that this, sometimes a fairly common attitude, ignores. First, any responsible organization, particularly in the public services, has its reputation and goodwill to maintain, both of which can be greatly enhanced by complete honesty towards suppliers. Second, and of greater risk from our viewpoint, the lack of an invoice may indicate fraud and corruption within both the recipient and the supplying organizations, though collusion will be required to perpetuate such a fraud.

Experienced auditors will notice that the questions above are far fewer and more generalized than those that typically make up an internal control questionnaire (ICQ). Also, important key questions that relate primarily to the wider objectives of audit are missing. If we were to list similar non-fraud-type key questions such as: 'Are all payments timed to optimize trade credit and prompt payment discounts?', 'Are all payment amounts accurately and fairly disclosed in the published accounts?', then the selectivity aimed for would be lost.

The purpose of a KCQ is quite different from the more commonly used ICQ. An ICQ helps the auditors to document the system by indicating procedures in detail and what controls are present. The purpose of a KCQ, as we shall see, is to identify the control or test objectives of the audit and thereby the key risks also. Two further examples of KCQs are given below in summary form.

Example 2 of a KCQ. This concerns a payroll system where the following questions may be asked.

1 Can only genuine employees be paid?
2 Are all genuine employees paid the correct amounts?
3 Are all 'leavers' actioned?

One might argue that the third question is not needed as an unactioned leaver would not be a genuine employee, but for the sake of simplicity it is included here.

Example 3 of a KCQ. This concerns a debtors' collection system. The questions here are the following.

1 Are all debts owed raised?
2 Are all debts raised owed?
3 Are all debts raised actioned, that is, paid, cancelled or written off?
4 Are all debts, cancellations and write-offs correctly calculated, coded and authorized?

Again, in example 3 the detailed arrangements for credit control and doubtful debts commonly associated with a full audit of debtors' systems are not covered in this approach for the same reasons of selectivity as noted with the creditors' KCQ.

KCQs are merely a useful first stage in formulating and expressing objectives of the system and its key risks. KCQs can be reworded as key control objectives, basically by expressing the questions as a statement. For the payroll system, example 2, the KCQs can be expressed as the following key control objectives:

Objectives

(a) All employees are genuine, that is, properly authorized.

(b) Only current employees are paid.

(c) Only due amounts are paid/deducted.

(d) All the amounts paid/deducted are correctly calculated.

Related KCQs

(a) = 1 and 3

(b) = 2

(c) = 2 and 3

(d) = 2

Thus the ability to, say, bring about an unauthorized regrading would mean that objective (c) was not met by the controls in the system. Objectives (c) and (d) are similar but should not be confused – a control may ensure all amounts are correctly calculated but not check that they were actually due.

The audit assignment objectives already outlined in Table 3.3 are, in most audits, too broad to assist the auditor in directing his effort when identifying and compliance testing internal controls or carrying out substantive testing of individual transactions. The audit requires system control objectives in line with the audit objectives. These should provide clear beacons toward which the auditor can direct his or her efforts. The control objectives help the auditor decide whether a procedure he or she has identified when documenting a system is simply one among many that are convenient for the processing activities to continue in an orderly manner, or whether the procedure is a key control. *Procedures without which one or more of the control objectives would be seriously impaired are key controls.*

In, for example, a wages system the allocation of a correct code for the paypoint may be required. If this is mis-allocated some payslips may be distributed to, say, the vehicles maintenance section rather than the central accounts section. This would cause some initial inconvenience and no doubt some urgent telephone calls but in the end each employee will get his or her wages and the wages clerk will get a mild ticking-off. This procedure has no material effect on any control objectives listed above and it is not a key control.

However, if the incorrect pay code relates to a point on an incremental grading structure which results in the employee's receiving an ongoing overpayment this would affect objective (c) of the due payment. If, to take another example, procedures relating to the setting up of a new employee and the cancellation of a leaver are not subject to internal controls, then the risk of a 'ghost' employee is substantially increased, affecting the first control objective. Procedures and arrangements that prevent these errors are clearly, in these circumstances, key controls.

If no effective controls are apparent, as is often the case in some smaller or poorly resourced systems, then the control objectives can be taken as test objectives and extensive substantive testing of transactions should be undertaken to achieve the test and thence the audit objectives.

If, as is normally to be expected, effectively designed controls are apparent then these should be compliance tested as part of the client's routine systems-based audit. During compliance testing the auditor tests the operation of the control rather than the detail of the transaction. Thus equal importance is attached to all errors, irrespective of the value of the items being tested. If £5 and £10 vouchers were not correctly authorized the auditor cannot assume that £5000 and £10 000 vouchers, processed in the same system and subject to the same controls, were correctly authorized.

Interpreting the results of compliance testing calls for skill and judgement. This point is of such importance it is worth repeating: the results of compliance testing will help determine the level of substantive testing to be undertaken. A system may, on initial evaluation and documentation, appear to have adequate internal control. But upon completion of compliance testing it may be found that the controls that were initially documented are, in practice, ignored or ineffective. Thus the ultimate effect of compliance testing is to determine the level of substantive testing. Management must be informed of any lack of effective control but only by substantive testing will the auditor know whether or not such lack of control resulted in any fraud or errors in the information produced by the system and used by management for taking important decisions. This is also a particularly important point for the external auditor who verifies information in the accounts. His or her professional reputation may be called into question if their opinion was based upon inadequate testing.

FRAUD AND CORRUPTION CHECKLISTS

These are usually no more than extractions of 'fraud and corruption tests' from the wider body of compliance and substantive testing that usually form the bulk of routine systems-based audits. Such checklists are aimed more at the latter stages of Table 3.4, serving two main purposes:

1 To bring together at the end of one or more audit assignments all those tests that will show the work done to guard against fraud and corruption. This is particularly useful if the risk of malpractice is considered relatively high. The checklist results should clearly highlight any items that give negative testing results.
2 Such checklists are often prepared for each main client body, department or function, as part of the requirements for corporate governance.

It is probably more helpful to use an example to show how such checklists might be compiled and we have done this in case study 3.2.

Summary

This chapter has introduced the reader to some basic audit approaches and suggested ways in which these can be fine-tuned to the requirements of preventing fraud and corruption. The basic ORC relationship is useful in many managerial contexts but particularly so during times of reorganization or other situations in which the relationship between risks and controls are sometimes ignored. The more detailed attention given to auditing may seem a little specialized to some non-audit readers and to auditors it might seem rather basic. But, the main stages – documenting systems, asking KCQs, identifying controls and compliance and substantive testing – are not solely the prerogative of the auditor. Certainly the stages prior to testing are suitable for any manager or other professional concerned to minimize risk of malpractice.

The approach is, at the start, akin to a general manager setting out his or her business objectives, then asking what effect if any the presence or absence of a particular procedure or arrangement will have on achieving these objectives. Those concerned with the operational effectiveness of such controls must then go on to undertake testing. This applies as much to opinions on the effectiveness of measures to guard against fraud and corruption as to opinions on many other aspects of management effectiveness.

CASE STUDIES

The following case studies are chosen to illustrate situations in typical systems-based audits. For readers who feel they need to appreciate a more fully documented SBA, this is given at Appendix 4 in the form of a longer case study, WACI.

CASE STUDY 3.1

CHECKING FOR GHOSTS

Payroll 'ghosts' are a well-known type of fraud. Yet they continue to occur despite all the warning signs. Managers, it seems, have to keep on relearning all the old lessons. The following case study outlines a pessimistic scenario in an attempt to emphasize the variety of possible ways these ghosts can appear.

This case assumes the auditor has come to the end of the full systems-based audit. The main parts of his or her report relating to their approach and detailed findings are considered, showing the control objectives and the inadequacy of internal controls. The case then goes on to discuss the ghost check implemented in response to these very disturbing findings. The ghost check reveals several payroll ghosts and the case discusses how these arose and what detailed precautions should have been taken. The main countermeasures are underlined and a summary of causes is given at the end of the case.

The Warranty Assessment Commissioning Office (WACO) is a (fictional) major agency of a central government department. It employs 3000 civil servants, 1500 at WACO HQ and 1500 at approximately 50 local offices. All officers are monthly paid salaried employees. During holiday periods temporary staff, often students, are taken on.

The chief internal auditor of WACO has received the following, rather disturbing, draft report from one of his or her auditors.

* * * * * *

CONFIDENTIAL REPORT TO DIRECTOR OF WACO

FROM CHIEF INTERNAL AUDITOR

PAYROLL AUDIT 20X4

CONTENTS

CASE STUDY 3.1 *continued*

5. Detailed findings
6. Conclusions *
7. Detailed recommendations *

Appendix 1 – Staff interviewed *
Appendix 2 – Systems documentation *
Appendix 3 – Related reports *

Reference: AB/LG 4007
Date:

* Not included in the case study

1. Introduction

This audit forms part of our agreed five-year audit strategy. The last major payroll audit took place almost exactly three years ago: Ref. DC/70301 dated 2.3 x 9. At that time our findings were generally reassuring and all our recommendations were agreed. Since 2.3 x 9 several interim audits have been undertaken and these are listed at Appendix 3.

3. Audit objective

To form an opinion on the reliability of the internal controls operating over the payroll system, and the accuracy, completeness and validity of the payroll information produced.

4. Audit approach

A full systems-based audit was undertaken. Officers were interviewed as per Appendix 1 and amendments were made to existing systems documentation, see Appendix 2. Internal controls were identified on the basis of control objectives to ensure that:

(a) all employees are genuine;
(b) only genuine employees are paid; and
(c) the amounts paid or deducted are due and correctly calculated.

The controls identified were compliance tested and a sample of the transactions processed were subjected to substantive testing. In this audit the control objectives were not met for the reasons discussed below.

5. Detailed findings:

5.1 The authorization and input to the computerized payroll (online and batch) is undertaken at WACO, although the mainframe computer is shared with several other government offices and is located at London. All output is received via screen, printout hard copy, or secure-courier tapes from which the pay-advice slips are printed. Salaries are paid directly by bank transfer into the payee's bank or building society account.

CASE STUDY 3.1 *continued*

5.2 Appendix 2 shows an outline of the system, including a ow chart on which are listed the key controls and weaknesses.

5.3 Several key controls that were operational during our last audit are no longer so. The main cause of this appears to be the partial introduction of online terminal links to the mainframe computer centre that processes the payrolls. Just over one year ago the first stage in the replacement of batch processing with online terminals was completed. Due to several technical difficulties and inaccurate budget forecasting the second stage, which was due to be completed by next month, has only just started. The third and final stage has been put back until the latter half of next year.

5.4 This means that there are three separate categories of payroll processing currently operating at WACO; online, batch processing, and partial online processing. All payroll processing is also subject to some common procedures and controls irrespective of which category is chosen.

5.5 The staff involved in payroll processing have in many cases changed from our last visit. The general feeling of malaise and confusion generated by the failure to implement changes quickly and effectively is in stark contrast to our former impressions.

5.6 Management's attention should be drawn to the serious weaknesses in internal control identified during our initial evaluation and testing. Additional substantive testing is being undertaken in view of these findings and this may lead to further communications over the coming months.

5.7 Main area of weakness in internal control:

5.7.1 *Insuf cient separation of duties* Several examples were noted of temporary staff having been employed without implementing the usual recruitment procedures involving the personnel department. Examples were also noted of payroll officers with complete responsibility under the online system for inputting starters, changes, leavers, and so on and confirming the accuracy of the consequent output, including salary advice slips. In general, management seemed aware of these breakdowns in separation of duties, and excused them by the need to speed up procedures to deal with the growing backlog of work.

5.7.2 *Inadequate input validation checks* The new software for on-line processing omits any headcount comparison – of staffing levels authorized per division or section – to staff paid per division or section. Under the old batch system of processing this was done automatically prior to production of a payroll. It is also noticeable that no upper-limit checks are performed on individual payments.

5.7.3 *Lack of clearly de ned responsibilities (audit trail)* Apart from the usual difficulties in maintaining an audit trail through the computer, the trail of responsibility for authorizing and processing changes was not always apparent in the 'manual' parts of the system. Although most key documents contained sections for the initials or signatures of the officers responsible for calculating, entering dates, or authorizing changes these were seldom completed by

CASE STUDY 3.1 *continued*

payroll processing sections. Copies of the forms going forward for batch processing were rarely, if ever, sent back to the line division manager or section heads for confirmation that their requirements were being met. This was particularly noticeable in respect of the frequent overtime or 'substitution' duties where it is reasonable to assume that any overpayments to staff would probably remain unnotified.

5.7.4 *Poor control over key documents* Key documents used to input changes were not prenumbered. These documents could easily have been obtained and completed by any one of nearly 100 officers including some with no direct payroll duties. Ideally these documents should be subject to the usual 'secure stationery' controls including stock control sheets with initials of officers issuing and receiving stock. Some key documents were very badly designed, particularly time sheets on which overtime payments were based. These documents contained space for far more entries than were ever likely to be made and none of those examined had been ruled-off prior to or during authorization. Several entries were made in different ink and may well have been written in after signed authorization had been given.

5.7.5 *Lack of direct supervision and management information* In all but one case, team leaders were expected to supervise 8–10 team members without any ability to observe directly the operations carried out. Team leaders were unable to review the documents processed by team members and were in effect no more than team advisers preoccupied with attending to difficult queries from line departments or from the team members themselves. No attempt to monitor work in terms of volume, overtime, or allocation of payroll changes was undertaken, and no attempts to review the changes input by team members were apparent. Management information regarding transaction processing time, volume, or allocated workloads, and so on, was almost completely lacking. The management checks previously performed and recorded (evidenced during our last visit) seemed to have gradually lapsed over the past year to the point where they are no longer undertaken.

* * * * * *

COMMENTARY ON THE REPORT AND ACTION TAKEN

The conclusions and recommendations of this audit report go on to outline the rather obvious improvements required to 5.7.1 to 5.7.5 above. To illustrate how 5.7.1 to 5.7.5 above may be involved in cases of payroll ghosts we shall assume that the chief internal auditor, by now seriously worried about the integrity and accuracy of the payroll, decides to supplement the increased level of substantive testing with a full reconciliation of authorized staff in post to payroll – a so-called ghost check.

This is often not as difficult as it sounds, though it can be rather tedious for the auditor actually performing the reconciliation. Allowing for any peculiarities of organizational structure the following basic steps will usually be undertaken.

1 Choose, say, a recent payroll (any payroll may be chosen but the most recent is usually easiest).
2 Divide into departments (this is usually already done).
3 Obtain staff-in-post listings from personnel department or individual departmental managers as appropriate.
4 Deduct from 3 above any of the chosen month's and subsequent month's starters who could not have been included in the chosen month's payroll. For starters during the chosen month it will be necessary to

CASE STUDY 3.1 *continued*

know the precise date of starting. A computerized payroll will probably require some days' advance notice for a starter's pay to be calculated and included in that month's pay run.

5 Add to 3 above any officers who were officially classed as having left the organization but who were owed money during the month chosen.

It is usually quite difficult to obtain full details of all leavers who are still owed money. Arrears of pay may be discovered several months after an employee has left. The auditor will probably be left with a number of discrepancies relating to payments to former employees, each of which must be investigated. This is one important reason to pick a recent payroll. Also, staff, especially temporary staff recently laid off, may be retained on a payroll and a payment advice – but no cheque – produced each month in anticipation of their re-employment a few months later on.

At this point it should be possible to start reconciling staff-in-post to payroll. In most organizations the above information will be classified departmentally and it may be easier to take each main department at a time. In this case however inter-departmental transfers of staff will need to be identified to avoid double counting. Such an exercise could take several days in a medium-sized government department or local authority depending upon the number of queries.

The ghost check is only reliable when independent and accurate listings of staff-in-post are available. If all listings are prepared by the personnel officer, then any collusion between this officer and the payroll section could invalidate the above steps. If such collusion is suspected it should be possible to perform the ghost check provided that prime documents authorizing staffing levels have been agreed by senior management or political members. In extreme cases of collusion every authorized job description may need to be examined.

Assume that for this case a reliable staff-in-post listing was readily available and that the following ghosts came to light.

COMMENTARY ON THE PAYROLL GHOSTS

A. Realscam

In this, possibly the worst case, one of the payroll team members was able to set up a completely fictitious employee.

A temporary employee, for which only a brief, forged, note from the line department is required on the pay file, was set up. No signature was required on the note and given the accepted lack of separation of duties between personnel and payroll functions no other clerk would be likely to question Realscam's origins. The team member had complete control over input and any changes to the pay details of Mr Realscam. It was a simple matter to open a fictitious bank account in the required name. The lack of supervision and management checks meant that the file created was unlikely to be queried from above. Even if another team member input a routine change to Realscam's pay whilst the perpetrator was, say, on sick leave nothing suspicious would have been apparent. No audit trail of responsibility existed, so when Realscam was revealed by the ghost check the perpetrator(s) could not be identified. Several team members recalled Realscam but no one had any obvious reason in the circumstances to doubt his authenticity.

K.E.E. Pongoing

This was possibly the simplest case to arise. Mr Pongoing was laid off but was not taken off the payroll. Originally this was an oversight, but the clerk who distributed the pay slips took advantage of the situation.

After several months had elapsed without Mr Pongoing notifying WACO

CASE STUDY 3.1 *continued*

of the continuing salary payments into his bank account he was paid a visit by the clerk. Pongoing, who was unemployed, receiving disability allowance and other welfare payments, had by this time spent most of the erroneous salary payments. During a subsequent court hearing he claimed that he had offered to repay what had by then amounted to several thousand pounds, in monthly instalments but had been told by the dishonest clerk that he had to repay the entire amount within 48 hours.

Pongoing panicked and offered a small bribe for the clerk to delay payment. Pongoing was easily intimidated by the clerk. Within a few more months he was to pay over to the clerk in cash almost the whole of each month's salary. The court found that most of the blame lay with the clerk who had misinformed and intimated the relatively vulnerable and gullible Pongoing.

Adequate supervision or selective testing and regular use of management information on payroll changes would almost certainly have detected or more likely deterred this case. Ideally, of course, payroll slips should not be distributed by one clerk on a continuous basis.

R.E. Turn

Mrs Turn had been one of the regular 'temps' with a long history of periodic employment, who was known to have recently left the area. It was not unusual for salary advice slips to be posted to temporary employees who may only work for a few weeks at a time.

A messenger whose duties involved regular visits to the payroll section obtained several loose copies of change authorization forms. The temporary employees were amongst those still subject to batch processing and it was a simple matter to reactivate Mrs Turn with the dishonest employee's address. He had often seen the forms left casually on desks and in files in various stages of completion and it was not difficult to work out how to fill in the correct boxes. No signature needed to be forged, though even if one had, his ready access to complete forms would probably have enabled him to do that too. Once he was satisfied he had completed the forms correctly, all that was required was for it to be slipped into a batch waiting to be keyed in. At this point, very strong batch controls might have detected the crime. But in WACO as in most organizations, if the batch total actually keyed in differs from the expected or recorded totals on the batch header slip it is assumed that an innocent error has occurred. The batch now containing the forged input was checked and the header slip amended. Inadequate input validation ensured no chance existed for the crime to be spotted on processing. Even relatively good validation checking may go no further than reasonableness checks over amounts and check digits, and it is unlikely to reveal anything worse than normal errors.

Once he had set up Mrs Turn the messenger stole more forms to authorize her temporary lay-offs and re-employments. Eventually the processed forms were returned to the payroll section, but as often happens with low priority filing, they were left unfiled for several days. Management said that the filing was delayed due to the backlog of work. In any event, there was plenty of opportunity for the false processed forms to be spirited away by the messenger.

So successful had his fraud become that the messenger had expanded his activities. By the time the ghost check brought them to light, the contents of his locker were found to resemble the payroll stationery cupboard. Three false temps and a full-time civil servant had been ghosted on to the payroll and all were recorded as residing at the messenger's address. The full-time civil servant had

CASE STUDY 3.1 *continued*

started off in the same way as the temps, but had been falsely promoted. This required a forged authorization signature on the false input form and in all probability would have led the messenger into more and more forged documents.

Given the general lack of control the auditors involved were of the opinion that this messenger could probably have continued his crimes undiscovered for some considerable time, though probably not indefinitely, had not the ghost check revealed them.

The most effective deterrent to Mrs Turn and her false colleagues is adequate control over stationery: all input forms authorizing starters, leavers and changes should be pre-numbered and a simple stock register of all issues and the receiving officers kept. Any spoils, cancellations, and so on, should be recorded by the officer responsible for holding the forms, which should be filled or ticked-off in numerical order upon return after processing.

It is often a remarkable fact that although organizations go to great length to safeguard, say, cash and leave a trail of responsibility for its handling, routine documents that can give rise to far greater losses are subject to quite inadequate controls.

The examples given above could be added to by many auditors familiar with payroll systems and the frauds sometimes involved. A summary of the causes of these cases and other plausible cases, brought to the author's attention at various times, is given in Table 3.5.

Table 3.5 Summary of possible cases of ghosts

The complete ghost

The lack of either adequate separation of duties or close supervision combined with complete autonomy over inputting major changes enabled Mr Realscam to be perpetrated. Even a completely false file existed on Realscam which though it may still have been compiled by a determined fraudster was made easier by the inadequate control of key forms.

Delayed termination

These cases like Mr Pongoing, are almost self-explanatory and are probably one of the most common cases of ghosts, especially when former employees are likely to be re-employed.

Back from the dead

This Mrs Turn type of case usually requires more nerve on the part of the perpetrator. Although it is similar in many ways to delayed termination, it can be made to appear accidental.

The partial ghost

These are variants on the above but a genuine payee exists. Usually the genuine payee is given a false promotion or special allowance, is laid off a few days late, or there is a similar partial enhancement of payment. Often an error can occur which leads a payee or payroll clerk – or both in collusion – to perpetrate the false payments.

The on-off ghost

This type relies on frequent changing demand for labour. Again, like the partial ghost it may occur by accident. But to be perpetuated on a significant scale or for more than a few payments at least one party must behave dishonestly.

CASE STUDY 3.1 *concluded*

The parts of the detailed report not shown in this case explain to management how the audit and control objectives relate to maintaining a secure system and achieving the laid-down management objectives. These parts of the report are heavily dependent upon the nature and specific objectives of the organization and go far beyond our concern for preventing fraud and corruption. For these reasons, and to maintain anonymity, the full report is not outlined in this case study. The measures underlined in the above cases largely correspond to the conclusions and recommendations of the report.

CASE STUDY 3.2

RISCASHIRE COUNTY COUNCIL

This case illustrates how a fraud and corruption checklist might be compiled, from audits undertaken throughout an organization. The checklist might be compiled at the audit planning stage to ensure that all areas thought potentially at risk are covered. But it is more usually compiled at the end of an audit, at the review stage, to give an overview of the total risk of fraud and corruption.

The external audit manager has embarked upon his final review of the X3/4 audit of this authority. One of the overall responsibilities is that every three years the measures and controls to guard against fraud are reviewed.

Her approach is to review all the audit programmes currently in use, including this year's amendments, selecting tests that are of particular relevance in guarding against fraud and corruption. She will need to assess the results of these tests separately from the rest of this testing. This is because testing is designed largely to give assurance on the accuracy of balance sheet and revenue account figures in order to satisfy her overall audit objective of forming an opinion on the accounts. She uses best judgement to rank each test result as per Table 3.6 with a 'score' depending upon the frequency and significance of compliance and substantive errors.

She scores the risk as 0 for no errors, 1 if the acceptable level is reached for compliance or substantive testing; 2 if the acceptable level is reached for both compliance and substantive testing; 3 if below the acceptable level is reached for either type of testing, and so on up to 6.

In addition to reviewing the audit programmes, the auditor also reviews any known areas of fraud or high risk from previous years' work and investigations and reports related to fraud.

It is not feasible to reproduce all the accumulated audit programmes that might be used on an external audit for a major local authority. An indication of the number and detail of such programmes is given by the Audit Approach section of the Audit Commission Auditor, available from the Audit Commission for local and health authorities in England and Wales. In practice many audit programmes and adaptations may be devised by internal audit sections, individual firms or district auditors, to suit the needs of particular authorities. The following examples, one of compliance tests and one of substantive tests, have been chosen merely to complete a realistic illustration of the stages involved from Tables 3.6 to 3.8, that is, ranking the error scores, using compliance and substantive tests, and preparing a summary checklist of the scores.

CASE STUDY 3.2 *continued*

Table 3.6 Error scores

	Score	*Compliance errors*	*Substantive errors*
High risk	6 5	Errors that indicate the controls tested did not operate throughout the period	Errors that contribute to breaching materiality for this account and likely to be recurring
Beyond acceptable level	4 3	Errors indicate control did not operate for a substantial period or over a substantial volume of items	Numerous or high value errors or errors likely to be recurring
Acceptable level	2 1	Very few errors that have affected only a few isolated low-value items	Very few errors of low value and unlikely to be recurring
Low risk	0	Nil errors	Nil errors

Table 3.7 Example test programmes

Compliance test programme capital works contracts

Prepared by: .... Reviewed: .... Encl. Ref: ....
Date: .... Date: .... File Ref: ....

Objective: To determine whether or not the internal controls identified in our systems documentation and evaluation (File x-3–4) have operated effectively throughout the period .... to ....

Control objectives	*Control reference (see Flow chart)**	*Test*	*Comment and cross-reference to working papers**
All contracts were necessary	Page 1 Point 3	1. Ensure each contract file has a feasibility and cost/benefit report if contract value exceeded £100 000. 2. For all contracts over £100 000 and a judgemental selection of those under that amount, ensure there was a full report to the relevant committee which recommended implementation.	
All contracts were adequately authorized	Page 1 Point 6	As test 2 above; 3. Each page of contract general conditions and detailed specifications is signed by chief executive and chairman of the	

CASE STUDY 3.2 *continued*

Table 3.7 – *continued*

Control objectives	*Control reference (see Flow chart)**	*Test*	*Comment and cross-reference to working papers*
		relevant committee after detailed scrutiny by senior architect/engineer/quantity surveyor as appropriate.	
	Page 1 Points 7 and 8	4. All variations to contract must be examined and agreed by architect/engineer/quantity surveyor as appropriate who must sign a variation order. All variations over £5000 or 5 per cent of contract value must be approved by the relevant committee.	
All contracts were let on a fair basis between contractors invited to tender	Page 2 Point 10	5. Procedures for inviting tenders are vetted for compliance with standing orders by internal audit who compile working papers on each. (Standing orders relating to contracts are already designed to encourage fair letting of contracts.)	
	Point 12	6. All select lists of contractors are approved by the relevant committee.	
	Point 14	7. At least 25 per cent of firms on select list must be invited for each contract. Each firm must be invited to tender for at least 25 per cent of contracts.	
	Point 16	8. Identical tender conditions and specifications are given on the same day to all firms invited to tender.	
	Page 3 Point 18	9. All tenders received are logged upon receipt by the 'post clerk'.	

CASE STUDY 3.2 *continued*

Table 3.7 – *continued*

Control objectives	*Control reference (see Flow chart)**	*Test*	*Comment and cross-reference to working papers*
	Point 21	10. All tenders received are opened at the same time by chairman of committee, clerk, chief architect/engineer and one other member or senior officer and a schedule of tender sums is prepared by the clerk and signed by all of the above.	
	Points 22/23	11. If the lowest tender is not accepted the reasons must be set down in a report to the relevant committee.	
	Point 25	12. The schedule and report at 10 and 11 are reported, in summary, in the public minutes of the relevant committee.	
All contract work conformed to contract conditions		As per 4 above;	
	Point 27	13. Each stage payment is checked and certified by a quantity surveyor.	
	Point 29	14. All contract final accounts are subject to checking and certification by a quantity surveyor.	
		15. All contract final accounts are subject to attestation audit by internal audit who check performance against contract conditions.	
	Point 33	16. A 'performance bond' of 10 per cent is required from the successful contractor.	
	Point 34	17. A retention of 10 per cent is made until the expiry of the 'defects' period.	
		18. Provision for liquidated damages is enforced.	

CASE STUDY 3.2 *continued*

Table 3.7 – *continued*

Control objectives	*Control reference (see Flow chart)**	*Test*	*Comment and cross-reference to working papers*
	Page 4 Point 40	19. All site visits by architect/ engineer/quantity surveyor are recorded and signed in site visit log.	
	Point 43	20. All contracts over 3 months duration have monthly progress reports filed by clerk of works.	
		21. All contracts have a post-completion assessment report signed by an architect or engineer not responsible for contract letting or performance prior to payment of final account.	

*Not reproduced herein

Substantive test programme grants for tree planting

Prepared by: .... Reviewed: .... Encl. Ref: ....
Date: .... Date: .... File Ref: ....
Objective: To gain direct substantive evidence of the accuracy, completeness and validity of the grant payment. .... to ....

Test objectives	*Control reference**	*Test*	*Comment and cross-reference to working papers**
	File H/3/3	Examine application forms; selected on a judgemental basis to cover the whole year and all areas of Riscashire. Check that:	
Only eligible applicants are approved for grant	H.17	1. Applicant is eligible according to statutory requirements (set out in H17). In particular:	4C
		(i) trees of species listed;	
Paper		(ii) location is close to a public highway (check with OS map* attached); and	4E
		(iii) land is not adversely affected by local plans.	

CASE STUDY 3.2 *continued*

Table 3.7 – *concluded*

Test objectives	*Control reference**	*Test*	*Comment and cross-reference to working papers*
	H.19	2. The applicant owns the land (see copy of title) or is a tenant with fixed leasehold of at least 25 years unexpired.	
	H.23	3. The applicant has certified and dated the claim.	
Grant is in accordance with laid-down condition and calculated correctly	H.25	4. An initial inspection report was prepared and signed by a senior officer to recommend or amend the applicant's claim and planting proposals prior to committee approval.	
	H.26	5. Committee approval (land and amenity) was given and that budget was not exceeded. Check the arithmetic of the grant claim and agree to committee approval for £X for the individual named.	
Grant is given to correct applicant for agreed works	H.28	6. Expenditure listed on output tabulation under code H21573-B agrees for each grant selected – name, amount, address and brief description.	
	H.35	7. A post-completion report was prepared and signed by a senior officer other than the one at 4 above no sooner than 12 months after the payment of the grant. This report confirms the locations, species and area covered as per original grant application and inspection report.	
		8. Inspect a selection of sites and compare to initial inspection report.	

* Not reproduced herein
• Tests 3, 4 and parts of 5 and 7 also relate to the compliance test programme

CASE STUDY 3.2 *continued*

One could continue thinking of examples of internal controls and compliance tests, especially in relation to capital works where procedures are usually both complex and tailored to meet the specific needs of each authority. To keep this case manageable the reader is asked to accept the above test as being adequate for Riscashire's circumstances.

For her checklist the auditor selects from the first example of the compliance test programme the following tests as particularly relevant in Riscashire's case in guarding against fraud and corruption: 2 to 5, 7 to 14, and 19.

In fact all the tests in this programme may, in certain circumstances, be relevant in helping to prevent fraud and corruption. Capital contracts are notoriously prone to fraud and the audit programme will almost inevitably include a large proportion of key tests designed to cover fraud and corruption. Those selected above have been chosen on their general applicability rather than the 'but what if' scenario of any particular fraud.

The next audit programme has been chosen to illustrate a case where relatively few tests relate to fraud and corruption.

Unlike capital works contracts it is usually the case that few tests relating to tree planting grants are designed primarily to guard against fraud and corruption and the auditor must be careful not to miss any that are relevant.

The auditor selects 1, 3, 7 and 8 for inclusion in her checklist. Although all of the above tasks might help prevent a particular instance of fraud or corruption only 3, 7 and 8 have significant general applicability in this respect. Most of the other tests relate to detailed statutory or arithmetical checks which, given the small value of any one claim, are unlikely to reveal serious errors in total.

The importance of 3 and 7 is that for a fraudulent claim(s) to be processed three individuals would need to collude – the applicant and the two reporting officers. This level of collusion, though possible, is generally considered unlikely due to the scale of corruption required. Certainly if such collusion occurred it is difficult to see how any system could prevent fraud.

The majority of systems are likely to fall somewhere between the two programmes outlined above.

Table 3.8 Summary of the scores from selected fraud and corruption tests

Systems test selected	*1st*	*2nd*	*3rd*	*4th*	*5th*	*nth*	*Average*
Debtors	0	0	0	1	0	0	0.29
Cash collected	0	0	0	0	0	0	0.13
Creditor	0	0	0	0	2	0	0.31
Central purchasing	0	0	0	0	0	0	0.09
Salaries	0	0	1	0	0	0	0.03
Grants (trees)	0	0	0	–	–	0	0.00
Wages	0	5	4	0	0	0	1.25
Grants (students)	0	0	0	0	0	0	0.03
Loans	1	0	0	0	2	0	0.27
Capital works	0	1	0	0	0	0	0.73
Investments	0	0	0	–	–	0	0.00

CASE STUDY 3.2 *concluded*

Let us assume that in this case the auditor has examined the main systems for Riscashire and selected compliance and substantive tests judged to be particularly relevant to her checklist.

She has reviewed the results of testing for each test and uses a method of scoring along the lines suggested in Table 3.6. Setting out her results in the matrix illustrated in Table 3.8 immediately highlights any potentially risky areas.

In this case high risks are indicated by two tests in the wages system. The matrix also gives some measure of overall comparison between systems – the average score. By comparing the results of such checklists over several years a relatively comprehensive fraud risk profile of each main system might be constructed.

Concluding points

It was necessary at the beginning of this chapter to outline the systems-based approach to audit for the benefit of non-auditors. The adapted version of the systems-based approach enables the auditor or manager to concentrate on those aspects most generally useful in preventing fraud and corruption either during the audit or towards the close of the audit when most of the evidence from testing is available.

The two case studies have been set within typical audit situations which have been chosen to illustrate how weaknesses in the system may lead to examples of fraud and corruption. It is most important that the manager or auditor appreciates not simply how the examples arose in the case studies but what should have been done to prevent any repetition.

The overall message of this chapter is that a well-planned and well-executed systems and risk-based audit encourages a secure system and will go a long way towards preventing fraud and corruption.

Two appendices, 4 and 5, relate to this chapter, and are included largely for the benefit of the non-audit professional who wishes to gain a greater insight into SBA and typical internal controls. The first is a detailed example of the documentation used during a typical SBA, in this case the audit of weekly paid wages. The documentation used in practice will vary between auditors but it is hoped that the example here is reasonably typical of the genre. Comments on the actions taken and findings are made as the case proceeds. The second appendix is a series of internal control grids, which are designed to give a high level overview of typical internal controls against risks to typical corporate objectives.

CHAPTER

4 Capital Projects and Major Contracts

Introduction

This chapter is about major capital works contracts and revenue-based contracts for outsourced services. It also considers the relationship between the public and private sectors in undertaking these contracts.

Major capital works contracts are particularly important and often account for massive, long-term capital investment budgets in the public services. Revenue contracts, considered later in this chapter, are not tackled in quite as much detail as capital works because, once set up, they are more akin to ordinary purchases and creditor payments, both of which are dealt with more fully in Chapter 6. The main differences usually involve replacing the usual purchase order with a more formal and detailed contract entered into at the start of the contract period, and the need to monitor performance. The supply of refuse collection, computer services, or whatever, will usually be invoiced in the usual way and should be thoroughly checked. The checking of many revenue contracts for services can indeed be relatively complex, requiring procedures by the client to reassure themselves that the service is being delivered to the required standard. But essentially the risks of fraud for ongoing revenue-based payments can usually be considered in a similar manner to routine payments to any other creditors.

Major capital works contracts

These usually take up by far the most time in contract design, vetting, control and audit work. For many organizations they are of much greater risk and value than any other single area of expenditure, capital or revenue. Capital works contracts nearly always involve relatively high risks of corruption. The amounts of money (and potential profits) are very high and quite often a lucrative public services contract can mean the difference between financial success or ruin for a company. In these circumstances the pressure that can be brought to bear upon public servants and their political masters may be enormous.

Any major capital contract from irrigation schemes to road building, but particularly building works, can be split into ten convenient headings. These are discussed as this chapter progresses.

The headings often cover activity over several years, from establishment of needs to past contract assessment. Anyone, manager or auditor, seeking to prevent fraud and corruption should consider all stages. Unfortunately familiarity with all stages of a project is unlikely to be maintained by a single manager. (Figure 4.1 outlines in very broad terms the main activities covered under the headings excluding freedom of information and planning issues, which are considered in the text.)

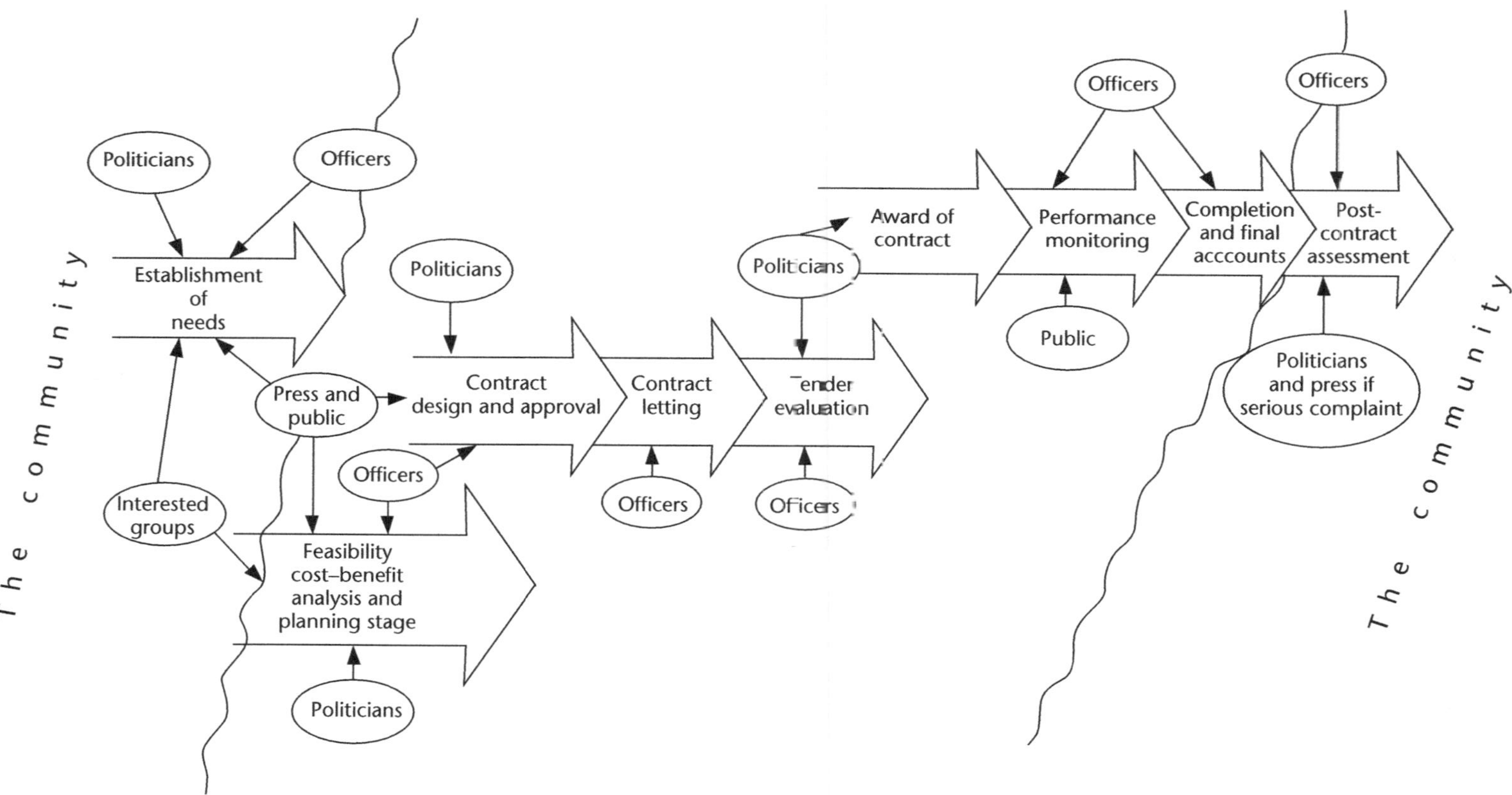

Figure 4.1 The main activities covered in major capital works contracts

ESTABLISHMENT OF NEEDS

This is essentially a political stage although in practice many of the needs are of an uncontroversial and often recurring nature. Good examples of these are cyclical building maintenance works, which may be almost permanently enshrined as part of a basic property maintenance strategy. Very few politicians would question the need to maintain valuable housing stock, schools, hospitals, office buildings, drainage facilities and so on, whether they ultimately intend to retain or dispose of these assets.

The need for new capital works – hospitals, sea defences, military installations, roads and tunnels – is, in contrast, often highly controversial.

Political debate on such new works may well extend to any future capital and ongoing revenue implications.

FREEDOM OF INFORMATION TO INTERESTED PARTIES

Provided debate is informed, open and democratic the risk of corruption in the conventional sense can be reduced quite significantly. It may be argued that a project will benefit few at the expense of many, or that it is an act of unjustified waste, or whatever. Many politicians interpret the deeply held views of others to be, say, a corrupting in uence on society, or harmful to the natural environment. Such stances cannot be ignored, but they are outside the scope of this work and it is left to the reader to exercise his or her own values and principles. Nevertheless, the opening up of debate on the needs, costs and motives of a capital project to close political scrutiny can act as a deterrent to overt favouritism and various other corrupt practices.

Occasionally public officials may, despite the normal low of the launch, encounter significant attempts or pressures to sti e information – information that, if it is not covered by the Official Secrets Act 1989, would normally be openly available to the press and public. Such attempts to sti e information may well be driven by financial corruption.

At this point it is interesting to consider the oft-mentioned differences between central government and most other public services organizations. Any organization is likely to recoil at the thought of its errors, omissions, follies and (assuming they occur) frauds or acts of corruption being made public. Those in positions of power may try to bring pressure to bear to sti e embarrassing information. Central government bodies can bring serious threats of prosecution and imprisonment to bear on any insiders who release such information – consequences that reach over and above any of the more usual threats such as loss of current job or promotion prospects. This undoubtedly places central government departments and the ministers in charge of them in a far more powerful and less accountable position *vis-à-vis* corruption than other public bodies.

It is true that in other public bodies officials, acting perhaps under pressure from political members or appointees, may also act to suppress information that would otherwise be treated as being in the public domain. But apart from a very few exceptions (such as sections of the Local Government Act 1972 applying to council meetings where matters relating to the confidential affairs of individuals or companies are to be discussed) the law gives more support for the freedom of information from other public bodies and makes suppression of embarrassing information more difficult than would otherwise be the case. For example, the Public Interest Disclosure Act 1999 covers 'whistle blowing', the Data Protection Act 1998 guarantees the right of access to computerized personal records in most circumstances under which these are held. The Local Government (Access to Information) Act 1985 also gives the public certain rights of access to local government.

The important question in most circumstances is: does the act of withholding information constitute or encourage fraud and corruption as generally understood and defined by the Acts discussed in Chapter 1? The dividing line between corruption in a financial sense for personal monetary gain and corruption in a more general political sense is easy to miss. In the public services the manager and the auditor must be sensitive to this distinction.

PLANNING AND RELATED ISSUES

This question of withholding information is part of a wider question of taking corrupt or unfair advantage of information, whether or not it is eventually released. Large-scale developments that require planning permission and are subject to building control regulations will involve tenderers in complex exercises estimating the costs of work to arrive at their final bid. The officers handling such developments can have access to valuable information which should be kept secure at all times.

An obvious con ict of interest arises if a politician or public servant has a fiduciary interest in any of the companies attempting to obtain planning permission or to estimate the costs of work or the value of rival bids. Many of the examples of fraud involve collusion between private firms and public servants. Such hidden interests are virtually impossible to uncover, unless things go wrong for the colluders (or their friends, colleagues, family, and so on) and they start talking to the press, police, senior managers or others. Various official lists of the interests of politicians are indeed held. Public servants are generally required to declare any interests they or their immediate family may hold in outside firms who do business with public bodies. But it is very unlikely that anyone, politicians or officials, would declare an interest if they intend to perpetrate a fraud. Of course the requirement for such declarations may have a deterrent value but this value, if it exists, is virtually impossible to measure.

Both freedom of information and, at the planning stage, general publicity and public awareness of interests and intentions, are an inherent, if still limited, safeguard in avoiding the opportunity for corruption. Where appointed members or public officials have it within their own powers to decide on major developments involving large sums of expenditure the risk of corruption is increased. All these considerations apply before the decision to go ahead and they can involve a high level of risk. After this decision the number of opportunities for fraud and corruption are generally increased, though it is often the case that many of these opportunities relate to lower value frauds.

FEASIBILITY AND CONTRACT DESIGN

For new projects these two closely related stages (Figure 4.1) are very important. There are always risks that consultants or in-house professionals will undertake or recommend work that is not really required or recommend specifications that are likely to give advantage to a contractor they favour, possibly their own colleagues. This is particularly so if the client has not set out detailed, clear and unambiguous requirements. To a large extent issues of corruption at this stage of a major project overlap with issues of value for money (VFM). Feasibility should involve a cost–benefit analysis – how do differing designs compare? What are the likely future revenue implications of the designs? If good VFM is being achieved the scope for corruption is generally reduced. Specifications that are limited to genuine needs, rather than included merely in the hope of deterring competition with or from particular firms, are more likely to produce a design that is cost-effective. Whether or not the cost can be afforded or is less than the potential benefits (that is, cost-efficient) is of course entirely another matter, more the concern of the management accountants.

CONTRACT LETTING

At this stage measures to prevent fraud and corruption change from broad consideration of principle and overall arrangements, such as freedom of information and open debate, to more detailed considerations of individual procedures, in particular procedures that constitute key internal controls.

At the outset of contract letting decisions must be made about the number of firms to be invited and the basis of tender. To some extent the law lays down requirements; for example, European Community directives currently adopted by the UK require contracts over a certain amount to be advertised in the *European Journal*. The amount is varied over time according to the exchange rate between the pound sterling and the Euro.

Tenders are sometimes invited on a purely open or public notice basis. It is often argued that this is the fairest method. Provided sufficient notice and reasonable details of the value and nature of the work are widely notified in, say, the professional journals applicable to the type of contractors, all contractors who might possibly be interested get a chance to make their interest known. However, unless the work required is of a very specialized nature or the market supply is, for some other reason, hard pressed to meet existing commitments, then most organizations usually restrict detailed tendering to a limited number or select list of contractors. This is often quite reasonable on practical and cost grounds, though the list may well be selected from the most promising replies received from a public notice. For this reason the selection procedure must be fully recorded, for example, by committee minutes, and seen to be fair. Quite often those who replied to any initial notice will be sent a project specification, including computer hardware requirements, building designs and materials, safety requirements and so on, depending on the nature of the work. At this stage some initial respondents may withdraw.

Sometimes permanent select lists are maintained of firms who are approved for work within certain categories and to certain cost limits. All or some firms may be chosen from the lists by various selective methods. At this point it is not difficult to see the risk of corruption starting to increase. How does a firm get approved? How does a firm move from a relatively minor list for, say, small value property repairs to major construction projects? Who selects the firms to be invited to tender from the current list? Who decides the criteria for regular selection? Who decides when a firm is dropped from a list and the reasons? The issue of who makes such decisions – an individual senior officer, a group of officers, a committee – become less critical the more the reasons for the decision are fully documented and guided by objective criteria.

Consider for a moment the relative risks of a senior officer, perhaps an architect, accountant or engineer, or perhaps a generalist civil servant who is given complete freedom to choose firms (or even a single firm where market response is slow or unpredictable). Compare these risks to the risks where he or she (or they) are required at least to:

1 include in a list any company given a positive financial vetting by an independent party, for example, internal auditors or credit rating agencies;

2 include the company that won the last similar contract let and was not significantly penalized for poor work or failing to meet deadlines;
3 include at least four other firms on a rotating basis so that all the list is covered, for example, over a given number of projects years and so on depending upon the nature, value and complexity of the work, past histories and any legal requirements.

In both the private sector and the public services, practical requirements and past experience often dictate the need to select firms to tender. But in the public services, often lacking a motive to maximize or optimize profits, the old adage about 'all power corrupting and absolute power corrupting absolutely' is particularly apposite. If this seems to necessitate a less efficient organization bound more than most by red tape the appearance is a short-term view. In the long run dishonesty in public services affairs usually leads to even greater inefficiencies than a little red tape. The important point is not who selects firms to tender or even if every possible interested firm is invited. Rather it is how the selection is undertaken and how it can be shown to be fair. Impartiality must be shown from the decision to use contractors for all or part of a project to the compilation of a shortlist, to the final awarding of the contract, whether 2 or 200 tenders are received. To help achieve this, certain procedures and precautions are (or should be) virtually standard throughout all public bodies:

1 The tender should be in a standard form for all tendering firms. In many building and engineering works standard forms are issued by the Joint Contracts Tribunal (JCT), the Institution of Civil Engineers (ICE) or the government where conditions such as Government Conditions – GC/Works/1/2 and so on – are used. These certainly make it less likely that disputes will arise and the room for fraudulent behaviour (by either party) is reduced. However, non-standard tenders are also used, especially for projects at the upper end of the cost scale or where the client does not have requirements normally catered for by building and engineering works contracts. Projects of a 'design and build' nature are becoming increasingly popular, particularly among local and health authorities. In this case the final specification that would otherwise have been part of the standard tender documents varies between each contractor according to the design. Various gradations of specifications from basic building specifications laid down by an in-house design team to short policy-type statements may be used. An important point in minimizing risks of corruption is that identical initial specifications are given to each contract at the same time.
2 Any pre-tender site visits should be strictly controlled and open to all contractors. This is also true when tendering for service contracts such as cleaning, leisure services or catering. If all contractors are not shown the whole site and conditions at the same time or at least subject to the same facilities and constraints over inspection some are likely to complain at a later date that they were treated unfairly. This precaution is rather in the same vein as freedom of access to information mentioned earlier.
3 If a contractor requires additional information and this request is granted, the same information should, for obvious reasons of equity, be sent to other contractors.
4 All tenders should be received by a specified deadline and held securely and unopened until a specified opening time. Opening should be in the presence of independent officers, that is, not officers representing any in-house team or involved up to that point in the tendering process. Usually a senior executive, a political member (such as a committee chairman or junior minister) could be expected to be included in membership or a tender

committee for major contracts. Some organizations send identical envelopes inside which the tender should be returned, thus hoping to make it more difficult to spot and presumably delay or destroy a particular tender. In practice this is unlikely to occur once tenders have been received and in any event most tender envelopes will have differing postmarks.

5 The tender documents should be signed by all members of the opening committee to avoid any risk of substitution at a later date.
6 The bottom line results are usually summarized and most importantly sent to each firm that asked to tender (without the names of rival bidders). In this way if a tender has been altered or prevented from arriving on time or at all, the firm concerned will be able to raise the alarm.

TENDER EVALUATION

Contract letting merges into tender evaluations as soon as the details of the bids or the presentations of the schemes are known. Evaluation may be a brief arithmetical exercise to find the contractor with the lowest cost or highest offer. However, even fairly simple cases can involve casting and cross-casting rates and bills of quantities to ensure the final summary used to compare each contractor is arithmetically correct. If this is not the case the client organization then needs to decide if any inaccuracies are immaterial and do not affect the result of the comparison. It is not usually considered unfair to contact the contractor for clarification if in the final analysis it is merely his arithmetic or typing that is in question, always provided he is not given any indication of the results of the tender comparison.

At the other extreme, evaluation of tenders can be complex and highly subjective. Cost–benefit techniques may help give politicians and other decision-makers an idea of the measurable costs and benefits involved in, say, a design and build scheme. But different contractors may submit different designs and in any event many of the matters finally debated by political members are unlikely to be easily quantifiable. Hence in all but the most simple of schemes evaluation is thrown back into the political arena and freedom of information and open debate should once again provide a measure to help prevent fraud and corruption.

It is often the case that questions of corruption arise some time after any debate or evaluation. For this reason any evaluation, particularly any cost–benefit analysis, should be fully recorded as should the minutes of debates. Any accusation however apparently trivial should be documented together with the action taken. These measures are as much for the benefit of the parties accused as any reply to the party making the accusation.

CONTRACT AWARDING

The actual awarding of a contract might appear a simple matter of writing to successful bidders and notifying them of their good fortune and the date from which the contract is to commence. But even here risks can arise.

If the start date has not been set out precisely in the specifications any delay could prove costly. Even if it has, only a severe delay is likely to be worth a retender. Quite a high proportion of building contracts are delayed at the start. These initial delays and any subsequent delays may be the subject of claims for 'liquidated damages' usually at so much per day. Site access, working conditions and disturbances to nearby land and property should, ideally, all be covered in the contract. It is surprising how, once the contract has been awarded, ironing out arrangements for such items as works sanitations, hours and conditions of work, commencement date, access to site by client employees, and so on can lead to costly delays. It might be asked: what have these issues to do with fraud and corruption? The answer is, hopefully, not much. Yet the dividing line between poor drafting or poor management and deliberate and possibly fraudulent delay is often difficult to define.

PERFORMANCE MONITORING

Similar difficulties in interpretation and measurement can arise throughout the monitoring of a contractor's performance. The split between the client and the contractor(s) must be maintained at all levels if a public services body is not to be accused of unfairness and corruption. Throughout the period of the contract the client officers will come under pressure, often from former colleagues and others with whom they have done business for many years, to overlook contractor error, agree to extensions of time, and so on. Disputes will arise between client and contractor as to the nature of the blame for, say, delays or poorly provided services. It is common practice to issue warnings and penalty points against a contractor for failing to meet such performance standards as response times in emergency work, meeting completion dates, and various quality measures. In these circumstances certain key controls should be in place throughout the period of the contract.

Separation of duties between client and contractor

This may seem obvious beyond need of reiteration, but many contractors offer consultancy and other expert-related services in design and management of contracts. If the client is tempted to employ these or is unaware of the links between an apparently independent consultancy and a contractor then serious con icts of interest will arise. Separation should be maintained when an in-house team such as a works Direct Services Organization (DSO) wins the contract. Separation may be more difficult when client and contractor staff share the same premises but, unless it is decided not to invite other contractors, then a lack of separation will almost invariably give rise to accusations of bias and unfairness if not of outright fraud. This is particularly so when certifications such as for variation orders are prepared and a quantity surveyor, architect or engineer certifies the reasons for extra work. All such measurements and calculations must be done independently of the contractor.

Site visits

Details of all site visits by client managers, auditors or other non-contractor experts should be fully documented, signed and dated. In any later dispute such records may, though not compiled for the purpose, shed important light on an argument. This is in any event good management but the lack of properly documented inspection is a great encouragement for any potential fraudsters.

Management reports

Regular and timely management reports (including summaries of cost against budget, variation orders, extensions, claims for damages, betterments and quality controls, and so on) should be received and evidenced as to the action taken. The first sign of fraudulent activity is often failure to meet work schedules or overruns of cost without reasonable explanations or even without signed variation orders or time extensions. Even worse, contract management may rely upon exception reporting, usually by professionals who themselves may rely upon exception reporting by their juniors. The great disadvantage of exception reporting is that the reporting official is required to stick out his or her neck and carry the full blame for drawing attention to poor or corrupt practices among their colleagues. This is entirely different and requires a great deal more independence and strength of character than making out a regular report that is a normal part of one's job. The main advantage of exception reporting applies to automated or regular processes whereby (assuming exception does not become the norm) senior managers are usually forced to act.

Exception reporting on major contracts is not like exception reporting on automated industrial or clerical processing. On major contracts time budgeting and production measurement involve considerable subjective judgement and an unplanned overrun can often be genuinely unforeseen and no cause for alarm. The precise stage of completion of a major building work can rarely be specified to the same level of precision as the production of a mechanical component or the processing of a benefit claim. This is even more the case where major public works are of an unusual nature, indeed possibly unique. For these reasons regular management reporting is generally of more value in combating fraud and corruption than exception reporting, provided of course management take properly recorded action.

Site records

Site records should be up to date and available for inspection. Site visits – arranged with senior management – should be at short notice and all records should be available for inspection. Inspection details will vary enormously between contracts but some attempt should be made to verify stage payments to date and work in progress.

Deliveries

Deliveries to site, requisition from stores and stock control of site stores should be authorized and controlled as described in Chapter 6. Basically all deliveries, stock measurements and any damage/returns should be subject to signed authorization with appropriate delegations of value.

Performance bond

It is fairly standard practice for the contractor to provide a performance bond. This is unlikely to prevent or deter fraudulent actions but may provide some recompense if a fraud on the part of the contractor can be proved to have had a detrimental effect on the client.

Unusual payments

Various unusual payments and claims, for example, for unforeseen circumstances, ex gratia amounts, direct payments from client to subcontractors, should be treated with caution and only authorized by the highest level of client management. If monies are being paid that were not even envisaged in the original contract then the chain of public accountability from politician, via the officers acting as client to the contractor may be broken. In short anything that does not come within the direct scope of the bill of quantities, certified variation orders under the term of the original contract or any specifications forming part of the original contract should be fully explained and agreed by senior managers and, if significant, by political members.

COMPLETION AND FINAL ACCOUNTS

Final accounts, despite being the accounts of the contractors, may be prepared by senior in-house specialists such as quantity surveyors or third party consultants. This is one significant area where internal auditors may undertake attestation audit, that is, they attest or certify the accuracy of accounts. (Major claims by or accounts of subsidiary organizations are other less frequently encountered examples.) In most situations quantity surveyors, engineers and architects of the client (or their consultants) and interim audit work will provide documentary evidence to back up the final account sums. Site visits, if appropriate, will have been undertaken during the currency of the contract as will audit of any interim certificates. Ideally, the auditors involvement will have been intermittent throughout the contract period at key stages to test the controls identified so far. (Auditors sometimes refer to this as current contract audit or CCA for short.)

For major capital projects CCA is very desirable, but unless an audit section is exceptionally well resourced or few capital contracts are undertaken a CCA approach may not be feasible on all capital contracts. Nevertheless, attestation of the final accounts can still provide a worthwhile insight into the likelihood of irregularities in the tender evaluation and performance of the contract. Unfortunately, earlier stages, such as the need for the project, the suitability of the design and the selection of contractors invited to tender, are often beyond any significant independent appraisal at this late stage.

With the likely need in mind to delve as far back as possible prior to the final accounts stage the checklist in Appendix 6 was compiled. The final accounts work carried out by the auditor and indeed by the quantity surveyor preparing the account is basically one of checking arithmetic and facts. Are all rates in accordance with original bills of quantities? Have all subtotals been brought forward to summary schedules and ultimately to the finalaccount itself? Readers particularly interested in this aspect of the work or of the wider considerations of auditing major contracts are referred to the Bibliography.

It is difficult to pick out particular checks that guard against fraud and corruption at this final accounts stage, as the whole of the preparation and audit of the final account is in a sense a control against fraud and corruption, but the following items should be particularly noted:

1 Any alteration to the original published contract conditions, schedule of rates, bill of quantities, and so on should be initialled by both parties.
2 Any alterations to the final accounts, interim accounts, variation orders and other documents submitted in support of payment should, unless they are obvious errors of a typographical nature, be initialled as above and explanation provided in writing.
3 All final accounts and interim documentation should be submitted to the client in the original (not photocopies), typewritten or in ink without using erasing uid.
4 Missing vouchers, particularly in support of variations and time extensions should be investigated and, if at all possible, duplicates sought from contractors/suppliers. If necessary the client should refuse any payment due.
5 Daywork records especially timesheets should be signed by site agents, the clerk of works or quantity surveyor (QS), appointed by the client.
6 Correspondence files should be fully examined, particularly for matters relating to subcontractors' appointments, any complaints and disputes. In particular, any details of

negotiations that took place before and after tendering should be available on a correspondence file. It should be standard practice to keep all letters exchanged, quotes, requoted sums and notes of any arrangements agreed by telephone.

7 Quite often sums tendered in the first instance turn out to be higher than the sums estimated and set aside in capital or revenue budgets. A retender could be costly and cause delays, and unless the sums are far above the budget, it may not be worth redesigning the project or searching for finance from other sources. Contractors should be invited to lower their bids, possibly indicating any easily attainable savings they feel could be made in respect of, say, specified materials, delayed start dates, and so on. At this point written evidence should be retained that:
   - ensures all contractors who originally tendered are given equal opportunity to renegotiate on a fair basis. For example, if one contractor is allowed to substitute a less expensive quality of material all others should be notified of the change in specification.
   - ensures none of the contractors are given any details of other tenders or of the relative positions of the different companies.

POST-CONTRACT ASSESSMENT AND RELEASE OF MONIES

This stage is usually the least well performed. Release of retention monies is often a formality upon certification by an architect or engineer that the capital works have no significant defects, perhaps after minor improvements and rectification are negotiated with the contractor. Yet, though little can (nor should) be done to prevent final payment to contractors in most circumstances, this is the stage at which management should ask: 'Did we make the right decisions during our earlier stages, identifying the needs, the feasibility, and the best contract design? Did we choose the right contractor?' A good letting system does not guarantee the contract is let to the best or even a suitable contractor. Most importantly, does the final product meet the envisaged need? Essentially, such questions are of a value for money or operational nature. But all too often indications of poor VFM are indications of possible fraud and corruption. This point is tackled in more detail in Chapter 9 when we will consider some of the problems of public services accounting.

Revenue and other contracts

Contracts let under competitive tendering for service provision or for facilities management are an important issue throughout the public services. Sometimes lay people and politicians are surprised to find that most public services organizations have had many years' commercial experience of competitive tendering, at least from the client standpoint.

Although, traditionally, the audit and investigation of contracts has been directed at capital works these skills are being used increasingly to investigate and assess other major contracts. Most public services bodies enter into numerous contracts every month if not every day. A purchase order for the supply of stationery or a subscription to a trade journal implies a contract in law and many order forms have contract conditions stipulated on the reverse. It would be extremely costly to audit all purchases using the same approach as that for capital contracts. But the approach outlined can nevertheless form a sound basis for protecting other major contracts against the risks of fraud and corruption. It would be impossible to consider all types of other contracts for lift maintenance, office cleaning, consultancy work, supplies of computer hardware, software and so on in this chapter. Many are, as explained above, best considered during Chapter 6. However, additional comments are called for on certain aspects that are widely applicable to contracts not of a capital works nature.

CONSULTANCY CONTRACTS

Contracts with firms of specialist consultants pose particular risks in respect of fair appointment and the confirmation of work done. The appointment of consultants may:

1 Form part of a larger project (particularly consultant architects, engineers or quantity surveyors as part of a capital works project);
2 Be an ongoing arrangement for regular work at certain limited times for which permanent employment is uneconomic; and
3 Be an ad hoc commission usually for specific advice in the form of a report or training.

The appointment of consultants should follow procedures similar to other contractors. Unfortunately consultants are often required at fairly short notice. Their personal relationship with and understanding of the circumstances and requirements of the organization can be of critical importance. This often puts them into a far more specialized relationship with their clients than, say, the average firm of building contractors. Many organizations continue to re-employ consultants on the basis that they understand that body's particular requirements better than a new firm would. A so-called professional relationship is built up that involves trust, a degree of flexibility of working arrangements (especially during unanticipated problems) and the like. As stressed throughout, the public services manager must bear in mind that he or she is acting in the interests of the wider community, and as in so many respects already discussed they must be seen to act fairly. Most public services bodies that use consultants in the regular way described above generate sufficient work to build up a worthwhile relationship with several firms. Moreover, any reasonable consultant is likely to appreciate the position of a public servant as being quite different from, say, that of a local manufacturer. For these reasons it should be normal practice to complete a list of consultants and offer work on a competitive basis. If nationally laid down standard fees are offered by all for the same work then rotation of commissions on a systematic basis can usually ensure that firms where standards fall are no longer invited, without risking any accusation of favouritism. Problems can occur when work of an unusual nature is required. In these cases it is fairly standard practice to ask an appropriate professional body to recommend accessible members from its lists.

Official terms of engagement should be made public and clearly laid out in contracts or exchanges of letters that can be readily checked against the fees charged.

A formal post-assessment should be recorded for each consultancy report or other work, with reasons clearly stated for criticism or recommendation to use or not to use the firm for future works.

VOLUNTARY COMPETITIVE TENDERING AND OUTSOURCING SERVICES WITHIN BEST VALUE

Voluntary competitive tendering (VCT) is in many ways a child of compulsory competitive tendering (CCT) which was peculiar to local government during the 1980s and 1990s when public bodies were often required, by law, to invite tenders for different parts of its activities. The wide use of CCT and later VCT has been based on the assumption that competitive tendering will force public services to compete with private sector providers, driving down costs and encouraging more efficient working practices. It was politically unacceptable given their opposition to CCT for the incoming Labour government of 1996 to retain CCT, and yet it wanted to retain the efficiencies that CCT had encouraged. The answer appeared to lie in a more complex regime that sought to retain the improved efficiency, effectiveness and best working practices of competition, in line with achieving value for money – always a high profile consideration in public services. At the same time the government appeared to be offering more freedom and exibility to local government to choose the methods by which efficiencies and best working practices would be achieved. The new regime came to be called simply 'best value' and involved local government making a wide range of best value plans, to be monitored by a special best value inspectorate with formal assessments of their progress against the plans. The actual best value regime is in fact diverse and complex and seems to becoming overtaken by later developments such as comprehensive performance assessments (CPAs), none of which will be covered in this short chapter. The essential point is that all these developments still seek, to varying degrees, to utilize competitive tendering, outsourcing, and commercial comparisons, and so on in various forms.

Underlying all attempts to use and encourage competitive tendering and outsourcing of services is a need for fairness and the vital requirement to minimize any risk of corruption. Fairness is a very subjective concept. If the public official does not act in a way that is generally perceived to be fair and, as far as he or she can ascertain, in accordance with the law, it is almost certain that the official will be thought to be acting corruptly (see the earlier discussion of the assumption of guilt at page 6–7). For these reasons outsourcing puts public servants in an even more delicate and difficult situation than usual.

Peer pressure is likely to be exerted from colleagues whose jobs are at stake, as is political pressure from elected representatives who may well have staked their political careers upon either the success or the failure of the planned outsourcing.

CLIENT AND CONTRACTOR ROLES

In such circumstances a rigid and effective separation of duties between the client and contractor's roles is one of the few controls likely to be effective against fraud and corruption. Sometimes it is difficult to identify the client. Ultimately the taxpayer/elector is the client. The minister or committee appointed to oversee the service subjected to competitive tendering/outsourcing is the political client. But for all practical purposes officials must perform the role of the client. They must decide the detailed method of selecting contractors, evaluate the tenders or designs or even, depending upon the nature of the service, evaluate quite different business proposals.

The reasons for the choice of contractor must be made public. For most cases this will be the lowest cost or highest revenue offered subject to varying measures of service quality. The latter can prove to be a potential minefield both politically and professionally. It is often very difficult to even quantify service output in agreed terms. Social services, education services and support services in general are examples. But even a service as apparently quantifiable and well-established as refuse collection can cause problems when comparisons of output and quality are made. Numbers of collections, times and routes can involve such qualitative factors as the effects of traffic congestion.

For the reader's purposes the important point is not the desirability of competitive tendering and outsourcing or the measures used to judge success or failure. Rather it is that measures, particularly of costs (direct and indirect) and performance, should be clearly defined and agreed by political representatives well in advance of drawing up the tenders. Any changes of mind once tenders have been opened or are to be evaluated should be fully and publicly explained and recorded.

The highly charged atmosphere that may surround such policies in some public bodies means that decisions that are normally routine for an officer must be confirmed at the highest level or even outside the body concerned. This might entail advice from lawyers, the advice of an auditor or at least second opinions sought from colleagues in other public bodies.

Summary

Capital projects follow a basic progression as outlined in Figure 4.1. It is essential to encourage free and open public debate and to have public access to information right from the start. Once the needs have become established, strict controls should be enforced over the conditions of contract letting. The final evaluation of tenders should, like the establishment of needs and the design of the project, be subject to open political decisions.

Whether the project is a building, an ongoing public service or simple debt collection, a clear separation of duties between the client and the contractor should be maintained. All variations should be fully explained and documented and costs monitored by the client. The final accounts stage is a crucial control, bringing together supporting documentary evidence of all stages of work, though controls of a physical or procedural nature and non-documentary evidence cannot usually be examined at this stage. The end of the project is not the end of its assessment, nor of the risk of fraud and corruption, and management should take steps to ensure that any defects, shortcomings and the like are rectified.

The most risk-prone aspects of a major project are often considered to be:

1 Conception and political approval (including granting of planning and building consents) often more associated with pressures on politicians than officers;
2 Tendering procedures;
3 Certification of work done/variations; and
4 Recognition of inadequate performance.

CASE STUDIES

Possible case studies are very varied in this area, though widescale fraud and corruption in contract performance are, arguably, far more difficult to prove in a court of law than petty purchasing or benefit frauds. The first case illustrates the early stages of needs assessment, conception and planning; the second that of a final accounts examination.

CASE STUDY 4.1

BURNUM CITY COUNCIL CREMATORIUM

The need for a new crematorium had been debated at intervals in the council chamber for the past two years. Burnum was a relatively small compact city with very little land available for additional cemetery spaces. A privately run crematorium already existed but the need for extra capacity was evident and agreed by all political parties. Outline planning permission had been agreed on a site owned by the council. An outline specification was drawn up bearing in mind the size of the site; landscaping; likely throughput (Burnum had a relatively large elderly population especially in the more run-down inner city estates); technical requirements such as height of chimney, access (by car, bus) requirements and the opinions of local communities and interests.

Advertisements were placed in the relevant professional journals and in the *European Journal*. The initial response was very encouraging, indeed it was overwhelming. Almost 100 enquiries were received and the detailed specification had to be photocopied many times.

Surprisingly few potential contractors showed much interest in completing the detailed specifications. There was little doubt that, as with most competitive contracts, contractors often seek a detailed specification to familiarize themselves with the market long before they have firm intentions of competing.

In due course three firms sent in detailed specifications completed and priced. The design details within the specification varied and one of the three was felt to be totally unsuitable. Both members and officers agreed that this scheme offered the highest costs with the lowest quality of building and surrounds. Unfortunately the two remaining schemes, while broadly comparable in costs and benefits, were both in excess of the budget provision for the scheme. Timescales can be very difficult to predict and costs can rise, often erratically, during the stages of conception, design, planning (including planning permissions), any public enquiry and the detailed mechanics of contract letting. Such a project may well take one or more years to be approved. At first this may seem rather bureaucratic compared to commercial organizations. Political accountability, including the need to report to and obtain approval from committees that may meet only infrequently throughout the year, is a major cause of delay. Also there is an element of political unpredictability. In debate, sometimes involving sides only too ready to score points, no tenderer or officer can assume the feeling of the politicians will remain as it was. Opinions previously expressed may turn out to be swayed by speeches during debate. In local government, resolutions of committees may still need to be adopted by meetings of the full council during which further debate and delay may occur.

Let us assume, as is often the case, that senior officers are asked to negotiate on behalf of the council with the two applicants with a view to reducing the cost of the scheme to within the budget approvals.

Had several firms all put in tenders for roughly comparable amounts in excess of the budget it would have been more efficient (and probably politically acceptable) to amend the materials, design, timing or other ingredients of the scheme and, despite the increased costs of delay, invite retenders. But with only one or two firms interested, negotiation on an individual basis is more cost-effective and not unusual. In local and health authorities this method will generally require suspension of some standing orders and financial regulations to allow senior officers to undertake the negotiations. Such officers will have to tread carefully. In one sense by placing them in the spotlight, so to

CASE STUDY 4.1 *continued*

speak, where their actions are deliberately beyond the norm and invite query, the risk that they will succumb to any corrupt in uences (whether from tenderers or of their own volition) is reduced. However, negotiations inevitably give more power and discretion than straightforward arithmetic evaluations and used on a regular basis they introduce significant additional risks. It is from this point onwards that events at Burnum wove a web of corruption.

Three senior officers, an architect, a civil engineer and a quantity surveyor were chosen to conduct the negotiations on the council's behalf.

Company A, a medium-sized company with similar establishments at nine locations throughout the country, could only meet the cost restriction with significant reductions in the capacity and landscaping of the scheme. Company B, a smaller, more recently formed company were able to offer a design that met almost all the original requirements but extended the completion time from approximately 12 to 15 months. The officers had no hesitation in recommending company B, which was duly awarded the contract. A year-and-a-half later the half-completed project lay abandoned; Company B was in the hands of the official receiver. The taxpayers of the city were paying about double the original costs of the scheme (partly due to large increases in interest charges) for its completion at short notice by a completely different contractor. Not surprisingly the external auditor's attention became focused on the debacle.

The auditor was, at first, concerned mainly with the VFM implications of the cost overrun. However, as he called for the correspondence files and background information on the contract, and as he started to interview the officers concerned, the following points emerged:

1 None of the contractors were subject to the usual level of financial appraisal. (Bank references were sought but these are notoriously easy to come by.)
2 Company B was basically a 'shell' company set up to take advantage of new business opportunities. No parent company guarantee had been sought. In fact because no financial appraisals had been undertaken, officers were able to claim that they had no knowledge of the true nature of company B, which appeared, on the surface, to be a normal trading company. Financial appraisals were not enshrined in the standing orders or financial regulations of the council though most organizations would be expected to undertake at least a company search, seek a credit rating and ask their in-house accountants to review the company's latest annual report and accounts.
3 The figures quoted by company B were exceptionally favourable and the cost was far below that offered by other contractors. A profit share clause was offered to the council for the first five years' trading on condition that the council did not give planning permission for any further new crematoria during that time, a condition that was virtually certain to arise in any event. This clause, though virtually worthless, had probably sounded quite attractive to members and at the time the minutes of meetings revealed that the three negotiating officers had presented it as the 'icing on the cake' of their negotiations.

At first the auditor was tempted to assume nothing worse than incompetence on the part of officers of the council and of the company which had by this time gone into liquidation. However, an examination of the capital payments of the scheme revealed that for the first 12 months stage payments had

CASE STUDY 4.1 *continued*

been made on a quarterly basis for work done and certified by the same architect, senior engineer or quantity surveyor (QS) as had been involved in the negotiations. After this time most work had come to a halt. This meant that it was doubtful whether company B's parent had actually lost any significant sum on the bankruptcy of its subsidiary as virtually all the costs to date had been covered. In fact a site visit left the auditor with the general impression that the payments, certified by the QS and engineer, had probably erred well on the side of generosity.

A standard performance bond had been deposited with the bank but the monies were small in relation to the outstanding liabilities to subcontractors and the work still remaining. In any event obtaining possession of the bond would probably require complex litigation.

The auditor was suspicious of company B's role and the motive of the parent company. Suspicions of the role of the negotiating officers also arose. The lack of financial appraisal was difficult to explain. The likelihood was that company B's inexperience in this (or any) type of work would almost certainly have come to light during negotiations.

It was also difficult at first to understand the motive of company B's parent. Eventually this became clear from perusing that company's annual report and in conversation with officers of authorities who had offered, or were proposing to offer, similar contracts for which company B's parent had been invited to tender. This market was particularly difficult to break into without a track record. Few authorities were prepared to offer work without being able to know that contracts had already been won by the company. In fact the site at Burnum had been held up as a model design. The showpiece aspect of the Burnum scheme had, according to company B, been one of the factors in deciding to reduce the cost of its initial tender. This fact in itself is not unusual, but the lack of any concern for the likelihood that the scheme would fail financially most certainly was. As soon as company B had (largely on the basis of the Burnum contract) won a contract for a similarly designed crematorium with another authority at more realistic prices it lost interest in the Burnum scheme. By the time they had won their third contract they were fully prepared to let the Burnum scheme lapse and let company B (effectively set up and assigned merely to that scheme) go into liquidation. The more profitable schemes had already been purchased by the parent company or they had been entered into by that company even though company B had been involved in negotiation and fronted the deals.

In this case it would be very difficult despite the great likelihood of corruption that any of the officers could be successfully prosecuted. However, the external auditor may have had the power to surcharge members and officers whom he or she considered to have acted irresponsibly. In this case the officers did not seek parent company guarantees and they signed certificates for work that had been completed in the knowledge that even if the work referred to in the certificates was completed it was virtually worthless. There could have been little doubt that company B could not have fulfilled its contract right from the start. Without the contractual obligation of the parent, or some other party, to support it until more lucrative contracts were won, company B was virtually bound to fail.

It is very likely, given the urban environment of Burnum, with relatively high land prices and the higher than anticipated bids from genuine companies that the crematorium project was uneconomic from the start. Burnum City Council should have arranged for the joint funding of a

CASE STUDY 4.1 *concluded*

crematorium in another more rural authority, or undertaken the project itself, at a loss, if the local electors were so determined. The members, it seems, wanted to be able to control the development for reasons of civic pride, political ego or whatever. When, despite all odds, company B offered, or appeared to offer, options at a price they could afford they were, like all recipients of hoped-for news, only too willing to believe it.

In this case the main controls absent from the tendering procedure were:

1 financial vetting of companies;
2 parent company guarantees; and
3 a more competitive and open form of tendering instead of negotiation by officers.

Other controls, particularly over examination or certification work completed or in progress are also likely to have been inadequate. But any one of the three key procedures mentioned above would have been almost certain to have avoided any serious corruption with the taxpayer having to bail out the partly completed project at vastly in ated costs.

CASE STUDY 4.2

MINISTRY FOR LEGAL AID

The ministry had decided to computerize its main information recording system. A system requirement specification was drawn up and six major manufacturers were invited to tender. The data was quite straightforward but the access requirements of users were complicated. Each user needed to be given access permission to the data at different levels. (A user may not be able to call up on screen any records other than those that he or she needs for their work.) This meant in practice that virtually all officers involved in information processing and reporting would need a separate terminal. Despite this the total cost was not considered excessive.

The company eventually successful in supplying the hardware and software were engaged to provide training. Inevitably, a strong working relationship grew up between this company and the civil servants during the course of the implementation of computerization, based on the trust of the latter and the superior knowledge of the former.

It is often the case that officials, however well they may understand their own needs, are far less well versed in the latest information technology. The ministry was no exception. In such situations the hardware and software suppliers are in a very powerful position; in this case it was one that they abused.

In fact, despite the initial opinions of the auditors, no serious fraud had, legally speaking, been committed. Nevertheless what took place would undoubtedly have been considered dishonest and devious to say the least.

Quite simply much of the equipment was not what had been ordered. The precise make and model of terminals, disc packs, personal computers and laptops were not made completely clear to any of the staff either during installation or during the training seminars. Everything supplied was, in fact, adequate for the work required and the level of security expected. The system specification was met. The project did not run over budget. No complaints beyond the usual teething troubles were expressed by

CASE STUDY 4.2 *concluded*

the ministry. Yet between a quarter and a third of the cost was swallowed up by hardware and software of an inferior quality to that actually agreed in the contract. Slightly earlier versions of software (particularly software for generating interrogation reports designed for ad hoc use by management) were provided in place of the latest versions. In some cases managers had subsequently been persuaded to authorize purchase of updated versions by sales staff of the very same company that should have provided this in the first place.

The same principle applied to some of the hardware. The hardware, rather than the software, first brought this fraud to light when a clerical assistant was charged with completing an inventory. The inventory was inspired by a change in accounting principles and the subsequent need to revalue all fixed assets. Normally the supplier company could have expected equipment including IT purchases to be checked only upon delivery. Provided the delivery passed unquestioned and maintenance or replacement of faulty items was promptly carried out, it was very unlikely that the delivery would be queried at a later date.

The clerical assistant compiled the inventory from hardware she found being used at the six ministry sites. Her curiosity was aroused by the fact that not all sites had exactly the same equipment for the same job. She had, in any event, intended to scan quickly through the orders just to make sure no significant single items or numbers of smaller items had been omitted. This she thought might happen if she had not known of a section or been told of any recent deliveries. When she obtained the orders she found to her surprise that neither the orders nor indeed the delivery notes bore out the significant variations in model of equipment between sites and sometimes between offices on the same site.

The company apologized and eventually agreed to replace some of the items called into question. However, it pointed to a minor sub-clause inserted in the contract, though precisely when no one seemed to recall, that allowed it to replace items not immediately available with others of similar quality at the same cost. The clause also provided for the ministry to be notified. This notification, it was claimed, had been sent but a revised and updated version was now being prepared.

Although deliveries were signed for at the ministry by the officers who unloaded and stored the equipment, they were generally unable to verify the order at that point. In fact most hardware was not unpacked until installation and this was often done by the company. Some of the ministry staff had, it later transpired, been aware that they were not getting the very latest versions of the hardware and software supplied. Some even queried this with the company but, most importantly, none of these officers were sufficiently senior to have responsibility for the contract or for any of the IT budget.

It is doubtful if any single officer would have been aware of the fact that the ministry was being eeced had it not been for the inventory clerk. In fact, given the rapid change in IT technology the same dishonest procedures could have been followed during upgrades. One key (and rather old-fashioned) control was missing from the ministry – adequate checking of delivery to contract or order. This is a commonplace weakness for IT equipment delivered through usual channels. Where complicated and valuable items are involved it is essential they are checked by an in-house expert prior to payment.

Concluding points

This chapter has dealt with the more common contracts and typical capital works projects. The issues implicit in these major areas of expenditure apply throughout an organization, though for smaller projects they rarely come to the fore unless something goes wrong or a major change occurs. Is there a real need for ? If so, how should it be provided and by whom? Can the quality, completeness, and effectiveness be monitored? How, and by whom? Can the cost be monitored against the budget and against alternative sources of provision? These are essentially no more than questions of good financial management but, as Chapter 9 outlines, good financial management is one of the strongest defences against fraud and corruption.

Great stress has, rightly, been laid upon those procedures that are likely to form key internal controls and on those that open up the organization decision-making to public scrutiny and accountability. These are important considerations throughout this book. But of equal importance in guarding against fraud and corruption is substantive evidence of the value, legality, completeness and accuracy of expenditure, income, assets and liabilities. This is particularly true of capital projects and outsourced revenue contracts. Officials are always at risk to temptation and pressures. A company that would never consider putting undue pressure on a public official for a few hundred or thousand pounds of revenue expenditure may act differently when many millions of pounds are at stake. Likewise an official that would never consider acting improperly when he can affect the outcome of a mere £1000 purchase may have a change of heart when far larger sums are involved. The sheer magnitude of what is at stake makes it imperative that client management participate directly in monitoring performance and in verification of work done and service quality.

CHAPTER

5 Information Technology and Management

Introduction

This chapter considers various effects of information technology upon the measures needed to guard against fraud and corruption. It also considers the legal framework that has come about since the 1980s in an attempt to bring the law in line with developing technology, though this legal framework stretches beyond the narrower criminal concerns of fraud and corruption. Appendix 9 is used to set out key aspects of the legislation.

The subject would without doubt merit a separate work of its own and there are already some fine examples of such. Computer-related fraud can be intermingled with any of the circumstances considered in other chapters as some of the case studies show. This chapter seeks to draw attention to specific fraud-prevention measures related to computers and to consider some, often fairly traditional, measures in a computerized working environment.

Why should computers demand special attention?

After all, most significant systems are computerized, especially in the public services. The general systems-based audit approach, identifying key controls that help lessen the chances of fraud occurring or remaining undetected, can be applied equally to both manual and computerized systems, or to a mixture of both.

Computers can sometimes hide actions more effectively than written records, particularly if a fraudster uses software or an operating system developed in house or that is generally unfamiliar to others. Computer systems can be rendered unaccountable by a determined fraudster, hidden from effective management control and review that in a manual system would simply be provided by physical access to bound ledgers. Frequent changes in technology are difficult to keep up with, offering added scope for the criminal mind. Many frauds, especially those involving the unauthorized transfer of funds by computer, can be perpetrated far more speedily than would have been the case prior to computerization.

Computer-related fraud tends to be perpetrated by trusted employees, often disgruntled, whose superiors or peers have not previously envisaged information technology being used in such a way. Computer technology is still relatively new as well as being in a constant state of change. Each advance in technology may present additional risks or enable extra safeguards. The objectives and motivations of the fraudster remain the same, or almost so. Some evidence points to the human ego and a misplaced sense of challenge as additional motivations in computer crime, a point we will discuss later.

Every three years or so since 1981 the Audit Commission for Local Authorities and the National Health Service in England and Wales (The Audit Commission) have published a wide-ranging survey of computer fraud and abuse, covering both the public and private sectors (see the Bibliography). These show a depressing trend of increase over the years not just in conventional computer fraud but also in varieties of IT abuse, particularly disruption of business caused by virus infections. Also depressing is the finding that failures in basic controls are still a major problem despite increasing anti-fraud awareness at the strategic level in organizations.

The remainder of this chapter cannot provide a proven methodology for preventing particular crimes in particular installations. But by directing attention to special features and giving extra prominence to well-tried preventative controls, it seeks to limit the occurrence of premeditated computer-related fraud.

Segregation of duties

This type of control is important in any computerized system involving financial transactions or the movement of assets. Although nowadays the use of mainframes is proportionately less widespread than in the past many organizations, particularly in the public services, still use this and networked approaches. Where a computer manager and support unit is available a reasonable separation can usually be maintained via:

User Data entry/user at terminal or linked personal computer.
Programmer Protection and maintenance of operating systems, software and hardware; development and amendment of programs, databases, and so on.
Operator Handling and custody of value documents such as cheques or licences.
Operator Data updating and security, including any library, holding, or distribution function.

Segregation is a genuine problem for stand-alone personal computers (PCs), many relatively small sites or so-called open systems involving computer networks of linked PCs or terminals connected to a secondary processing unit. Supervision, strict password control and a readable, non-erasable audit trail may overcome the risks inherent in a lack of separation in most cases. However, lack of separation can increase the risks of collusion and this is one of the most difficult methods of fraud to detect.

Following transactions around the computer

This involves checking actual payments, transfer of assets, and so on processed by the computer against the prime documentation evidencing the reasons and authority for the transaction. Be above board and open about this – it may well have a deterrent effect.

In the early years of computerization auditors were encouraged to use this approach, treating the computer as a 'black box' simply because they were not computer literate and probably a little frightened of these new machines. Such days are long gone. All the same, following transactions around the computer can still be useful, though it is usually sufficient to select a sample of transactions possibly at each stage. If a system is working as well as it should then different stages of processing should result in the update by debiting and crediting the accounts in a correct and predictable manner and no amount of complex processing should be allowed to obscure this. Any failure to reconcile, even on a sample basis, complex stages in processing is a fraudsters 'dream' in the technical world of transaction processing and no one should trust the system itself to be completely self-reconciling and tamper-proof, if they are seriously concerned to prevent fraud.

At a macro level computer output, in particular hard-copy reports, can often be verified in total, or with minimal problems of reconciliation, to another computer-produced or manual output of a feeder system that provides the input to the computer. For example, with a payroll system, see Figure 5.1.

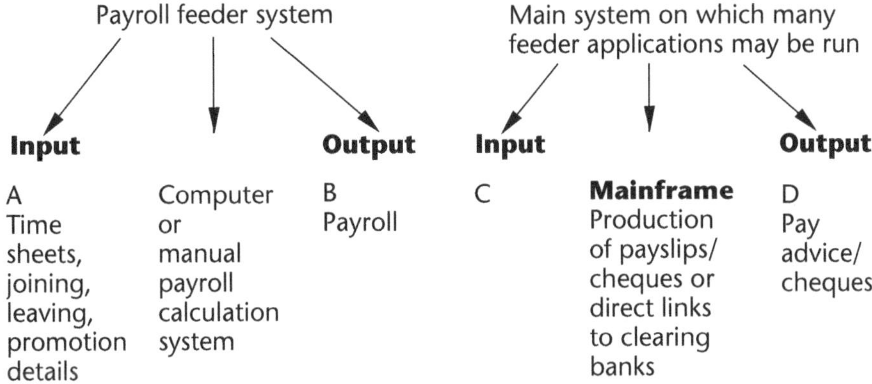

Figure 5.1 A payroll system

A mainframe computer, as shown in Figure 5.1, would usually be used for a variety of other purposes each with its own feeder system. An ideal verification may take place between A and D either in total or on an individual sample basis. Most systems are capable of some reconciliation between B and C or C and D, as in most systems the relevant management, for example, the payroll supervisor, manager or the accountant at the next level above, would need to know that his or her instructions to, say, pay 5000 staff a total of £4 732 000 were followed once they had left the feeder system. Verification, whether in total or on a sampling basis, should be conducted confidentially but openly and above board. Staff, including any potential fraudsters, should know that regular and unpredictable checks are carried out but that all their personal information is treated in the strictest confidence.

Similar overall reconciliations between systems should be undertaken for other main transactions, such as debtors, creditors, and so on. This element of control is discussed again in Chapter 9 on the main accounting arrangements.

Data input arrangements

However many computerized systems are used to process data, at some point an original input of manually provided information or raw data will have initiated the processing. This initial input data may be in many forms, for example time sheets, invoices, stores requisitions, or computer-produced documents provided by, say, an outside supplier. But at initial input no direct link between computer systems will exist. This initial input stage is one of the most vulnerable, high-risk points to fraudulent manipulation. It may help to identify particular risks by asking the following questions:

Would the objectives of processing be compromised by unauthentic data? Obvious examples would include application forms such as for passports or hosing benefits. If so, who will ensure the authenticity of the data?
Is the raw data held securely and in a tamper-proof manner prior to input?
Can input be linked to responsible individuals? By secure passwords for example?

Risks at input require preventative controls that cover at least the authorization and initial vetting of raw data.

THE AUTHORIZATION OF INPUT

This should be done by the user at a defined level of responsibility and in a form that cannot be amended or overwritten. Signed hard-copy vouchers, printout produced from a feeder system or input control sheets are often the most secure. Ideally, input totals produced from manual or computerized feeder systems should be capable of being easily and directly cross-checked to output totals produced by the system that has been updated, that is, cross-checked from A to B to D in Figure 5.1. After documents have been input the originals should be kept for audit and verification providing a final trail of management responsibility. The time of retention will vary depending on the nature of the documents, but in financial transaction processing this could be up to seven years.

INITIAL VETTING

Data should be subject to immediate validation checks as soon as they are input. These may, for example, include checks over maximum or minimum monetary values for individual transactions; agreement of the total values or numbers of items against a batch total for organizations where batch processing is still in operation; comparison of input records to lists of unacceptable parameters such as blacklisted addresses, suspect VAT numbers or unacceptable transaction dates. Whatever the procedures for programmed vetting of data, generally speaking the sooner this is undertaken the less risk of fraud.

Data updating and processing

The data that are input will usually be used to update standing information on suppliers, debtors, rent accounts, and so on. It is crucial that access to this standing data, or master files as they are often called, is securely controlled. If standing property details, rent accounts, tax accounts, and so on, are deleted or interfered with fraud may run into millions of pounds and go completely unnoticed for an indefinite period. By comparison for the transaction data being input, an unauthorized interference would usually have to be repeated and risk detection time and time again to create comparable mayhem.

Ideally, the data user or data controller should monitor or carry out regular checking of the information held on the standing data master file. This may be difficult especially where the user is a small department with little time available for review or checking, or a user-friendly print of the master files data may be difficult to obtain. In any event the master file and the arrangements and controls covering amendments thereto should be regularly reviewed by a senior programmer, analyst or computer auditor not involved in the design of the operating system or the application to which the master file relates. This is particularly important where a database is being used, possibly for numerous purposes, see also page 105.

During an updating run of a major mainframe processing system, say a weekly or monthly payroll run, programming and system design staff should be kept clear of the operation. This involves a standard separation of duties between operating staff (including data preparation, input and control officers) and programming staff. This separation of duties often breaks down on a day-to-day basis as programmers are consulted about malfunctions in software they helped design or install. In practical terms, given the tendency of many organizations to move away from batch processing mainframe situations to networks and PC-based systems, this control is often difficult to impose. Nevertheless every time the separation breaks down the potential risk of fraud is increased, as indicated by the increasing computer crime statistics. Management should consider what other controls can compensate for the lack of separation of duties.

Among the other possible controls are regular reviewing of management control information related to:

1 programme amendments;
2 data amendments; and
3 access (or unsuccessful access attempts) to live data especially during updating runs.

Additional supervision and the encryption coding of sensitive or valuable data to be transmitted or updated are other possible control features that may compensate for inadequate separation.

Data access and output

ACCESS CONTROL

The use of individual, confidential and regularly changed password control is of course the primary control over access. Access control also implies control over the level of access allowed to different classes of user, with differing authorities to read and amend different types of data. Clearly authority to change standing data such as bank details and addresses is critical and needs to be reviewed on a regular basis. Controls may include the recording and authorization of all amendments to key databases, programs, and so on. Sometimes it may be necessary to make certain fields permanent or tamper-proof once they have been changed or updated, thus making it impossible for the person, even if they have made a mistake, to conceal any change to a value or authorization they have made. This will leave a clear trail of every event including any errors and their corrections.

Physical access also needs to be reviewed particularly, as is so often the case in the public services, in areas open to the general public. Screens should not be left on and visible in public areas, staff should log out when leaving their desks and restricted areas should be clearly marked.

OUTPUT CONTROL

Final output (as opposed to intermediate output to magnetic media used for further updating) can be on screen, on printed hard copy, or even be recorded voice output.

Screen output is largely controlled via access controls that apply to input and output at a terminal or PC screen. Access control is very much dependent upon physical security of the terminal/PC and password protection over the software.

Quite often, a read-only facility is available to numerous users and has a relatively low level of password protection. The risk is often that relatively junior officers who would be denied access to sensitive manual records or hard-copy reports, will have access to data from which the reports were compiled. Even if no fraud is possible, the Data Protection Act (1998) must still be borne in mind and personal data should not be released to users who do not have a genuine and legal right of access (see p. 116).

EXCEPTION REPORTS

In Chapter 4 we mentioned some of the drawbacks from which exception reports suffer in respect of capital works programmes. Capital projects are varied; each one is usually quite different from others even when they are of a repeatable nature such as housing improvements. Computerized bulk processing of transactions and online updating of standing information are, however, events of an ongoing type with little variation in nature. In fact, many of the uses of a computerized system are akin to the industrial production-line processes and lend themselves to the use of exception reports as a means of internal control; for example, computer production of payroll – summary reports, payslips, cheques, and so on – or of stock item movements – purchases, issue, returns and stock-in-hand – or of hospital bookings; in fact most types of regularly required information. For these types of information exception reports can play a useful role as a key control. The regular monitoring of progress and the output from different processing stages may, if left to accumulate, become a useless mass of statistics. In such circumstances management would normally wish to view only the exceptions and the overall trends. In these circumstances exception reporting may well be the only practical answer. Indeed effective management is often characterized by the ability to discern the important exception reports and interpret what they mean. Thus, taking the examples mentioned above, exception reports of payroll payments over a certain value, high volume stock movements or trends in emergency bed usage may be a useful internal control. Exception reports may well accompany key trend totals such as monthly management accounts or, say, bed or stock usage totals.

ACTION AND RELEVANCE

For exception reports and any other computer output to be an effective form of control they must be relevant and actioned. This may seem too obvious to be worth saying, yet in many IT frauds information that may have prevented or at least ended a fraudulent activity was delayed or ignored until it no longer seemed relevant. Critical information may sometimes be directed to an irrelevant destination, produced in an irrelevant or unintelligible form or simply available but not actioned. Lapses in checking computer usage logs are examples of failures to action output.

SECURITY OF OUTPUT

The security of output (in whatever form) should be considered in the wider context of its relevance and who should action it. Since the first Data Protection Act in 1984 (now replaced by the 1998 Act) additional weight has been given by most organizations to the relevance and security of the output of personal data. Confidential hard-copy output should be recorded and, if necessary, signed for by the intended recipient.

Various security measures include:

1 password control for access to screen output;
2 printers located in a high-security area;
3 logging of all copies of reports and their intermediate and final destinations; and
4 review of emails and retention of email listings of sensitive output reports.

The system manager

We are concerned here with the interface between the central processing unit (CPU) and the applications that are run by users. At the basic level of a PC the system manager is of course the user – he or she determines the controls, changes the passwords, runs the programs, manages the files and so on. This will clearly be a risky concentration of duties if a vital system (for example, in some organizations payroll, lending, and so on, may be vital) are controlled by a single user on a stand-alone PC. At least in such a situation regular management review of the work undertaken might offer some level of compensating control. On a larger scale the system manager situation becomes more complex but offers more scope for independent control. Most larger networks and mainframe environments have a dedicated individual as the system manager who will control the issue of passwords, access levels, the running of programs and so on. Such individuals can be in a powerful position and the focus of potential risk. Certainly any potential fraudulent action or collusion involving the system manager will be particularly threatening and difficult to trace. To counter this level of risk most systems managers will be under the direction of a senior manager such as the computer centre manager who can exercise direct supervision of their work. Usually a tamper-proof log of the system changes and actions by the system manager and other users will be available for scrutiny by the computer centre manager or other independent high level managers.

Database management

The database function is sometimes likened to a library and the database manager, who may also be the system manager, to the librarian. The database enables information entered once to be accessed by different users for different systems, which can be very efficient compared to transferring or re-entering data for different systems. Such a database is clearly vital to guard against fraud and corrupt use or corruption of the data itself. The database is a particularly high-risk asset and one of the possible key controls is likely to involve security and validation of data entry, such as rekeying and reconciliation procedures and also the regular testing of the accuracy of the database. The physical security of the database is vital and it may need to be duplicated at a remote location.

Access to the database is a key issue not just for prevention of fraud and data corruption but also in respect of the security of personal data. Fraudsters may seek to alter personal data to their own or another's benefit or misuse confidential personal or commercial information. But there are also many wider legal implications covering personal data which we shall consider below under the Data Protection Act.

Systems development, operation and maintenance

The traditional input–processing–output scenario is generally discussed as if it operated within a steady state of affairs. This is seldom if ever the case. New systems are being developed and existing systems are being enhanced and maintained all the time. From an auditor's objective it is often permissible to take 'snapshots' of the current state of the system at various audit visits. These may be adequate to help form an opinion of the balance sheet values or the overall reliability of the system's internal controls, particularly if sufficient audit testing is undertaken. But this conventional audit approach offers only minimal assistance in preventing fraud and corruption.

If one is determined to prevent or at least keep to an absolute minimum any risk of fraud and corruption then all new developments, user support measures, system enhancements and routine maintenance must be both independently assessed and monitored by management. This would require far more effort and resources than a periodic (say annual) audit which is usually directed only at specific applications being run on the system, and more than the usual management checks and controls. Indeed, it is arguable that much more effort would be required to reduce the risk of fraud to a minimal level on a computerized system than on an equivalent manual system, though nowadays this argument is becoming increasingly difficult to prove as so few sizeable systems are not computerized. In a manual system all concerned usually recognize the prime importance of staff attitudes, morale and, quite simply, the way the system is used as a factor in preventing fraud and corruption. In a computerized system far more reliance tends to be placed upon the design of the system (security over access to hardware, or software facilities guarded by complex levels of password control are typical and essential design features). But most computer fraud seems to be made possible by designed controls being allowed to lapse, deliberately bypassed or simply not built into the final system. When a computer, especially a mainframe, is relied upon by those seeking routine reports, calculations, updates on events or whatever, they are largely unaware of the attitude of its controllers, designers and maintainers. If the same information was being sought from an army of clerks, or even a few key personnel, their attitudes collectively and individually would usually be recognized as crucial. In such non-computerized systems, human attitudes conducive to fraud and corruption are far less likely to remain unnoticed by those seeking information.

All this points towards a need for greater resources if a computerized system is to be secure. But why spend the money? Basically, because computers introduce risks on a magnified scale. Often a single relatively junior official may commit crimes or wreak havoc that it would be difficult to have imagined in a pre-computerized era. Entire payment runs can be duplicated, access to very large sums of money can be gained and used for fraudulent manipulation often via a single password, credit transactions or information highlighting debtors can be suppressed, sensitive information can be hacked and sold. Many examples have come to light in recent years, often involving relatively few fraudsters in each case.

Because risks of computer-related fraud depend very much on attitudes and motivations and these are often obscured by technology, issues concerning the selection and motivation of staff must be given extra emphasis. During any system design or enhancement and when reviewing the controls over system maintenance, including so-called change control procedures, senior management should ensure that the new system or changes can at least satisfy the security requirements of the old system, and key personnel involved in design, testing, operating and maintaining the system should be subject to adequate pre-assignment vetting, separation of duties, and performance review (see Assessment of key personnel on p. 113).

SYSTEMS DEVELOPMENT CONTROLS

The public services has acquired an unenviable record of poorly implemented large-scale systems development probably bordering on the corrupt, near fraud situations, discussed in Chapter 1, where the level of overspending and apparent incompetence begs the question of whether collusion with corrupt suppliers, individuals working for suppliers and contractors has resulted in 'manipulated' overspends. To some extent this may be unfair, as large scale IT developments in the private sector are not immune from disaster and gross budget overruns too. But in the public services such blunders are more open to public scrutiny and easy prey for the media.

Rather than being a clear source of fraud, the problems often revolve around poor project management, public services clients who lack top IT project implementation skills and experience, lack of developmental control processes and, basically, poor VFM, particularly poor control over cost and efficiency. Yet this is just the sort of environment that attracts fraudsters or encourages otherwise honest staff to act corruptly. The pressures are on for suppliers to win contracts with a low bid then recoup the profit: pressures that can easily be translated into manipulated cost overruns, extra work that was not envisaged and is not strictly necessary, even outright bribes. Sometimes both client and contractor managers, who may be outside consultants or otherwise very skilled and highly mobile, develop an interest in keeping the development complex and going for as long as possible – and possibly 'jumping ship' to develop new projects elsewhere in the industry before the worst aspects of the current one become widely appreciated.

It is nearly impossible to prove fraud and corruption in such circumstances. But in recent years many public services developments of this nature have been burdened by extreme levels of apparent incompetence, resulting in massive cost overruns, very significant delays and revisions, even complete abandonment of projects, which while not often resulting in 'prosecutable' fraud have certainly exemplified serious abuse of taxpayers' money.

Clearly, one broad failing in recent systems developments has been the general lack of controls, whether general processes or specific control arrangements, to guard against foreseeable risks. Figure 5.2 sets out some of the issues for a major project development.

SYSTEMS DEVELOPMENT: POSSIBLE CONTROL FEATURES AT THE EARLY APPROVAL STAGE

It is important to set a sound example of developmental control and counter-fraud features at the initial inception and approval of a new systems development project.

Elected politicians or appointed board members should have some ultimate, recorded approval of major capital expenditure on IT projects. Prior to this approval written reports are 'owned' by named senior officials and discussed and minuted at the political/board level. Examples might include the following:

Evaluation of user needs and justification of the development in principle.

Evaluation of the different systems and hardware/software available to meet those needs.

Various estimated cost–benefit analyses of the different options in principle.

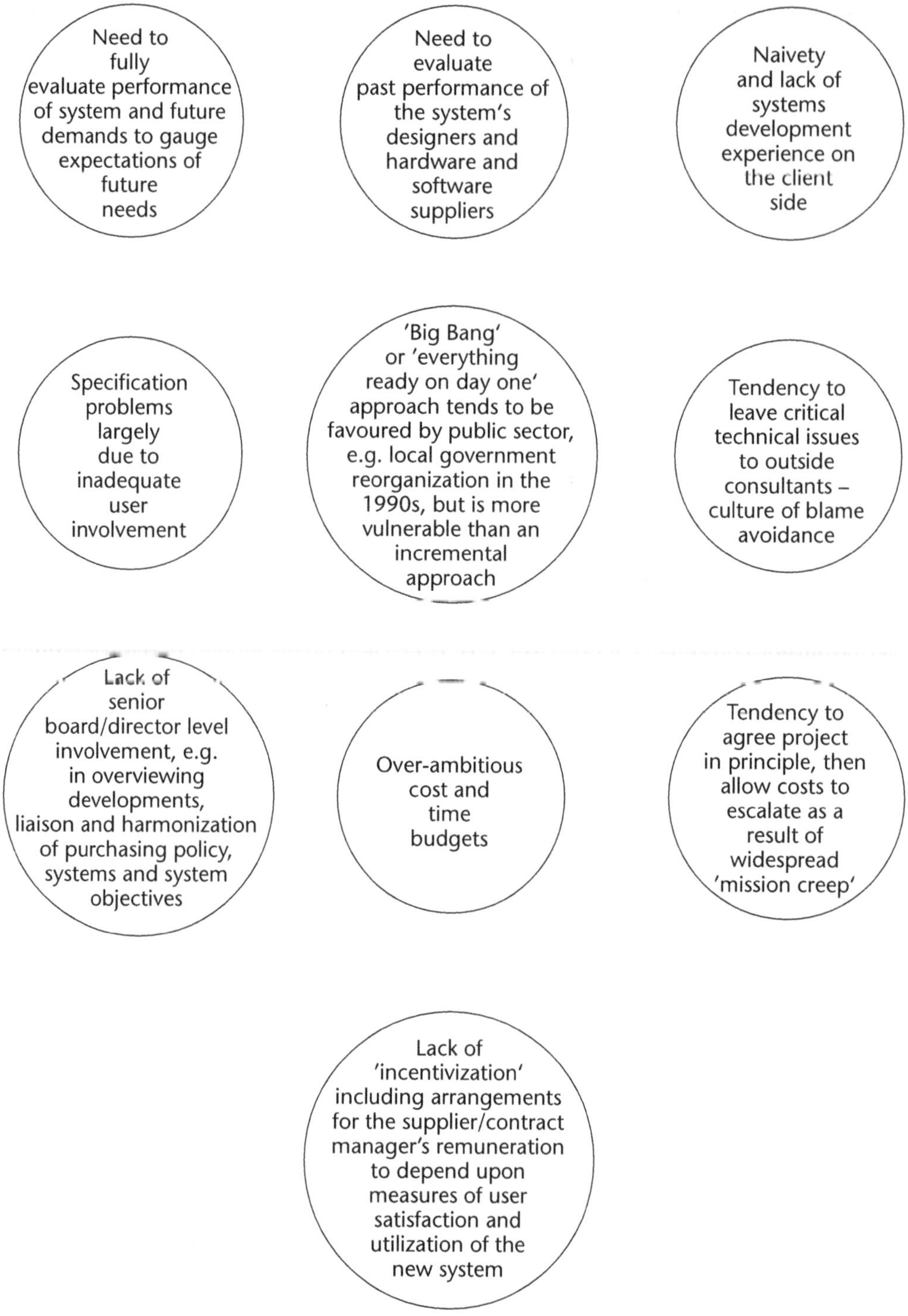

Need to fully evaluate performance of system and future demands to gauge expectations of future needs

Need to evaluate past performance of the system's designers and hardware and software suppliers

Naivety and lack of systems development experience on the client side

Specification problems largely due to inadequate user involvement

'Big Bang' or 'everything ready on day one' approach tends to be favoured by public sector, e.g. local government reorganization in the 1990s, but is more vulnerable than an incremental approach

Tendency to leave critical technical issues to outside consultants – culture of blame avoidance

Lack of senior board/director level involvement, e.g. in overviewing developments, liaison and harmonization of purchasing policy, systems and system objectives

Over-ambitious cost and time budgets

Tendency to agree project in principle, then allow costs to escalate as a result of widespread 'mission creep'

Lack of 'incentivization' including arrangements for the supplier/contract manager's remuneration to depend upon measures of user satisfaction and utilization of the new system

Figure 5.2 Public sector IT project development – key risk issues

- Detailed and fully budgeted system design, with agreement by both IT managers and line-user managers that this will best meet user needs.
- Detailed project implementation plan, stages and times, with statement of feasibility 'owned' and signed by the project manager(s) and signed agreement by user management that this plan will meet their needs.

Key developmental controls at this stage involve the setting up of an audit and responsibility trail:

- the recorded ownership of the decision at political/board level;
- the recorded ownership of the supporting reports by senior IT and user managers;
- the detailed budget, 'owned' and recorded at senior financial and at political/board level (usually capable of being exed as the project proceeds, but with all budget variations over a minimal level accompanied by recorded explanations to and agreement from the 'owners');
- the statement of feasibility with named project management 'owners';
- a fully costed variation-approval mechanism for variations to the implementation plan (cross-referenced to, or an integral part of, budget variation approval), with recorded agreement by IT, user and political/board level 'owners', but with possible delegated powers to approve below a deminimus level.

CONTRACT LETTING AND ONGOING PROJECT MANAGEMENT

It is important that the above controls are in place before any contracts for supply of hardware or software are drawn up or the project gets underway. One of the main risks is that agreement in principle will lead to authorization of expenditure before proper controls are in place. In the early stages of a new systems development different managers may have a wide variety of desires for a 'piece of the action' and if reasonable developmental controls are not in place the tendency to overspend, or to make unauthorized expenditure, is often strong.

This stage of the project management is best controlled along the lines already discussed in Chapter 4. Although that chapter was not specifically directed at IT situations, many of the control features can be copied quite seamlessly to this topic; in particular performance management, separation of duties between client and contractor, the respective roles of each, consultancy contracts and Appendix 8.

POST-IMPLEMENTATION REVIEW

Although this work can not take place until well after the initial implementation it should continue long past the completion of the new systems project. Often it is long after the new system has been in place that fraudulent activities come to light, some of which can be traced back to the initial system implementation stage. Adverse reactions by line users and sometimes quite small systems failings can be indicative of more deep-seated problems of system manipulation. Regular and wide-ranging post-implementation review can provide a limited but important countermeasure both in helping to spot irregular system usage and deterring potential fraudsters from abusing the system. The following control questions may provide useful examples:

Does the new system fully meet initial specifications?
Were the initial systems specifications the best ones given the user's post-implementation experience and the use of hindsight?
Are all the system controls, see for example pages 100 to 109 above, in place and have they been positively compliance tested?
Have all non-conformance occurrences been recorded, investigated and fully explained?
Have all corrective actions been implemented and tested?
Have the performance of the contractors, project implementation team, and any training/support services been evaluated and any subsequent needs/actions implemented?

Computer-related reviews

This short section is intended to act rather like the fraud checklists considered in Chapter 3. Often management are unaware of the risks involved in the computerized system or parts of systems for which they are responsible. It is very important that the management should sometimes be able to stand back from the routine (of ensuring the system output or product is completed and arrives at its intended destination on time) and undertake a fraud risk review along the following three main themes:

1 Review the impact of potential financial loss and loss of sensitive data.
2 Review internal controls in areas highlighted by 1 above.
3 Review the key personnel (numbers, grade, performance, and so on) in the light of 1 and 2 above.

Of course the management, usually in conjunction with the internal audit service, will often undertake disaster recovery planning which assesses such impacts and the associated preventative actions relating to the loss of computing facilities, for example, reviewing the impact of terrorist attacks, fire and so on.

Given the specific objectives of combating fraud and corruption each review will probably appear narrower than a full audit or managerial review and will be weighted towards selected key control procedures. Each of the above three themes is considered below.

LOSS AND SENSITIVITY ASSESSMENT

What is proposed here is essentially a continuation of the risk modelling discussed in Chapter 3 taking account of the concept of materiality. The element of risk refers both to financial risk and to confidentiality. Some computer files will contain confidential personal data and although commercial confidentiality is less critical in many public services it too can be important.

For example, hospital patients' treatment data, tenants' rent arrears, council tax data, Inland Revenue details, and so on, all are confidential and sensitive and likely to fall under the provisions of the Data Protection Act 1998, which will be discussed later. Sometimes the impact of deliberate or accidental release of personal data can be financially very harmful in terms of compensation to data subjects, in any event unauthorized use or release of personal data may result in criminal conviction.

Many computerized systems will handle transaction ows of material significance. The concept of financial materiality historically stems from the concept of the risk to an external auditor of not uncovering errors that would affect the readers' interpretation of the accounts, that is, although the auditor can not be expected to spot all errors, a material financial error(s) would call into question the auditor's 'true and fair' opinion on the accounts. Thus an external auditor attempts to assess the 'materiality' of the balance being audited. For a set of accounts with a balance sheet total of, say, £120 000 000 and revenue expenditure of £90 000 000 over the year, a year-end provision for bad debts of the order of £10 000 would, other things being equal, be immaterial. Of course some audit effort would be required to verify the £10 000 was not hopelessly undervalued but it is unlikely that extensive audit testing or system evaluations would be undertaken. Perhaps, for these particular accounts the auditor may use his professional judgement to decide that the 'materiality' would be set at any balance or annual system throughput of less than say 0.005 per cent of £90 million for revenue and £120 million for balance sheet, that is, £450 000 and £600 000 respectively. The auditor would probably take additional notice of any major system that gave rise to an unexpectedly low value and the potential sensitivity of any particular figures. For example, expenditure directed at subsidizing, say, a controversial local hospital unit may amount to only £250 000 but require special attention by the auditor because a serious over- or understatement could undermine the credibility of the local politicians and call into question the auditor's own attention to sensitive detail.

This brief account of materiality in an external audit context belies the complex professional judgements that may be required to take account of monetary values and perceived risks. Nevertheless it can provide a useful model when applied to computer systems. Every installation and the software application used on it should be compared in the following terms:

1 The total value of transactions, including movements in value of assets, processed over a given period. (Higher priority, given the usual scarce computer audit resources, should normally be given to higher values.)
2 The number of important accounts balances or other management information totals affected by the system. (A major system that handles purchases, stock balances, losses, damages and produces year-end figures for current assets is likely to be more crucial in terms of fraud and corruption than a system that records and updates employees' training and qualifications records, though of course the latter will have some data protection and human resource management implications.)
3 The total number of transactions processed over a given period. (If, say, all but a few large commercial rental transactions relate to hundreds of peppercorn values of way-leaves, the few large ones can be isolated and quickly verified.)
4 The handling of personal data, especially any data of a sensitive nature relating to, say, income, illness or debt recovery. Apart from the risk of prosecution under the Data Protection Act, employees, contractors or suppliers may be blackmailed by others or tempted to access and amend their own records if these are not protected.
5 The political sensitivity of transactions in relation to known or anticipated areas of controversy such as repair times on empty properties, hospital waiting lists or funding of military research programmes. (This may have little direct practical effect in terms of fraud and corruption though politicians may be motivated to massage figures, leaving them exposed to corruption with wider fraudulent consequences.)

Such a loss and sensitivity assessment will usually, of course, be undertaken irrespective of the degree of computerization. In fact such considerations tend to be in the mind of any auditor, particularly at the planning stage of an assignment. When applied to computer systems and to the allocation of management effort in planning, organizing and controlling computer installations and running the necessary applications, the five points above prove useful in minimizing the risk, and maximizing the likely detection of fraud and corruption.

KEY CONTROLS REVIEW

The important systems identified from risk and sensitivity assessment are likely to vary from a laptop with software that records data relating to AIDS cases at hospitals, to a mainframe installation dedicated to the processing of a common payroll for several government departments or agencies. Some commonly recurring questions of control are listed below. In practice every installation and software application will require individual attention.

1 Are *control totals* produced and independently reconciled to ensure the completeness, accuracy and correct disclosure (accountability) of transactions processed between initial input and final output; for example, between manually produced timesheet totals by value and number and hourly paid wages payroll; or between changes in letting of domestic properties and weekly or monthly rent account totals?

2 Is a *separation of duties* maintained between staff who control the input of data (nowadays with increased PC use and networks these are often becoming the data users) and staff who act as programmers, software designers or systems maintainers? In general, control of the installation and running of software may be in the hands of a computer department. Where independent PCs are provided or networks are under the control of departmental mangers this separation of duties is plainly more difficult to maintain and needs to be compensated by regulatory controls. Corporate policy/regulations should lay down both the operating systems used and the software applications to be run on the computers. At corporate level too a computer security-type policy should determine appropriate controls, along the lines discussed earlier in this chapter. It is vital that individual users are not left to decide such policy and controls outside any corporate guidance and regulation, combined with regular and independent computer audit. The risk of fraudulent and illegal use of software and data is always increased by unregulated use of PCs and networks. In a mainframe batch processing situation the operational and programming staff in particular should be separated including, if possible, physical separation of office accommodation.

3 Are controls in place that *independently verify input* for example, along the lines discussed earlier in this chapter? Traditional bulk batch processing often involved all input data being separately keyed in and verified. If, as is often the case today, this is not feasible, are for example, samples of input verified by supervisory or managerial staff?

4 Are controls in place over *access to the system*, particularly while live data is being handled? Examples might include password controls, usually at different levels of authority, so that while junior officers can read files, only supervisors or a separate group of staff can enter transactions and only management can amend key fields such as debt redemption dates. Other access controls include, for example, physical measures such as high-security rooms, or key-operated switches on terminals.

5 Are separations (mentioned in point 2 above) and other key controls maintained at times of *system changes or malfunction*? Computer staff may require access to live data, particularly to standing or near-permanent data such as addresses, account numbers, and

so on. Given that additional maintenance may be carried out on a regular basis it is not unknown for computer staff to have relatively frequent access to live files and for any separation in duty, often carefully set up by the user, to be in effect overridden by computer staff with subsequent risks to the integrity of the data.

6 *Is all access traceable to the responsible individual* (including failed attempts) and any consequent data amendment? This is often best maintained by ensuring that every person who can gain access is issued with a genuinely confidential, regularly changed, password. Ideally, the use of his or her password automatically records that person's name or initials in a field which cannot be subsequently amended and is reproduced in any hard-copy computer activity log.
7 Are independent *'change control authorizations'* kept for any changes to software or key fields and key data? This is particularly important when changes to access permissions or amendments to standing data are authorized.
8 Are adequate and remote *back-up copies* of all work, client accounts, and so on, kept? The traditional 'grandfather-father-son' level of copies is adequate for most situations.
9 Are the *physical security controls*, particularly access to any mainframe site, regularly reviewed by an independent security manager, auditor or equivalent? Many so-called computer frauds result from conventional theft of data or high value printed output such as cheques.
10 Is all *sensitive or high value printed output* subject to control such as stock control records, transfer authorization and, where appropriate, shredding after use?
11 Are *electronic funds and sensitive data transmissions authenticated*? This might, for example, be achieved by subsequent telephone calls, automatic confirmation such as that used by automatic bank transfer systems or the use of passwords between recipient and sender.
12 Are controls set up to ensure *all exception reports are actioned* by appropriate managers or technical officers? It is particularly critical for obvious reasons to ensure that arrangements continue operating during sickness, holidays, and so on.

For the sake of brevity and impact the author has limited this review section to the dozen points above. If any manager considers that systems judged of high priority in the first review are significantly deficient in any of the above he or she should consider taking urgent advice and action.

ASSESSMENT OF KEY PERSONNEL

Recruitment, retention and career development measures can, depending upon the particular circumstances, play an important role in minimizing fraud and corruption. This is particularly true of computer professionals. Such staff are often exceptionally mobile with specialized skills and often employed on a contract or ad hoc project basis. Although professional bodies exist, many IT professionals are often unrestrained by the possibility of professional censure or risk of being struck off from any professional membership:

1 References should always be followed up, if necessary telephoning the referees to clear up any ambiguity. Organizations often wish to avoid acrimonious dismissal, particularly prosecution and any attendant publicity resulting from computer fraud. Some organizations have been accused of giving unwarranted and misleading references simply to ensure corrupt personnel leave with the minimum of fuss.

2 New and temporary staff should be prevented from gaining access to and control over high value data, the transfer of significant assets or sensitive information.
3 Staff should be made fully aware of where their IT duties begin and end including comprehensive and up to date desk instructions and work manuals.
4 All staff should be made aware of their responsibilities under the Data Protection Act 1998.
5 All holidays should be taken. (Fraudsters are often reluctant to take leave and risk any replacement gaining access to their work.)
6 An agreed procedure for review of career and performance and for counselling employees should be maintained. Computerization can introduce additional, often boring, routine into previously interesting work patterns (although sometimes the reverse is true). Some positions involve little more than minimal intervention by operating staff into an automated procedure. Such circumstances can engender a feeling of achievement in managing to beat the system. This may manifest itself in nothing more serious than altering human work routines to enable a few hours' sleep during a night shift or using a PC to play games. Or it may, by only a few incremental steps, lead to malicious diversion of funds or theft of data.

Using computers to directly combat fraud

Many of the reported cases of computer fraud give the impression that the information technology revolution has worked mainly to the advantage of the fraudster. It is impossible to say what position we would now be in if there had been no such revolution. Certainly such developments have changed the face of business and financial management, but many developments have worked against fraudsters and other criminals, and computerization has often encouraged controls to counter normal human fallibility, for example, individual computer passwords are relatively simple and secure controls that protect records more conveniently than restrictions on physical access to ledgers or filing cabinets or locks on office doors.

More directly than as a spin-off from IT aimed at business needs, several developments have proved particularly helpful in directly preventing, deterring, investigating or otherwise combating fraud. These are all forms of more general computer-assisted audit techniques (CAATs) and the ones selected below are by no means an exhaustive list, simply those that have already been established as reasonably useful.

SPECIALIST AUDIT INTERROGATION SOFTWARE

There is a wide variety of audit packages available on the market; most are updated by the suppliers on a regular basis and it would be unfair to single out any for special attention. Some include all or most of the subcategories of CAATs listed below, most will be able to compare files, extract data that falls within given parameters, offer sampling facilities, provide reports geared to routine investigations such as transactions related to particular suppliers, time periods, budget holders and so on.

PERSONAL DATA MATCHING

One has to be careful to remain within the law and use data matching responsibly, seeking the latest guidance issued by the Office of the Information Commissioner. The Audit

Commission has issued a code of practice for local authorities. It is vital to ensure that there are valid reasons or grounds for investigating the relationships between two or more sets of personal data, for example benefit claimants and temporary workers, or student awards home addresses from different education authorities and so on. There have been examples of successful data matching exercises using data from different local authorities under the coordination of the Audit Commission but this is a technique that can be used by individual internal auditors, benefit inspectors and others provided it is justified.

BULK TRANSACTION CHECKING

Nowadays specialist audit software or in-house report writing facilities can help to read through, recalculate/check and extract transactions with particular features. This means that some at least of the routine substantive testing can be extended or errors can be brought to the attention of management, though usually simple mis-keying errors will be spotted during basic data vet checks. Particularly useful in some situations is the ability to vet say, VAT numbers against a formula that checks if they correctly conform to the way such numbers should be complied, that is, not simply fraudulently made up. (Basically, list the first seven digits and multiply each by 8, 7, 6, 5, 4, 3, and 2 respectively, sum the answers, then subtract 97 from the total repeatedly, until you get a negative result, this should equal the last two digits.) Another use of bulk comparisons can be to see if invoices or other documents conform to 'Benfords Law', on the grounds that populations or parts of populations with fraudulent numbers will be more likely to stick out as not conforming and thus worth investigation. (Basically the 'law' predicts the frequency with which digits should occur in large, unadulterated, listings, for example, the first digit will be 1 about 30 per cent of the time and so on with higher value digits being less likely to come first and combinations of the first two or three digits having very low probabilities of occurrence.) There are many other possibilities for bulk transaction vetting, such as for the validity of various licence numbers, order codes, supplier names, postcodes, or simply unusually large payments or other suspect fields.

SAMPLING

Many statistical sampling routines are now available to auditors and fraud investigators, though these are not usually designed specifically to meet their specialized objectives, being provided as part of audit software designed for more general audit needs (see the Bibliography). Sampling routines are usually aimed at detecting innocent errors and control deviations among mass transaction ows and large balances, which is rarely of immediate use in the fight against fraud and corruption. Sometimes however, fraudulent transactions are uncovered by statistical sampling even though most sampling is undertaken on a random basis. Certainly given the relatively low probability of spotting fraudulent items among what are often small sample sizes, when these are uncovered they are likely to be indicative of a more serious situation. The use of statistical and non-statistical sampling is increasing and may well lead to improved counter-fraud measures among bulk transaction processing.

AUDIT TEST DATA

This is a well established technique involving the use of data deliberately designed to trigger off data vet controls and other parameter-based safeguards designed to reject data that does not conform to such predetermined parameters. Examples might include monetary values, certain originator codes, suspect suppliers and so on. The usefulness of test data depends very much on the ability of the auditors and investigators to design tests that re ect the intentions of potential fraudsters, always a difficult and imaginative task.

The IT legal framework

In Chapter 1 the reader saw something of how the law defines and attempts to make broad provision for fraud and corruption. Some of the statutes predate widespread computerization but three important exceptions are discussed below.

COMPUTER MISUSE ACT 1990

For many years it was held that the ordinary civil and criminal law was adequate to deal with computer crime, the basic characteristics of which do not differ from non-computer crime. The main difference was not the crime but the medium of its perpetration. The phenomena of computer hacking and viruses appear to be the main developments that discredited this view. Hacking refers to gaining unauthorized access to computer data, usually due to lack of adequate control over telephone links or insecure network arrangements. Hackers appear to come from a wide range of backgrounds and motivations and many appear to be young, well-educated and motivated in part at least by the thrill of what was, until 1990, not generally considered illegal even though it arguably amounted to a form of breaking and entering.

A computer virus is a programmed unauthorized alteration to operating systems or other data stored in the memory or back-up storage. Usually it arrives via email attachments or corrupted software that has been purchased or copied on to magnetic disc. Like an organic virus it reproduces itself as programs are executed and magnetic media are utilized for memory or storage functions. Perhaps its most worrying characteristic is the relative ease of transmission between organizations and sites.

Neither of these two basic phenomena appear to be adequately covered by existing law. Indeed there are claimed to be other equally serious omissions, such as a lack of measures to combat international computer fraud and the lack of a precise definition of a computer.

Nevertheless as far as hacking is concerned the Computer Misuse Act attempts to legislate against unauthorized access to computers in section 1 (the basic offence) and section 2 (the aggravated offence) and against unauthorized modifications (the virus offence) in section 4. Section 3 contains a separately worded offence to take into account Scottish law. Appendix 9 contains the relevant sections.

DATA PROTECTION ACT 1998

The 1998 Act replaces the earlier 1984 Act. The Act aims to help protect people's privacy and reduce the risk of misuse of personal data. It lays down restrictions in the way such data can be acquired and used. The 1984 Act applied only to personal data held on computers and automatic processing devices but this has been extended by the 1998 Act to related manually held data. Of the three main areas of legislation considered in this section the Data Protection Act 1998 is probably the most widely used in the public services.

The Act is not primarily designed to deal with fraud and corruption. Rather it aims to ensure that personal data, that is, data relating to living individuals, is held accurately, securely, in a publicly accountable manner and is used only for intended and registered purposes.

In practice almost every organization that has computer-held records relating to names, addresses, diseases, insurance policies, job descriptions or literally any data from which it would be possible to identify an individual should complete a registration document. The registration covers such matters as:

1 the purposes for which the data is held;
2 the types of data held;
3 the sources from which the data is obtained;
4 to whom the data will be disclosed; and
5 any transfers of data abroad and other details.

A summary of each organization's registration(s) is given in the publicly available data protection register, held at main libraries and at the headquarters of the Information Commissioner in Cheshire.

The Act also lays down eight principles governing the collection, holding, use and dissemination of computer-held personal data. Most importantly, from our point of view, the Act provides that data shall be held securely and used only for the legitimate registered purposes, though it must be said that purposes are often recorded, as least in the public register, in fairly broad terms. The principles are summarized in Figure 5.3.

In general the Act provides an additional, and sometimes unintended, layer of defence against corruption and fraud. The seventh principle is very useful as it requires adequate security. Most public services bodies are particularly sensitive to their statutory obligations and this Act brings computer security and secure systems within those obligations.

COPYRIGHT, DESIGNS AND PATENTS ACT 1988

This Act is relevant to issues of fraud and corruption in so far as computer-related fraud may well involve the illegal copying of computer software. This offence is sometimes rather glamorously referred to as software piracy. The 1988 Act lays down that for copyright purposes software programs may be considered in the same way as literary works and illegal copying can be the subject of civil or criminal redress in the courts.

Illegal copying from, say, a hard disc supplied by a software company to the purchaser's own diskette and thence to other discs, is likely to be far more costly for the copyright owner than illegal photocopies from the pages of a book or magazine. The cost of a single copy of a piece of software can run into thousands of pounds. By comparison few people are likely to copy an entire book. Several recent examples of legal action or cases settled out of court indicate that software suppliers are starting to find enforcement action is now well worth paying for.

Principles of Data Protection

The rules

Anyone processing personal data must comply with the eight enforceable principles of good practice. They say that data must be:

fairly and lawfully processed;
processed for limited purposes;
adequate, relevant and not excessive;
accurate;
not kept longer than necessary;
processed in accordance with the data subject's rights;
secure; and
not transferred to countries without adequate protection.

Personal data covers both facts and opinions about the individual. It also includes information regarding the intentions of the data controller towards the individual, although in some limited circumstances exemptions will apply. With processing, the definition is far wider than before. For example, it incorporates the concepts of 'obtaining', 'holding' and 'disclosing'.

The full explanation of the principles can be found on the Commissioner s web site, www.dataprotection.gov.uk

Figure 5.3 Principles of data protection

Corporate policy for IT security and data protection

Nowadays IT, like finance, is a function that permeates across the whole organization with implications for work practices in general and countering fraud in particular. Most public bodies have detailed corporate policy on financial control, regulations and security often found in 'standing orders' or 'accounting manuals' and the like. These policy and practice issues are usually appreciated by managers and staff beyond the finance function though they may still need assistance from financial staff at times. Such a detailed level of corporate wide coordination and appreciation is often lacking in respect of IT and data protection. Even when detailed IT and data protection policy, manuals and regulations are available they tend to be available and appreciated by relatively few specialist staff and awareness of the presence and implications is often minimal or absent among general managers and staff.

Although the importance of this lack of policy and awareness is not limited to combating fraud and corruption, it is in this respect particularly worrying. Fraudsters ourish in areas of complexity that also lack consistent policy and standards. Appendix 10 sets out one possible structure for such a policy, though it is important that each organization tailors this to meet their precise needs. In any organization such a policy will need to be reviewed and amended from time to time. Readers are also advised to consider IT security standards that have already gained wide acceptance by industry, public services and commercial firms such as BS 7799.

Summary

Apart from the technology involved in its perpetration, computer fraud is very similar to any fraud. The technology is changing all the time. Even the key controls outlined above gain or lose a little relevance with each new development. Despite these shifting sands the importance of separating key duties, of maintaining controls over computer input, processing and output and of independent control of the development, support and maintenance of all systems remains paramount. The chapter so far has outlined these features and attempted to identify review issues including key controls that can be widely applied to any computerized systems. The legal framework, originally mentioned in Chapter 1, has been further considered as it pertains to computer-related security.

CASE STUDIES

The first case relates to armed robbery and blackmail. It illustrates the need for close control of sensitive personal data. The second case considers the security and access controls consistent with large mainframe computer facilities.

CASE STUDY 5.1

THE GALLERY SPORTS CLUB

Beneath the headquarters of a government department, located in a basement, is a social and sports club, the Gallery. Members are drawn from a wide spectrum of the civil service, national health service and other public services.

A computerized membership and booking system has recently been introduced. The system handles advance bookings from members and non-members, cash receipts at the reception area, invoicing of debtors, cancellations, and – the weak link in this case – membership records.

Membership costs £90.00 per annum plus additional rates for specialized activities including the gun club. A typical membership record gives wide-ranging details of name, address, next of kin, job title, workplace, including quite often work contact telephone numbers and a membership number to which is suffixed a letter to identify any special activities; G for gun club, Q for squash, C for cycling, and so on.

The letter enabled each membership number to be used by the computer to calculate total annual fees owed and automatically invoice these to the member.

The entire system consisted of a small and rather dated processor, a printer and three terminals, two at reception and one in the club secretary's office. Neither the secretary nor any other officials of the club including the four part-time receptionists had any formal training for using a computerized system. The company that installed the hardware and provided the software did an adequate job of instructing their customer in using the system, but little if any guidance was provided in ensuring adequate security. The shortcomings in internal control and the contravention of the Data Protection Act (of which the staff were

CASE STUDY 5.1 *concluded*

unaware) only came to light when a wave of gun thefts took place.

As is usual in such cases the benefit of hindsight revealed a complete lack of computer security. Like so many small PC and network systems operated by relatively inexperienced staff, the following were among the serious inadequacies:

1. Inadequate password control over access. A single password was used to access the entire system, usually at the start of each day. It was normal practice to leave the terminal in the secretary's office switched on throughout the day irrespective of who was in the room at the time. The password had in any case not been changed since the system was installed and was widely known to staff and some members of the organizing committee of the club. Ideally passwords should be changed every few weeks.
2. No one was aware of the need to register the system with the Data Protection Registrar (exemptions might apply to private clubs but not in this case) or to operate the system in compliance with the principles set out in the Data Protection Act.
3. Control over output on screen or printouts was negligible. Summary printouts of members, fees outstanding, change of address details, and so on, were held in ring binders on open shelves either behind the reception desk or in the secretary's office. Both these locations were subject to access by members with enquiries and to sales people. Screens were frequently left switched on and unattended.
4. No facility was available for any of the screens to be 'blanked' without the user having to exit from the enquiry facility he or she was currently using. Thus customers or other visitors were often left alone with a live screen while the receptionist or the secretary went to obtain information or was called away to deal with an enquiry.

In this case it came as no surprise to the investigating police and senior civil service management that a printout of members' addresses with G suffixes (about 14 in all) had found its way into the hands of a criminal/terrorist gang who had raided most of the addresses on the night of the annual Sports Club dinner. Most properties were empty at the time but several members and their families had been tied up and gagged and one had been shot and wounded. During this one evening about 20 weapons had been stolen.

In addition to the theft of data relating to weapons, investigations revealed that the club had regularly disclosed membership lists (without suffixes) to a company selling sports goods. There was no risk of fraud here, but given the failure to notify members of the intention to disclose this information or to register the disclosure with the Data Protection Registrar it was nevertheless an infringement of the law.

Obvious lessons emerge from this case. The general attitude towards computerization and internal control was extremely lax. Access controls, control over output and a general attitude of care for and compliance with the law relating to personal data are obviously required.

In practice screens in an area visible to the public should be capable of being blanked, and operators should log off from the system when screens are not in use. Passwords should be reviewed regularly. Output should be stored in a secure manner. In this case a thief could have generated the list, stolen a copy already printed, hand or photocopied a list or even noted the details from a screen left unattended.

In respect of the Data Protection Act it is worth noting that where serious non-compliance occurs individuals as well as organizations may be the subject of legal action.

CASE STUDY 5.2

CENTRAL STRATEGIC HEALTH AUTHORITY MAINFRAME INSTALLATION

The Central Strategic Health Authority operates a major mainframe computer installation that offers its services directly to independent trust hospitals and other health service bodies.

Various applications are run on the mainframe which has, following several reorganizations in the health service, proved a popular facility. Two large mainframes are operated and a separate local area network advisory service (LANADS) is available to users at an annual subscription. Ad hoc consultancy projects are also undertaken.

A recent report by the auditors has pointed out that the current staffing levels are considerably higher than for other similar NHS organizations. Management do not dispute the auditors' findings but point out that while the computer unit are managing to cover all their costs from recharges they are reluctant to make staff cuts. Natural wastage will, they anticipate, enable staff numbers to be reduced. They also intend retraining some staff to cope with the small but growing advice and consultancy service offered to outside bodies.

At about the same time as the audit report an internal management report pointed out that the log of computer operations was likely to be inaccurate and was in any case incomplete for about a quarter of the past year. The same management report also pointed out that formal authorizations of 'change-control' procedures were unacceptable (authorization sheets were generally unsigned and the reasons given for a program change were too short to be meaningful). Copy programs and systems documentation, especially security copies, were not updated on a regular basis and exception reports had no evidence of any review or action taken (though on this point the computer manager insisted that actions were taken but agreed they were not adequately documented).

During a meeting between the management report's author and the computer manager the latter accepted the main points of the report. The management report also raised several points relating to physical security, as follows:

1 Physical access to the computer. A main corridor, lift and stairs used by all staff at central headquarters runs through the suite. The doors to the main computer room, though lockable, are frequently left unlocked as staff need to pass between the mainframes and the control areas. Smoke detectors are in place but these use an old-fashioned sprinkler system which if set off accidentally or maliciously would cause immense damage compared to modern gas-based extinguishers.
2 Magnetic back-up storage is on site rendering it vulnerable in the event of disaster.
3 Emergency back-up procedures in the event of accidental or malicious disaster have not been tested for several years and appear out of date.
4 The windows are of normal glass and though kept locked are considered unlikely to present an acceptable level of deterrence. The computer suite contains several million pounds worth of movable hardware (excluding the mainframes) and is located on the ground oor.

These points have been re-addressed by the auditors in a subsequent report.

The staff association has asked that computer staff receive a special market premium in addition to the annual negotiated pay settlement. They point out that staff turnover is relatively high and pay rates lower than several published surveys. Morale, they say, is generally low.

CASE STUDY 5.2 *continued*

In this particular scenario it is quite likely that the management and auditors would have continued to make gradual, faltering progress towards improving security and internal controls. Extra security costs money. Staff morale is already likely to be poor given the turnover and any extra red tape such as adequate descriptions and authorization of changes to programs set out in change-control authorization is likely to be treated with resistance if not contempt. The computer staff probably realize the site is overstaffed. For some posts boredom and the lack of challenge or job satisfaction may be an additional demoralizing in uence.

In such a situation a major event can often act as a catalyst to improvement. Ideally this might be a complete change in senior management or in management attitudes, introducing an ethos of greater professionalism, an ethos that encourages higher standards, if only perhaps because these are felt to be worth achieving for their own sake, despite the apparent acceptance of the current service quality by the users. If a new management outlook is not forthcoming then at least a more persuasive and hard-hitting audit approach might encourage managers to rectify the current problems before disaster strikes. In this case, not unusually perhaps, disaster struck first. It came in the form of a major fraud involving unauthorized use of computing resources by staff to develop private software and the embarrassing release of sensitive personal health data.

A senior programmer who had been forced to resign from her previous employment for perpetrating a similar offence on a lesser scale could not resist the temptation to start up in business a second time. No legal or disciplinary action had been taken by her previous employers, an insurance company, who had in fact provided a short and acceptable reference (probably because they were glad to get rid of her without any embarrassing disclosures). During interview the lady explained that she had left her previous employer to live close to her sick mother. Given her outstanding qualifications, no further queries were considered necessary.

Compared to her previous employment she found her new workload less demanding and the controls, especially the log of computer usage and controls over the testing of new or amended programs, were lax. Her illegal activities and those of her close colleagues to whom her corrupting in uence had spread, might have continued unnoticed. However, some of the test data used to illustrate the functions of the software being developed and sold contained, unintentionally, live records of recent patient treatment. One of these records was found, to the annoyance of its subject, to have been purchased by himself from a small independent company set up by the perpetrators to market their illicitly produced software. The subject took legal action against the Health Authority. His complaint was found to be well founded and he was awarded considerable compensation. The perpetrators were quickly dismissed, this time with considerable publicity. A great deal more public money was spent recovering patient records and compensating firms who had purchased the illegal software.

The main lesson from this case is, of course, that such a situation should not have been allowed to arise in the first place, but more than this, that we should look beyond technical issues of internal control, physical security, and so on, to the underlying corporate attitudes in attempting to understand the wider causes and risk. In particular new staff should be screened and existing staff (who were soon dragged into this case) must not be taken for granted. Regular performance review by senior

CASE STUDY 5.2 *concluded*

management, as suggested by the staff themselves, and career development counselling might well have revealed a bored and disgruntled workforce with a high level of unsatisfied skills and the opportunity and temptation to use these to ill effect.

Concluding points

This chapter has considered 'ordinary' fraud and corruption in relation to information technology. A computerized working environment has become a feature of most public services bodies. Certain familiar aspects of fraud and corruption and the appropriate countermeasures must be seen afresh.

Protection and control of physical assets and access to computer hardware, accounting for changes in program software and in key data, separation of duties, confidentiality of financial or personal data and password control – these are just a few of the important issues.

Certain standard procedures take on an added significance in relation to information technology, particularly with regard to staff recruitment.

The second case study illustrates the importance of an independent and detached frame of mind when dealing with or managing information technology. It is often worthwhile to turn one's mind away from the demands of ever-changing technological details to what appear to be the overall objectives of the computerized system. These objectives should be those of the people who control and operate the system, and of the organizations of which it is part. If they are not and, say, objectives of individual line management are out of synchronization with corporate objectives or the intended use of the system and this has been allowed to persist, then there is every chance that assets might be used corruptly and fraud occur without detection.

Usually the objectives of anyone, especially the auditor, wishing to prevent fraud will coincide with sound management provided such objectives are not taken to the extreme. Given the rapidly changing pace of new technology, more trust than usual may, unavoidably, need to be placed in the technical experts especially when new systems are being introduced. In many ways this means that all the more weight should be given to ensuring that key controls such as those described in this chapter are introduced and reviewed effectively. Such controls should be designed to meet as many as possible of the following objectives:

1 To ensure the new technology satisfies a genuine need in line with political policy, corporate strategy and management objectives (in that order).
2 To ensure technology is acquired and used honestly, economically, efficiently and effectively, that is, offers fraud-free 'VFM'.
3 To ensure the continuing accuracy, fairness (that is, objectivity) and relevance of the financial and management information produced by each system.
4 To ensure the adequacy and ongoing reliability of each system as a whole and all its controls (in line with 1, 2 and 3 above).

These objectives may apply, of course, to any non-computerized system and are, depending on the circumstances, likely to be interdependent.

A frame of mind that keeps these objectives in view often requires that the computer auditor should not consider him or her self as 'auditing computers' or the manager as 'managing computers'. Rather they should consider themselves as auditing or managing a part of the wider corporate system for say, maximizing the return from land and buildings, or processing salaries and wages, or ensuring a defence need is maintained, depending upon the audit or corporate objectives that apply to each. Given the need to keep up with changing technology, attaining such a frame of mind can present the manager or auditor with a genuine professional challenge.

CHAPTER

6 *Expenditure*

Introduction

The systems that facilitate routine expenditure on goods and services – broadly speaking, sundry creditors' payments and their associated activities – deserve special attention. Individual revenue payments may often be of relatively low value compared to capital payments (discussed in Chapter 4) but there is strong evidence that the revenue expenditure systems are among the most frequently abused and, in total, account for more fraud than most other systems. The only convenient published public services statistics come from the Audit Commission and expenditure-related fraud has figured prominently for many years, both in respect of the regular IT fraud surveys mentioned in the previous chapter and in the summarized individual cases published in the commissions updates and in *Audit Viewpoint.*

Whatever the correct statistics – which no one will ever know for certain – creditor payments is a critical area for fraud prevention. Almost any level of fraud discovered among the expenditure systems is often indicative of more widespread malaise and corruption. Sometimes frauds can be shown to arise solely in unusual circumstances or isolated locations. But, in general, the detection of just one or two cases of revenue expenditure fraud will indicate serious internal control problems.

A trail of responsibility

An audit trail or trail of responsibility should exist throughout the revenue expenditure systems, as shown in Figure 6.1. This trail should be clear throughout the:

procurement,
purchasing and
payment functions,

and be able to demonstrate:

1 who required a purchase to be made and for what purpose;
2 who ordered it and if possible at what estimated cost;
3 who checked it was satisfactorily received (or performed in the case of services); and
4 who authorized payment to be made.

At each stage from ordering through receipt of goods and invoice to actual payment, separate records of the individual quantities and values involved should be kept.

Ideally, the main duties involved, that is:

1 ordering and buying
2 custody and usage
3 bookkeeping and recording and
4 final distribution of any cheques, processing of BACS payments and so on,

should as far as possible be undertaken by separate staff. At times, particularly in smaller organizations or local offices, complete separation of duties may prove too costly to be efficient. Even in larger organizations staff may be unavailable when an urgent need is established or an urgent payment is required. In these circumstances, at least two people should be actively involved in the payment authorization prior to payment being despatched (whether payment is by post, electronic funds transfer, or even by handing over cash to a supplier).

An acceptable level of internal controls in a typical organization's revenue expenditure system would involve most of the following (or a high level of compensating, and usually costly, control activity such as direct supervision by senior management).

PROCUREMENT

Official requisition forms that are:

1 Pre-numbered with a record of all spoils or cancelled forms and the officer responsible for controlling forms Nos 1 to n; and
2 Signed and dated by the officer(s) authorized to requisition goods/services and, if different, the officer requiring the goods/services.

PURCHASING

The above will usually suffice for internal requisitions, for example, for goods already purchased and held in store. For external purchases, whether required to top up reorder levels or for ad hoc items control would normally include:

3 Official pre-numbered purchase orders (possibly using the same form as for internal requisition as in 1 above) also signed and dated by an authorized officer as for 2 above. Most importantly, a separation of duties should be maintained between the officer requiring the goods or services who initiated the order in the first place (or is responsible for confirming the need for regular reorders) and the officer undertaking the buying or purchasing of goods or services for the organization.
4 Delegated expenditure levels for individual ordering officers, or budget holders, or whoever is responsible for finally authorizing the purchase. Where, as is often the case, a central buying officer makes all purchases on behalf of numerous ordering officers these should have delegated expenditure levels set and made known to the buying officer.

If 3 and 4 are not feasible, possibly due to manpower budget restrictions or to the small size of the organization, a senior finance officer (or whoever is responsible for monitoring expenditure against budgets but is not directly involved in initiating purchases) should check all purchase documentation or at least a judgemental selection, depending on time available, to ensure:

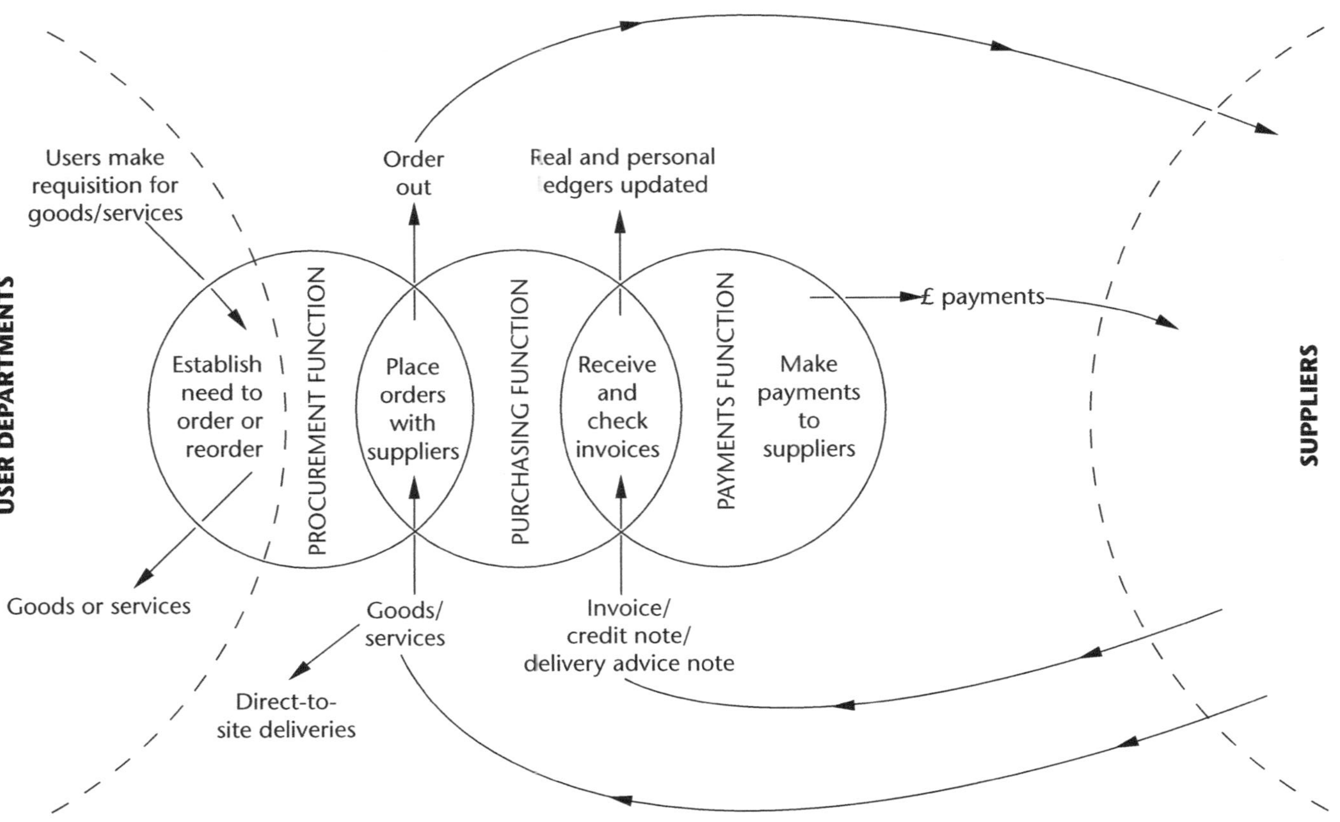

Figure 6.1 The trail of responsibility through the revenue expenditure system

(a) goods or services do not appear *ultra vires*, that is, beyond the statutory powers of the public body;
(b) the quantity and nature appear reasonable in relation to the ordering officer's duties;
(c) the order has been properly completed and signed and dated by an officer authorized so to do; and
(d) any delegated expenditure levels (per item or per budget ceiling) are not exceeded.

If possible any major physical assets should be verified by inspection.

DELIVERY

This is often the most difficult stage over which to maintain reliable control. Goods can arrive at various, often unexpected, locations sometimes direct to a building site or perhaps to a remote sub office. The carrier is often in a great hurry to get on with the next delivery and may not even be clearly aware of the nature of the goods he is unloading. The 'delivery' of services is often impossible to fully verify. Goods can at least be counted or measured but who is to say that a service engineer has accurately and diligently checked a piece of equipment, or that a professional legal opinion has been based on careful judgement? If such services are inadequate this will usually be revealed in time but not until long after payment has been made and little hope of recovery remains.

Despite these difficulties some of the more useful controls are given below.

5 Delivery advice notes for goods should be signed by the consignor or on his behalf by the carrier and by the consignee, preferably after the latter has checked the delivery. The author has yet to come across large deliveries of bricks being individually counted or reels of wire being measured before the carrier has left the site but should any queries arise once the materials have been checked an unsigned delivery note can cause problems. It is generally acceptable practice for the site foreman, storekeeper, night security officer or whoever to receive a delivery to sign 'for receipt only' or 'accepted not checked'. This is done on the understanding that undue delay would be entailed in checking at the time and place of delivery and a reputable supplier would take the word of a reputable customer on the odd occasion a discrepancy arises. Notwithstanding these obvious exceptions most goods can be checked and signed for without undue effort before the delivery advice note is signed.
   Very occasionally firms will deliver without an advice note. In such circumstances a photocopy order also signed, or a separate in-house goods received note must be made up.
6 The delivery advice or goods received note should be matched to the order and the order marked off. Again, this should if possible be done prior to the departure of the carrier. It is surprising how often invoices are subsequently matched to orders and paid while the delivery advice note is ignored. Often handwritten adjustments or only part deliveries are noted on the advice note but this information takes time to get back to the supplier's accounts payable department, who invoice on the assumption that full payment is owed. If the consignee has paid an invoice against an order that has not been matched and annotated to show any discrepancy, any attempt to chase up late delivery of goods still outstanding (that may have been paid for) is likely to run into severe delays. This problem may be lessened when combined delivery notes/invoices are used by suppliers but only if the purchase orders are carefully matched to delivery prior to payment.

PAYMENT AUTHORIZATION

This is, or should be, the stage at which evidence from all the foregoing stages is drawn together.

7 Each payment should be separately authorized. This statement seems fairly straightforward, though in fact several complications can arise. Varying methods of payment must all be subject to a common standard of authorization, for example:
   (a) cash;
   (b) computer-produced cheque runs;
   (c) ad hoc cheque payment;
   (d) automatic bank transfers;
   (e) credit notes issued; and
   (f) payable orders issued by HM Paymaster General.

In any one organization several main methods are likely to be used; regular cheque runs and bank transfers are very common. Throughout, central government payable orders issued by HM Paymaster General are commonly used. Other media affecting payment or transferring credit may be used but a common standard should ensure the following.

8 Whatever method of final authorization for payment is used (signature, official seal/stamp, computer password/code) the authorizing officer should have been able to examine evidence, usually in the form of a subordinate's certification upon the invoice showing:
   (a) that the goods or services were ordered and the order was crossed off cancelled/marked as part-delivered or otherwise annotated to show the goods/services delivered were in fact required. Apart from ensuring an important defence against fraud this control ensures an excessive or even mis-delivered consignment is spotted before payment. It is useful in ensuring no duplicate payments occur. Many firms will re-invoice if payment has not been promptly received. Suppliers commonly telephone organizations to speed up payment. If the person they speak to does not have their invoice conveniently to hand, another or a copy is quite likely to be hastily despatched. Unless the invoice is compared to an order which has to be annotated (or all invoices are dealt with by only one clerk with an infallible memory) there is a very high probability of two invoices going through the system and resulting in duplicate payment;
   (b) that the goods or services were adequate;
   (c) that the prices charges were as agreed or as advertised;
   (d) that the arithmetic (including VAT, cost centre code, and so on) has been checked; and
   (e) that any other specific requirements of the body have been performed such as dual authorization of amounts over a certain value.

Points (a) to (e) above are fairly standard for most organizations. In any large organization several different officers are likely to be involved and each should sign to confirm the stage(s) he or she has performed. This will evidence a trail of responsibility. Wherever this paper trail disappears into a computerized system the person(s) responsible for processing payments, or confirming that their part of stages (a) to (e) has been completed, must be able to evidence their authorization in a secure manner. In this respect secure password control is essential.

When only one person has responsibility for authorizing a particular computerized stage the part of the system affected must be protected by a password unique to that person. However, when more than one person can have responsibility for authorizing a particular stage, for example checking goods received or checking the arithmetic of the invoice, then secure authorization becomes more difficult.

In such circumstances each operator must be able to generate a unique password. Once the system has been accessed, using this unique password, evidence should remain on screen and printout – without revealing the password – of which officer accessed and amended the data. For example, each password once keyed in should automatically generate the initials or name of the password owner in a predesignated, tamper-proof field.

Unfortunately when several passwords are being used the chance of one becoming known to an unauthorized person is increased. Reasonably frequent password changes help, as do limitations on attempted system entry – points which were discussed in Chapter 5.

The complaint is sometimes raised that evidence that points (a) to (e) above have been certified prior to final authorization will mean 'mountains of paperwork' for the manager to wade through before signing the authorization or pressing the keyboard. This, in fact, would only be a real problem in a poorly managed system. The authorizing officer would normally be expected to rely on the signatures present on one summary document. This usually means the supplier's invoice must be forwarded to each relevant officer controlling stages (a) to (e), usually with a 'grid' stamped clearly on the front or (less securely) an authorization slip stapled to it.

PAYMENT PRODUCTION AND DISTRIBUTION

The final part of the payment stage is yet to come and this is the part most often ignored by management once they have completed their authorization.

9 Controls should exist to ensure that what has been authorized – and only what has been authorized – is paid. A cheque run, sometimes involving the production of thousands of computer-printed and presigned cheques, will usually be produced. Electronic and automatic funds transfer from the organization's own to possibly thousands of recipient bank accounts via BACS, CHAPS, GIRO or similar clearing arrangements are also common. Superimposed on these procedures will be urgent, usually manually produced, cheques and sometimes even large cash disbursements. Some of the more common controls are as follows.
   (a) Separate (manual) validation of input is still used in many batch input systems. Though this method of inputting information to the computer is becoming less and less efficient in the face of online updating it is often maintained simply because it works and the immediate risks and costs of change are perceived as high. Usually a batch 'header' slip is initialled by the officer who verified it. A single batch may consist of hundreds of payments though most batches are smaller.
   A wide range of computer controls are discussed in Chapter 5. But manual procedures may still have a key part to play.
   (b) At some point an overall reconciliation must take place. Usually this takes place in a central creditors section but it may be performed by devolved budget holders. The key question to ask is: 'Has the computerized payments system done what it was "told" to do?' Computer managers will usually say 'Of course. The system can only

do what it was told to do.' But all too often by 'system' they simply mean the hardware or at most the hardware and software. Hardware can malfunction, software can be poorly or corruptly designed or altered and both hardware and software are only as good as the people operating them. Where batch inputting is used payment schedules will usually be made up, perhaps for the whole organization, perhaps by division or section. Output reports should be available with payment totals that can be reconciled to the input schedules. Ideally this task should be undertaken by an officer not involved in the payment system up to this point, otherwise it should be undertaken by the budget holder or the officer making up the payment schedules. For a devolved online creditor payments system, where no schedule or batches are prepared, the budget holder, who may indeed be the authorizing officer, should be in a position to reconcile output. A cheque production run will normally take place no more frequently than weekly or at most daily and printouts or screen displays should be made immediately available to the officer responsible for reconciliation. It is important to realize that many exception reports made available by systems that carry out automatic reconciliations from input to output are rarely sufficient to deter fraud. Automatic reconciliation invariably depends upon the input being correct and untampered with in the first place and then being adequately vetted by processing controls within the system software. A mis-keyed amount, fraudulent amounts entered while terminals are left unattended or amounts produced by software that has been 'bugged' are unlikely to come to light through exception reporting.

10 As part of the final procedures of payment systems within most organizations come controls (if any) over posting out. Post rooms can be the scene of frantic activity towards the end of the working day but as a general rule someone must find time to take responsibility for counting and agreeing the number of creditor payments to be posted out. These should be signed for on transfer between cheque production (and possibly enveloping) and transfer to post room. Even if these duties are all undertaken immediately after cheque production it is still valid for the number of payments to be counted. The number of individual payments posted should be agreed to the cheque production run – usually a single figure at the end of a printout. For automatic bank transfer, payment statements should be received from the banks to confirm the completeness of receipt of a transmission or the completeness of receipt of payments processed on tape or other magnetic media. These statements should include total debits and credits by value and number, which should be agreed to in-house payment listings or be forwarded to budget holders and authorizing officers to be agreed in the same way as cheque runs.

11 Ideally, the distribution procedures, especially for cheques and payable orders, and so on, should not 'backtrack', that is, involve officers who have initiated or certified any stage or finally authorized payment. Thus if a false payment is generated it must be 'forced out' of the organization. The perpetrator of a fraud would then need a false address, or risk using his own address at which to collect the cheque or similar. Otherwise it is a simple matter for him or her to take possession of the cheque as it comes back into the system. Any exception to this rule, such as cheques that have to be handed over personally, during perhaps an exchange of legal documents, should be clearly sanctioned by senior mangers.

Key expenditure risks and controls

This is a convenient point to summarize the key areas of internal control in the basic procurement–purchase–payment system in the light of typical fraud-related risks. Plainly, this summary can not be exhaustive and each organization needs to evaluate the key risks and controls for its own circumstances, along the lines discussed in Chapter 3. But it is nevertheless hoped that the following may provide a useful starting point and a prompt for more detailed work.

GENERAL OBJECTIVES FOR EXPENDITURE SYSTEMS

The objectives of most routine payments systems are fairly standard, that is, that all payments relate to valid commitments, are due, and correctly and completely calculated and recorded. In general the risks are simply the reverse of the objectives. Looking at risks and controls simply in the light of these general payments objectives will help, but when it comes to fraud the detailed risks need to be specified according to particular processes and arrangements for each organization. Let's look at some typical examples.

TYPICAL EXAMPLES OF FRAUD AND CORRUPTION EXPENDITURE RISKS

Internal perpetration (with or without external collusion)

Obtaining or diverting goods/services improperly:

1 Directly ordering and obtaining of goods/services for improper use via false written orders (unauthorized or authorized), and so on.
2 As above but via telephone or email orders.
3 Over-ordering on an otherwise genuine order (with or without collusion with the supplier).
4 Diverting goods directly from safe custody in stores, offices and so on. (This risk is included for the sake of conceptual completeness but it really relates to the physical security arrangements rather than purchasing/payments.)

Obtaining/diverting payments improperly, essentially risk of overpayment:

5 Use of fictitious suppliers usually requiring false paperwork.
6 Collusion with suppliers, which could involve any of the above mentioned scenarios.
7 Directly generating/diverting false payments and overpayments with or without documentation and often in collusion with suppliers.
8 Generating duplicate payments often in collusion with a supplier.

External perpetration, essentially risk of overpayment:

9 By directly sending false invoices/demands for payment (including duplicate invoices) to 'customers'. (As in points 7 and 8 but externally initiated.)
10 By delivering goods or services not ordered by the customer and claiming payment.

TYPICAL CONTROLS TO COUNTER THE RISKS

Although it may not always be practical to have all the suggested controls in place at all times, managers should be careful that at least one well operated and sound control is in place to counter each of the risks above:

1. Pre-printed, pre-numbered and signed authorization required for requisitions and ordering. All staff must acknowledge their awareness of the requirement to use only these forms and any urgent telephone or email requisitions or orders must quote the number on the form, which must be despatched immediately. (A record of the issue of all pre-numbered stationery should be kept so that all such forms can be accounted for.)
2. No creditor invoice or other request for payment to be processed without the person responsible for authorizing payment checking and agreeing that the invoice, and so on, quotes a valid order number (see also points 4 and 7 below).
3. Delegated expenditure levels combined with independent budgetary control. Although budget holders will usually be expected to review and explain their own budgets, some level of independent accountability will help reduce risk of over-ordering, particularly regarding repeated small quantities. Usually the budget holder will be separate from the ordering process and the buying staff will be trained to query repeated or apparently unnecessary orders, otherwise the budget holder's reviews must be reviewed again by senior management. Sometimes accounting software will be able to identify and report on pre-judged suspicious ordering activity such as repeated orders to particular suppliers, orders over regularly reviewed levels, orders to unusual suppliers and so on.
4. Separation of duties between requisitioning or otherwise initiating the request for goods or services to be ordered from suppliers, undertaking the buying/ordering, authorizing and recording payment, taking custody of goods or receiving a service. These divisions are more difficult to maintain in some smaller bodies and at times of downsizing and reorganization but separation between the buying and the payment processing is particularly important for countering false creditors and collusion with suppliers. Point 5 below is bound up with this control.
5. Matching of deliveries to orders and marking the latter to show the deliveries were received and by whom (any subsequent over-delivery should be spotted easily).
6. Matching of invoices to orders and marking both as paid (any subsequent duplicate invoice should then also be easily spotted).
7. An identifiable chain or trail of certifying officers (by signature or computer password controlled and retained fields) responsible for checking each stage of payment as at points 4 to 6, culminating in the final signed authorization of payment.
8. Separate final authorization of each payment, that is, no proforma or 'listing' arrangements where junior clerks prepare unchecked/unsigned schedules of (usually numerous smaller) payments for senior staff to 'sign off'. Point 9 below is bound up with this control.
9. Reconciliation of input of payments by value and number to output totals of cheques, and so on, produced. This control is bound up with point 10.
10. Agreement of cheques produced to cheques posted out. This control is bound up with point 11.
11. No 'backtracking' of payment, that is, no cheques or direct debit payment authorizations/request for bank details to be routed back via the staff involved in

initiating and processing the orders or payments (to reduce the chance of false payments generated within the organization to be commandeered by the fraudster).

Figure 6.2 below links the above risks and controls in a grid format. It attempts to link the key control(s) that relate to each risk, though in practice other listed controls may help reduce the level of risk and in many practical situations managers may bolster up the effectiveness of particular controls or use other controls not listed here that work effectively in their situations.

Control→	1	2	3	4	5	6	7	8	9	10	11
Risk↓											
1	o	o			o	o					
2	o				o	o					
3			o								
4					o						
5				o	o		o		o	o	o
6				o	o		o				
7				o	o		o		o	o	o
8						o					
9						o		o			
10					o						

Figure 6.2 Risk/control grid for expenditure

Summary

Expenditure is always a risky area, particularly in the public services, which are often expenditure-driven. The key risks and controls are very maintenance-orientated, and even when one thinks that the systems are well controlled and risk of fraud is low or non-existent, new staff and the natural human tendency to take short cuts and deviate from the laid down procedures start to raise the levels of risk. It is fair to say that although the grids given in this chapter summarize important risks and controls, what is most important is to avoid complacency where expenditure is concerned.

CASE STUDIES

Two case studies follow. The first is very brief but typical of an increasing problem.

The relatively high risk of fraud in a poorly controlled expenditure system is generally recognized. As was mentioned at the start of the chapter, this is an area particularly prone to fraud. No system can give complete assurance against deliberate and planned fraud especially if collusion occurs. The rewards of a successful fraud in this area can often be very large and tend to involve an element of recurrence. This means, as will be illustrated in the second case, that dishonest staff may be prepared to accept an element of risk that in other systems might act as a deterrent and that once a method of perpetration has been devised it will be tried over and over again. Similar features of high risk/high reward apply to capital works payments (discussed in Chapter 4).

CASE STUDY 6.1

THE PUBLIC ORGANIZATIONS DIRECTORY EXCHANGE (PODE)

PODE is a fictitious example of a fictitious billing organization, though the mode of operation has become all too realistic among public services in recent years. The usual aim of false billing agencies is to obtain a large number of relatively small payments from as many organizations as possible who are, most importantly, a safe distance beyond realistic recovery action. They rely on poor internal controls in the organization targeted on appearing credible at first sight. For example:

1 They have names and logos similar in sound, spelling and appearance to genuine suppliers;
2 Their services are difficult to validate in a tangible manner and the goods will have been consumed, processed or passed on prior to the arrival of their invoice; and
3 Their bills are timed to arrive when workloads are high but budgets are largely unspent; when regular managers and senior staff are likely to be on leave; when telephone calls and emails between organizations often go unanswered due to staff shortages. Mid to late December is often a favourite 'targeting' time.

The PODE was set up in Zurich using a post box address. It distributed invoices for inclusion in various so-called 'international directories'. Typically, no sales promotional literature accompanied the invoice, which was usually phrased in terms of renewal of an existing subscription. This avoided placing the staff on whose desk the invoice eventually landed in the position of having to decide if the 'service' offered was actually worth having. Someone it seemed had already set the precedent last year, or the year before perhaps. The amounts involved were usually small – under £50 or perhaps £250 – as many relatively junior budget holders have limits set at such levels and often small amounts are less likely to be questioned anyway. Invariably, to increase the pressure to make payment, such fictitious invoices are described as overdue or subject to prompt payment discount if paid within a few days.

It is very difficult for the payee organization to prove one way or another whether the directory actually existed. No copies are ever sent out. Though, no doubt, if the perpetrators behind PODE were ever forced into court a listing of some sort would be produced. In the meantime the person(s) authorizing payment could well be expected to forget the matter or assume that a directory had been sent to the legal or perhaps the public relations departments. Figure 6.2 gives an example of PODE invoices, though the format was often amended to appear familiar to different types of targeted bodies.

CASE STUDY 6.1 *concluded*

PUBLIC ORGANIZATIONS DIRECTORY SUBSCRIPTION RENEWAL

TELEFAX SERVICE

SUBSCRIBER

Office of Consumer Affairs
Regional Distribution Centre
Ride Street
Dudhampston IXYZ 2AB
GREAT BRITAIN

TELEFAX NUMBER

000012345

DATE 01 . 12 . 2001

EDITION 2002

THIS SPACE IS PROVIDED FOR ANY EVENTUAL AMENDMENTS OF THE TEXT

SUBSCRIPTION FEE YEARLY AMOUNT ▶	GB£ 110
DISCOUNT BY PAYMENT WITHIN 21 DAYS ▶	GB£ 15--
TOTAL NET AMOUNT ▶	GB£ 395--

PLEASE KEEP YOUR ORIGINAL FOR YOUR BOOKKEEPING AND SEND US THE COPY WITH YOUR CHEQUE
Or transfer to our account

P.O. BOX
CH - 9475 ZURICH

The above text serves as a model for your listing in the exchange for Directory. If you agree to the print of your text, please remit the amount soonest, so as to ensure your entry in good time. We reserve the right to place your order in a Directory of our choice. After printing you will receive a copy of the Directory on request.

Figure 6.3 Example of a Public Organizations Directory Exchange invoice

The main control or countermeasure in such situations as PODE simply requires staff to stick to formal authorization procedures with a named budget holder taking responsibility for each individual amount. It is helpful if several such examples arise for a 'blacklist' of fictitious invoicing names (possibly with examples) to be circulated among relevant staff and similar public service providers.

CASE STUDY 6.2

GREATER HARMBOROUGH COUNCIL

This authority has been enlarged recently by the expansion of the old Harmborough City Council into its rural hinterland, swallowing up large parts of neighbouring rural districts to form a single unitary authority.

Greater Harmborough already operates a centralized purchasing system. The purchasing arrangements for a housing area local office inherited from one of the disbanded districts has been grafted onto this system.

The housing area local office (HALO) is one of five decentralized offices based among the larger estates owned by the new council. The other four were part of the original city council. HALOs allocate properties to families on the waiting list, make rent collections and authorize routine jobbing, that is, day-to-day repair. Each HALO has its own budget allocation.

The deputy director of housing has been concerned at the past three monthly expenditure returns of the new HALO. These show almost 70 per cent of its annual budget allocation has been spent by the end of the first quarter. The area housing manager in charge of the new HALO has explained that the former authority had been far more generous in its budget allocation and his staff were finding it difficult to adapt to Harmborough's more stringent regime. This issue has become a source of growing con ict between the director and the area manager, to the extent that the latter has hinted he may resign if more funds are not forthcoming. Most of the overspend relates to jobbing repairs contracted out by the HALO, either to the Council's DSO or to local firms, on a craft basis each year. Currently the DSO craftsmen have won the contract for non-emergency plumbing and electrical work while all emergency repairs, carpentry, bricklaying and other trades are undertaken by local tradesmen and builders. The director's suspicions of fraud are aroused when a property condition survey undertaken by his staff reveals that the new HALO's property is in an abysmal state of repair compared to the other four HALOs despite all the extra expenditure. Also, some streets mentioned by the area manager as having been the recipients of many jobbing repairs to gutters, roof tiles, and windows appear to be in the worst state of disrepair according to the survey.

The director approaches the chief internal auditor. A routine evaluation of the systems for undertaking jobbing repairs is carried out. Figure 6.4 gives a ow chart summary. Key controls questions used by the auditor are:

1 Are all repairs needed by genuine tenants?
2 Are all repairs correctly assessed, for example, as emergency, non-urgent?
3 Are all repairs carried out adequately and at the right time?
4 Are all repairs (that is, by job) correctly costed and coded? (Labour plus materials plus any other cost or agreed charges.)

In the case of the new HALO a serious control weakness was identified (as shown on Figure 6.4). The independent confirmation of the work was totally inadequate.

Very few pre-inspections were undertaken and post-inspection was limited to about 50 per cent of jobs that were effectively selected by a receptionist.

Tenants would telephone or call into the HALO which employed one full-time receptionist who, although she might not receive all the incoming calls or visitors, was usually called upon to deal with repair enquiries. Over several years she had built up expertise in the relatively complex task of summarizing the tenants' description of damages and the necessary action to be taken plus likely materials needed. These

CASE STUDY 6.2 *continued*

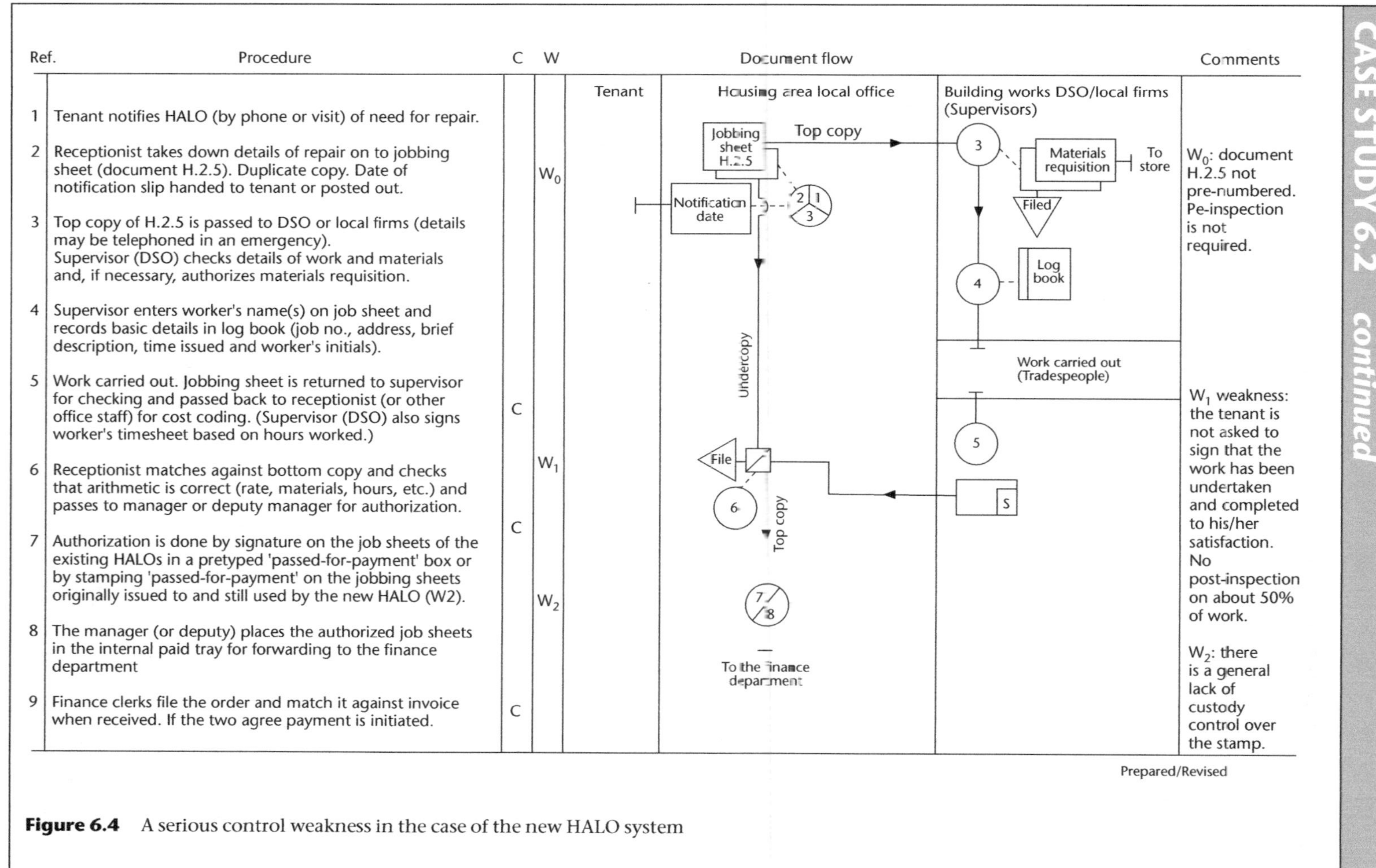

Ref.	Procedure	C	W	Comments
1	Tenant notifies HALO (by phone or visit) of need for repair.			
2	Receptionist takes down details of repair on to jobbing sheet (document H.2.5). Duplicate copy. Date of notification slip handed to tenant or posted out.		W_0	W_0: document H.2.5 not pre-numbered. Pe-inspection is not required.
3	Top copy of H.2.5 is passed to DSO or local firms (details may be telephoned in an emergency). Supervisor (DSO) checks details of work and materials and, if necessary, authorizes materials requisition.			
4	Supervisor enters worker's name(s) on job sheet and records basic details in log book (job no., address, brief description, time issued and worker's initials).			
5	Work carried out. Jobbing sheet is returned to supervisor for checking and passed back to receptionist (or other office staff) for cost coding. (Supervisor (DSO) also signs worker's timesheet based on hours worked.)	C		W_1 weakness: the tenant is not asked to sign that the work has been undertaken and completed to his/her satisfaction. No post-inspection on about 50% of work.
6	Receptionist matches against bottom copy and checks that arithmetic is correct (rate, materials, hours, etc.) and passes to manager or deputy manager for authorization.		W_1	
7	Authorization is done by signature on the job sheets of the existing HALOs in a pretyped 'passed-for-payment' box or by stamping 'passed-for-payment' on the jobbing sheets originally issued to and still used by the new HALO (W2).	C	W_2	W_2: there is a general lack of custody control over the stamp.
8	The manager (or deputy) places the authorized job sheets in the internal paid tray for forwarding to the finance department			
9	Finance clerks file the order and match it against invoice when received. If the two agree payment is initiated.	C		

Figure 6.4 A serious control weakness in the case of the new HALO system

CASE STUDY 6.2 *continued*

details were entered directly on to a job sheet and classified by the receptionist as emergency, high priority or low priority depending on the nature of the damage. Virtually no guidance was available defining the types of work to be put into each category – this was left to the discretion of the receptionist and the vociferousness of the tenant. If the receptionist was on leave a building inspector was normally called upon to deal with repair enquiries.

The receptionist was able to accept bribes from local firms and tradesmen to:

1 make out false job sheets for work that had not been requested. Later the invoice would be matched to the job sheet by a clerk in the finance department and paid provided the receptionist had stamped 'passed for payment' on the job sheet;
2 classify genuine work that was medium or low priority as emergency repairs for which a higher rate per hour was paid; and
3 exaggerate the amount of work required on a genuine job.

She also accepted bribes from some more desperate tenants.

The job sheets were not sequentially pre-numbered and the receptionist was trusted by the building works inspectors employed by the architects' department to send them undercopies of all job sheets. The inspectors were under the false impression that they pre-inspected all non-emergency work and post-inspected all jobs.

The 'passed for payment' stamp used by the receptionist was intended to be kept and used only by the HALO manager and the building inspectors. This was strictly the case at all other HALOs but at the new HALO the manager had, in his previous authority, been in the habit of delegating his authority to authorize payment to his deputy and other officers, and the stamp to authorize payment was kept unlocked and freely accessible among other stamps for general use in the office.

All the false job sheets were stamped and the top copy sent to the finance section a few days prior to the firm issuing an invoice. In the unlikely event of a query from finance the first point of contact would be the receptionist. In fact, the finance section held the new HALO in high regard because, unlike other HALOs, nearly all their works invoices could be easily matched to jobbing sheets; the amounts, dates and details always tied up (they were all made up by the receptionist) and they could be paid quickly and simply. Whenever documents from the old HALOs were missing or unstamped, the finance section would quote the new HALO as a model of best practice.

Once internal auditors had noticed the lack of control over the stamp and given the relatively high level of jobbing repairs and the known suspicions of the housing directors, they decided to check the diary of visits kept by inspectors against the addresses on the jobbing sheets. This revealed the extent of fraud almost immediately.

The simple but very important control lacking in this case was pre-numbered orders. Although the job sheet acted as an order it was probably not thought of in the same light as routine orders for stationery, cement, timber, and so on, which in all probability were numbered. Had the job sheets been pre-numbered then the inspectors would have noticed that they never saw half of them. Even if the sheets had not been pre-numbered but had been given sequential job numbers as work became available, this control would have prevented any significant level of false jobbing works.

The 'passed for payment' stamp should, of course, have been kept under the strict control of the person(s) authorized to use it. In this case the manager and probably

CASE STUDY 6.2 *concluded*

deputy manager should have kept safe custody of the stamp and not allowed it to be accessed by other junior officers. But stamps like this one often have to be passed to subordinates during sickness, leave, emergencies, and so on, and easily become common property.

Closer scrutiny of budgets could also have played a more important part in preventing or detecting this fraud. One is left to wonder whether similar frauds were in place at any other HALO in the authority to which the new HALO belonged before it came under the jurisdiction of Harmborough. Occasional comparisons to similar-sized operations at other locations might well have revealed the apparently poor value for many of the jobbing repairs undertaken at the new HALO. This, indirectly, was what happened on reorganization into Harmborough.

Custody of official stamps, pre-numbering of official documents – these are all very routine controls that often get overlooked. They can, depending upon the circumstances, be crucial in preventing fraud.

Concluding points

Whatever common elements are identified among the revenue expenditure systems of organizations, the scope for variety and for peculiar arrangements seems limitless. This means that it is often impossible to anticipate all the risks. In most large organizations the revenue expenditure systems span the responsibilities of several managers. Each manager, it seems, tends to assume that the others are carrying out more checks and controls than is usually the case, or at least the case when a fraud is discovered. Exceptions to normal best practice tend to be tolerated more than would be the case in other well-controlled systems.

Routine expenditure presents more temptation than most systems. The three most effective methods of deterring frauds in revenue expenditure systems seem to be:

sound internal controls including close supervision and separation of duties;
regular audit; and
management checks.

CHAPTER 7

Income

Introduction

Income is a particularly wide topic in which the scope for fraud and corruption is virtually unlimited. Because of their great variety, income frauds tend to be treated in isolation by auditors and managers. In fact, the lack of certain key controls is often a common factor in these frauds.

This chapter will be concerned largely with discussing these key controls and the basic risks involved in each of the main types of income.

There is an important difference between central government departments and other public bodies. The former, including a variety of related agencies, are financed largely by grant in aid or supply grant as it is called, voted by Parliament.

Tax revenues collected by the Inland Revenue, Customs and Excise and from other sources such as Vehicle Excise Duty are paid into the centralized consolidated fund managed by the Bank of England along with borrowings held by the National Loan Fund. These revenues are 'granted' to departments as the various spending programmes progress. Public bodies other than central government departments are often funded only partly by grants (such as grants paid over from the Department of the Environment to local authorities) and partly by local taxation, fees and charges. For these other bodies sources of revenue are generally far more diverse than for central government departments.

As far as transfer of tax-raised funds between public bodies is concerned there exists a vast and complex system; what an accountant might conceive of as a national bookkeeping exercise. Little in the way of cash or negotiable instruments actually changes hands and the risk of conventional 'income' fraud within this system is limited. However, once outside parties are introduced into the system, at the end point of, say, rent collection, fees and charges, or distribution of an income subsidy, many risks including the risks discussed in other chapters also apply. For most bodies, such non-transfer sources of income present the greatest risk by far. The first and often main scope for fraud and corruption, as with all income systems, occurs at the point of collection, that is, by initial evasion of payment.

National and local taxation

These areas will be dealt with quite brie y which, given the volume of money involved, may seem a little surprising. The main issue is one of tax evasion including corporation tax, income tax, the council tax, customs duty, value added tax, vehicle excise duty, fuel duty, and so on. Except for the few cases that may involve collusion with civil servants, this aspect of fraud and corruption is perpetrated within the private rather than the public services and thus outside the scope of this book. This is not to say that civil servants and local government officers never evade tax, rather that being almost whole salaried or waged employees, taxed via PAYE, their scope for evasion is immaterial compared to the wider and more diverse private sector.

Collection records can of course be falsified, but short of bribery on a massive scale, it is difficult to see the motive for any serious level of falsification. The main countermeasures against tax evasion involve completeness of data regarding the tax base and the ability of the collectors or inspectors to verify the details of statements and declarations. Take vehicle excise duty (VED) for example. On first consideration enforcement would seem fairly straightforward. The licensing agency (the DVLA at Swansea) keeps records of all vehicles, their 'keepers' and all drivers – a complete population. All details can actually be checked against the vehicle or, if required, against the driver for such things as age or medical conditions. In practice, though, even an apparently straightforward example such as VED can have many complications. Registered but unlicensed vehicles may be exempt from VED by being kept off the road and out of use. Numerous weight scales and axle combinations may be mis-declared by heavy goods vehicle operators which, unless the vehicle is subject to a spot check, are likely to go unnoticed on the road. Licences, which usually contain only small typed or handwritten vehicle registration numbers, can easily be transferred between vehicles. Provided that vehicles are not left parked on a public highway for any length of time few passers-by (traffic wardens excepted) are likely to read the printed detail of the licence disc. Perhaps the most costly form of VED evasion is the casual evader who does not bother to re-licence for a few months and then claims the vehicle was off the road. Such relatively simple evasion can cost tens of millions of pounds each year.

Tax evasion of local authority taxes (business rates and council tax) suffers from similar verification problems. Often a local tax requires a positive notification or declaration by the taxpayer. This is particularly true where a change of personal circumstances or use of premises occurs. If tax records cannot automatically be cross-checked to other data sources, and often for technical or legal reasons they cannot, then a tax debt may remain completely unrecorded. Here again completeness of the database or of the known population is the main problem. Enforcement agencies will carry out sample checks or circulate all known taxpayers which may well reveal unnotified changes but is much less likely to reveal a completely new tax debtor. Regular home visits are in most cases rather costly compared to the extra tax likely to accrue from discovering the occasional unrecorded lodger, for example.

Corporation tax evasion, or attempted evasion, by commercial bodies within the private sector, from small firms to multinational corporations, is on a vastly greater scale than what has been brie y touched upon so far.

Sales, fees and charges

Traditionally these are the areas most prone to public services fraud among the income-gathering functions of public bodies. The level of fees and charges will be set in most cases by statute or by resolution passed by the elected or appointed members of the public body. Occasionally discounts or special offers are available but, largely due to the need to be seen to be fair and electorally accountable, many common private sector marketing practices are not considered acceptable. However, income and expenditure accounts are becoming more like trading and profit and loss accounts and commercial-style management are in general becoming more frequently used. Often, this is on the basis of what might be called a stand-alone or self-accounting unit. Direct service organizations, NHS trusts and government trading funds are examples.

The basic consideration remains the same whatever the style of accounts produced and the risk of fraud and corruption is generally unaffected. However, certain detailed accounting issues are considered later in Chapter 9. Typical revenue income systems might be illustrated as in Figure 7.1.

Each of the three divisions of Figure 7.1 has its own serious risks and (hopefully) key controls to guard against these risks. Generally, separation of duty is difficult to ensure, except perhaps in very large organizations.

Ideally, separation should be encouraged between service provision, income receipt and accounting.

If, as often arises on small sites, a service is provided and cash or cheques are received directly by the person providing the service, risk of misappropriation is increased.

Staff often hand out tickets for cash, lea et sales or petty fines, for example. Pest control officers and others may accept cash on site. In theory a pre-numbered receipt or till roll should always be given when the cash is received. The customer can check the amount receipted agrees with what he or she handed over and the record of receipts issued can be agreed to takings. In practice few public service customers are overly concerned about their receipt, which may be little more than a till roll. The services provided are not often ones for which the customer may demand a refund, unlike counter sales in most shops. Most fees and charges are levied for services rather than goods, such as the hire of meeting halls, sports facilities, and so on. Compared with goods, inadequate services, unless they are persistently so, are far less likely to generate irate customers, who have kept their receipt, demanding back their monies.

The main risk in these types of situations is of course that once the income has been handed over without the issue of a till generated or pre-numbered receipt it will avoid any record being initiated within the system, and as services do not usually involve the diminution of stock the organization will never get any indication that it has lost income in the first place. This problem is particularly difficult to address in the public services and is one of the key risks discussed on page 145. For now though it is important to gain an overview of the situation. For many fee-paying public services continuous supervision of staff by managers is very costly or impractical; supermarket-style checkouts, or even nearby payment collection points are simply absent. Millions of pounds may be due for a wide variety of ad hoc services such as seaside car parks, cess pit emptying, pest control, home visits, and so on and even where the service is provided close to a payment point such as in sports halls it is sometimes difficult to prevent its consumption without payment. One of the main controls to counter this risk is the separation of duties mentioned above, so long as the customer is made aware via notices, application forms, and so on that payment must be made to someone or a location other than the person immediately providing the service. Even this control tends to break down in many public service situations, where the customers trust public servants to take charge of and pass on any payment and the staff themselves often fail to see the significance of such a separation in duties: it can appear particularly bureaucratic at times and encourages often relatively junior staff to ignore separations and collude to collect monies directly at the point of provision. This situation and such attitudes are most attractive to a fraudster and the level of such income frauds is very difficult to estimate. One of the few controls left in such risky areas is often the ability of other staff or managers to notice that their colleagues or subordinates do not appear to be generating much income compared to their level of activity. Some systems involve the regular recording and monitoring of income against a related variable such as staffing levels or incoming telephone

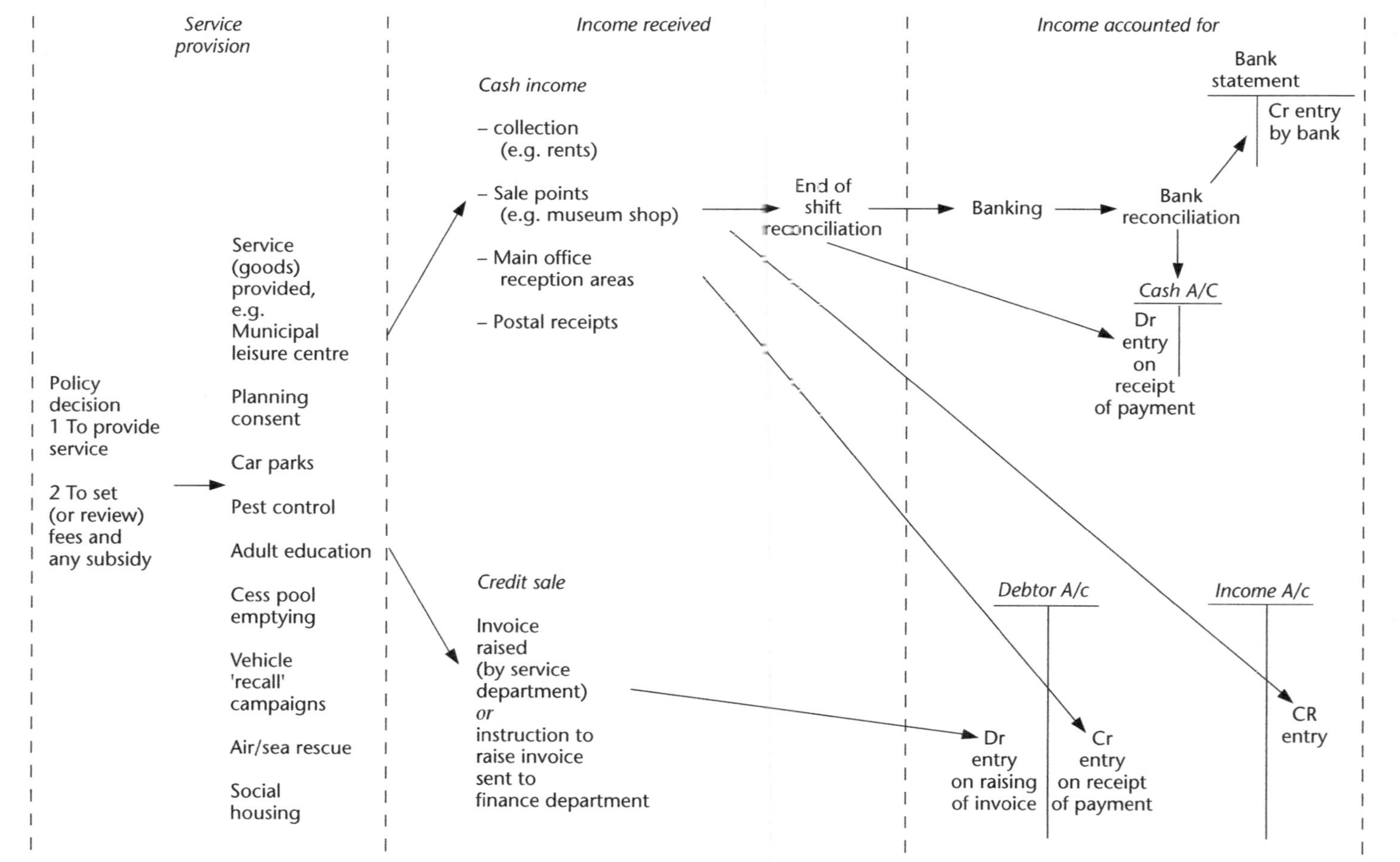

Figure 7.1 Example of typical revenue income systems

calls to spot any apparent peaks not supported by increases in income. But this control only operates at a macro level and persistent, hidden losses of individually small amounts can still build up into material sums and go unnoticed for many years. Perhaps the few remaining controls likely to deter a persistent fraudster are regular unannounced spot checks by managers or auditors, or sometimes CCTV surveillance.

Grants and donations

The major grants from central to local government present in general a very low risk of fraudulent abuse. Most are calculated according to formulae based upon the socio-economic characteristics of the local government area and its expenditure on various programmes such as housing or means-tested benefits. Errors can and do occur and some would say this area is particularly prone to errors, but the officers of the body giving or receiving the grant are unlikely to be able to siphon off any significant amounts. Again, as we discussed above, this source of income is but a part of the wider intergovernmental and agency bookkeeping. (Once grants are awarded to private sector and voluntary bodies the risk of fraud increases, as discussed in Chapter 8). Donations, particularly for disaster and similar ad hoc funds, are more capable of fraudulent misappropriation, and control over donations should be of a similar standard to income control in general. This is discussed below.

Key income risks and controls

Although ordinary errors are likely in income systems the two main risks in relation to these and to fraud are as follows:

1 That of not recording or bringing income to account in the first instance it becomes due. See also earlier comments on page 143.
2 The risk of subsequent diversion of income once it has already been brought to account. This is still of concern but usually less so than point 1 above because once recorded in the system there is usually less chance of its diversion going unnoticed.

TYPICAL CONTROLS TO COUNTER THE RISKS

An adequate level of internal control for revenue income systems could be expected to involve most of the following key areas of control – 1 to 11 in the list which follows – covering policy, accounting for provision, completeness of income received, accounting for income received and the role of senior management. All of the controls discussed below can be related to these two key risks and so it is less useful here to draw up a grid along the lines of Figure 6.2.

Policy

1 The fees and charges (including any nil charges) for all types of goods and services should be subject to periodic, usually at least annual, review. Statutory services or others that are funded by grant from another body – usually a central government department – should

also be included in such review, as should fully subsidized services provided by the reviewing body.

Such reviews may form part of a wider budgeting process such as a cyclical zero-based or regular activity-based budget review. The important control arrangement is that all actual sources of income and all potential sources of income are considered by an appropriate policy-making body, independent of the income-gathering and accounting processes. Local government is a good example. One community may tolerate direct charges for public car parks, galleries, meals on wheels, and so on, while its neighbour would fund these by full subsidy. Another important control arrangement is that staff involved in sending out invoices, collecting cash fees and so on are made aware of the review and its outcome, perhaps as part of the budget consultation process, and confirm this, thus reducing any scope or temptation to claim ignorance as an excuse for not following charging policies.

Regular political accountability also acts to reduce the risk of unintentional charges or subsidies; unintentional that is in the sense of not having arisen from positive policy decisions.

Political accountability also reduces the risks of such unintentional charges as might arise being improperly used or not fully brought to account. This might occur if some form of overcharging is made possible by deliberately or unintentionally allowing incomplete charging policies with an unbudgeted excess of income being used in an unauthorized manner; for example, an unapproved consultation fee that was used to finance bonus payments.

Accounting for provision

2 Review by policy-making bodies should be only the top level of a detailed budgetary review process by officers (usually accountants) not involved in day-to-day income generation or collections. Such a review should encompass:
   (a) the need and viability of charging for each service/product;
   (b) the amount and build-up of the charge or of any subsidy;
   (c) the amount of income or subsidy compared to the original budgeted estimates and any revised estimates.

It is important to note that the key control is in the separation between officers involved in income generation and collection such as property lettings officers, rent collectors and cashiers on the one hand and officers involved in the review procedures (a) to (c) mentioned above on the other.

Ensuring completeness of income received

3 A further and more detailed review of the trends of income from each source of collection is often undertaken: sometimes by an accountant, sometimes by a budgetary control officer, occasionally by an internal auditor as part of an analytical review. The objective is to identify and investigate unexpected troughs and peaks in sources of regular collection; for example, from direct sales of surplus military equipment or even from such mundane sources as car parks, seaside kiosks, and so on. Both unexpected peaks and unexpected troughs may indicate problems. Simple graphs of income over time may reveal sudden

changes with no obvious explanation. These should be the subject of discreet but probing enquiry. Should income have been higher in the past? Have staff changed or are better management practices now in place? Is a sudden drop due simply to bad weather, closure for repairs or some less innocent reason?

4 Also usually classified under analytical review are various stock and raw materials usage comparisons. These are generally more applicable to goods than to services. The basic approach involves identifying the mark-up or the relationships between the input cost and the income received. A simple example might be the sale of tennis balls at a leisure centre, as in Table 7.1.

Table 7.1 Main stock record – tennis balls

		Initial	*In*	*Out*	*Bal.*
Opening stock b/f	1.1.X1	AB			200
Issues to cash desk	2 boxes 3.1.X1	DL		24	176
Issues to cash desk	1 box 21.3.X1	DL		12	164
Issues to cash desk	1 box 7.8.X1	DL		12	152
Issues to cash desk	3 boxes 9.10.X1	DL		36	116
Issues to cash desk	4 boxes 17.11.X1	DL		48	68
Issues to cash desk	3 boxes 12.12.X1	CC		36	32
Purchased stock	10 boxes 20.12.X1	AB	120		152
Issues to cash desk	2 boxes 2.1.X2	CC		24	128

In this example AB is the centre's stores clerk who is responsible for the stock and keeps a card for all stock items. CC and DL are the cashiers, or other staff, who sell the balls.

If income is monitored over the period then, assuming the balls are a standard price, cash banked to the relevant income code can be agreed to stock figures and any peaks and troughs can be queried. In this example, at say £1.00 each, £24.00 (less any returns and stock in hand at point of sale) should have been credited to the relevant income code between 3.1.X1 and 21.3.X1. Peak sales occurred in late autumn and early winter and a marked trough occurred in the summer.

More sophisticated comparison may be required for most goods and services. Rarely is income credited to a single code or on the basis of a single price per unit. Halls may be rented at prices that vary according to the nature of the functions, the size of the party and at subsidized rates for, say, old age pensioners or charitable organizations. Average mark-ups may prove sufficiently accurate where goods or services are of a similar nature and the price range is relatively small. Reliable relationships can exist (even though exact checks of income owed cannot be made without detailed examination of prime documentation) where the auditor can be confident that error or fraud has not occurred on any material scale. Such a blanket approach to analytical review is often applied to changes in key parameters such as salary percentage increases, business rate poundages, increases in mortgage rates and the like.

Close management supervisory checks

Controls 1 to 4 attempt to offset risk 1, that is (see p. 145), the risk that income will not be fully brought to account, which often calls for even more direct internal control than the receiving and budget monitoring procedures discussed so far.

Services may be provided 'on the side' or charges may be levied when the service should be free – from relatively innocent tips to massive backhanders.

Surprise counts

5 A fraud at the stage of initial fee collections or levy is likely to be relatively straightforward in concept, such as not putting cash collected through the till or on to a rent card but, to make it worth the fraudster's efforts, such fraud must be perpetrated on a significant scale. So-called 'teeming and lading' whereby one day's (or other period's) receipts are used to cover up shortages in the previous day's takings can be perpetrated for a considerable time (see the Department of Trade's report on the infamous case of the Gray's Building Society) unless regular management or audit surprise checks of cash tills and banking are undertaken.

Receipts

6 One way for a significant fraud to continue is for the part of a steady income ow never to be recorded – either cash or credit owed – often when numerous services are being provided in complex situations. Once entries are made on till tolls, debtors ledgers or wherever the likelihood of detection is greatly increased. For this reason one of the most important controls at the initial stages of any income system is for the customer to expect and be issued with pre-numbered sequential receipts for goods and services. Receipts should be in at least two parts or copies. The top copy should be handed or posted to the customer. The under (or stub) copy should always be retained and can be checked by management via till rolls, or against income codes, and so on. Any missing copies will be immediately apparent.

7 Credit sales are in general a little more complex than cash sales but the same principles apply. The fee-payer should not go unrecorded at the point of agreement, that is, as soon as a debt arises. An invoice (or instruction to raise an invoice) should be made up or automatically printed out, particularly if the transaction has been generated over the telephone. Like receipts, invoices should be serially numbered and any missing ones should be fully explained. The invoice may itself act as a receipt when payment is eventually forthcoming by ensuring it is annotated with the payment's details. In some situations it is not thought worth the effort to physically mark 'paid' on copies of invoices issued once these have been paid (unlike invoices received) or even to show any trail of responsibility indicating the officer who actually agreed that the debt had been paid off. In most enquiries the existence of a computer printout or screen display showing the date of payment and possibly details such as an account number and debtor reference is sufficient to resolve any problems. But in any potential fraud enquiry resulting from income apparently being received (that is, a credit against the debtor account) but not actually being paid into the cash account, it can be crucial to identify the person responsible for entering the credit (or telling a junior clerk to go ahead and credit the debtor account).

As with authorizing an incoming invoice for creditor accounts payable (see Chapter 6) it is important to have signed authorization (or adequate password-controlled screen display) of all credits to outgoing invoices or debtor accounts.

It is often more secure from both the income collection side and the creditors payments side of a credit transaction for both parties to use BACS, as the authorization (see below) and the transaction itself are usually secure from interference from third parties. (This will in practice depend upon the arrangements in each organization as errors have been known to occur, for example if debtors enter the incorrect BACS payment recipient details.)

Accounting for income received

The importance of the trail of responsibility mentioned above applies equally as income is processed through each stage in the system.

8 All cash (including cheques, postal orders, and so on) should be accompanied by a detailed breakdown and be signed for on transfer. Ideally the transferor and transferee should count the cash and sign to say they agree the totals as broken down. If the cash is transferred in a sealed container this too should be signed for by the recipient. Thus if cash is transferred from a receptionist-cashier to a supervising officer for the day's takings to be banked then the till summary, usually an automatic printout, should be agreed to the takings (less any cash oat) by the receptionist-cashier and the supervisor, both of whom should sign. In any large cash office this will usually mean staggered shifts so that cashing up and banking can be completed in reasonable time.

9 A separation between the cashier, cash collectors and the officers preparing bankings should be maintained. Otherwise the officer preparing the bankings may be tempted to offset any of his or her cash shortages with another cashier's takings. The only reasonable exception to this rule occurs when officers have to bank directly, often in night safes, perhaps at outstations where the costs of enforcing centralized bankings would be prohibitive. A similar need may arise when officers collect cash for work done on site and cannot guarantee to be back at base before cashing up time. Night safe bankings necessitate reliance upon the integrity and controls of the bank. The author has encountered occasions when such reliance has been called into question.

10 Regular reconciliations should be undertaken between:
   (a) cash income recorded as banked;
   (b) the bank account; and
   (c) income accounts.

   Regular bank reconciliations, daily, weekly or monthly, will be undertaken in almost any organization and these should quickly reveal any failed or disputed bankings. Reconciliations of takings to the income account is not always undertaken but can be useful in preventing fraud. Reconciliation of (a) to (b) involved conventional cash account to bank account reconciliation undertaken weekly or daily in some organizations. Reconcilitation of (b) to (c) or (a) to (c) usually takes place less frequently. Sometimes this is made difficult because income is credited to the same account from cash and non-cash sources. Often income levels are monitored for each income code heading but against budgeted income rather than in total against cash actually received. This means that if cash is credited to the wrong accounting code (and then used for unauthorized purposes or to cover up fraudulent misappropriation) this will only be noticed if the accountant monitoring the budgets sees a significant and unexpected overpayment on one code and/or underpayment on another. If a debtor account has previously been raised, good debt collection procedures may reveal the fraud when the payee is chased up for debts he or she has already paid off. It is conceivable that neither of these events would occur (for some time at least) to reveal the miscoding of income. At various points throughout the cash-handing process it may be possible to misappropriate cash proceeds provided, as is often the case in direct fees income, no debtor account is set up. So long as the misappropriation is covered by diverting other (or excess) funds, again where no debtor account is set up, so that no serious drop in expected income is apparent to the budget monitoring accountants, a fraud may remain unnoticed for a considerable time. Eventually total cash and non-cash income should be reconciled to total income credited to the various income account codes allowing for cash in transit, accruals and timing differences with the bank, by which time it may be very difficult to substantiate who actually took the money. In most public bodies this task is further complicated by numerous year-end journal transfers between different expenditure and income accounts. Such accounts are often identified down to a very detailed 'source code' level to satisfy the demands of political members whose debates often lead to adjustments of the financial budgets. From the foregoing, three basic controls stand out as important (though certainly not foolproof) once cash, including cheques and other value documents have been received:

(a) the issue of prenumbered official receipts in duplicate;

(b) the signed (or otherwise evidenced) agreement of officers involved in transferring cash until it is banked; and

(c) frequent reconciliations between monies received, banked, and credited to income accounts.

The role of senior management

11 The involvement of senior management directly in controlling income varies greatly. Mostly direct involvement is limited to junior and middle managers. Yet a useful basic control, both before and after cash receipt, is a planned programme of senior management checks, as in the following two examples.

(a) Site visits during anticipated peaks and troughs in demand: do the figures for income appear consistent with conditions of demand encountered in the field? If undertaken unannounced this is one of the few control procedures that can be given any degree of assurance that income is not being intercepted prior to recording.

(b) Detailed testing of transactions from samples or selections chosen on a random or judgemental basis. When all is said and done the top managers may ultimately be held accountable for any fraud, especially in the eyes of their political masters. They should at least be aware of the main signatories who authorize and control income and the documentation involved. Are any handwritten invoices clearly made out? Are listings made of cheques paid into the bank? These are questions that in the event of a fraud might be asked by politicians, the public/press and, of course, the police.

Sometimes such checking by senior managers may be thought to have little if any value. 'The boss is just nosing about' will be a typical reaction. A deterrent effect may ensue in some, usually poorly run, organizations. If, however, planned management checking is carried out with tact it can have a motivating effect, as very senior managers are seen to have an interest in procedures at a relatively low level. In any event such a programme of checking should be reasonably discreet and, unless very poor practices are encountered, it should not need to be frequent. The dividends from such senior management checks come when things go wrong, as they will occasionally even in the best-run organization, particularly when fraud is known or suspected. In such serious circumstances senior managers who know, at least in outlines, of the day-to-day procedures and checks put in place by their subordinate (though often still managerial) colleagues are at a distinct advantage. They should already be able to view events from a wider perspective than the officers involved and so bring breadth and comparative knowledge to bear on the detail that they must then consider. Their learning curve, given their existing knowledge, should be very short, and their authority all the more credible. It must be stressed that this advantage can only be gained by checking and verifying evidence of events, not simply by meeting people and listening to their problems, necessary though this may be. The senior manager who actually examines, say, maternity leave records and work rosters (for the cash desk, the central accounts department, the licence issuing office or whatever) may see for him or herself that long-term maternity absences are causing a breakdown in, say, separation of duties: or alternatively that this definitely is not a problem. Otherwise these visits will probably do no more than confirm that babies are being born and junior and middle managers are finding it difficult (or not as the case may be) to allow their people maternity leave.

Summary

Income, like expenditure, in the public services often involves routine maintenance risks and controls and the tendency to become complacent. In the public services too, unlike most of the private sector, income does not equate to sales, rather taxation grants and so on are usually more important. This leads to a divorce between income and the incentive to be on the look out for any leakage of the income via inefficiency and fraud in its collection and allocation. The risks and controls considered in this chapter often relate to ensuring that all income due is collected and brought to account, hence the importance of reconciliations. But in practice it is often the quality and attitude of managers that will determine the ability of the controls to guard effectively against fraud and corruption. This factor is always unpredictable and makes the task of any auditor or counter-fraud specialist particularly difficult.

CASE STUDIES

The first case study of Oldtown Heritage Centre discusses a situation of 'over the counter' fraud. This fraud is generally thought to be more common in the private (usually small retail) sector, but as more commercial sources of income are sought it may well increase in the public services. The second case considers debtors arising from refunds due to overpayment, a situation fairly common in the public services.

CASE STUDY 7.1

OLDTOWN HERITAGE CENTRE

Oldtown Heritage Centre was originally the Oldtown Museum which also housed a collection of paintings of local artists, some of considerable repute. Oldtown itself was becoming increasingly popular among tourists and as a venue for the arts. Local councillors decided to have under one roof a subsidized museum, gallery, municipal theatre and tourist information centre – The Heritage Centre. This, it was anticipated, would cut the costs of running these as

CASE STUDY 7.1 *continued*

separate establishments. The centre would attract more visitors and trade to each function and to the town in general and provide an opportunity to offer refreshments, souvenirs, and so on at charges that would minimize the need for subsidy. The Heritage Centre contained gift counters which, among the postcards, bottles of Oldtown spring water and trinkets, sold copies of the official Oldtown guide at £1.00 each. This was a simple but attractive little publication with a centre double-page map of Oldtown, a guide to forthcoming theatrical events and the exhibits in the museum/gallery. Some of the costs of production were covered by a few discreet and tasteful advertisements for local hotels, restaurants and the like and the council hoped to make a small contribution from each copy. Unfortunately, the assistant manager, whose office contained a colour photocopier, had similar aspirations.

The colour copier had originally been very useful when notices, posters and programmes advertising public events at the centre and elsewhere in the local authority area ran out. Indeed its legitimate use in this respect, particularly for extra copies of the official Oldtown guide had, no doubt, put the idea of fraudulent use into the assistant manager's mind. The main obstacle to his intentions had been a rigid separation of duties between the cashiers at the two tills in the centre and himself. He or the manager made up the bank paying-in slips and the monies had to be reconciled to the end of shift printouts produced and signed by each cashier. He or the manager would countersign the printouts and sign the paying-in slips.

The assistant manager, had at first, considered collusion with one or both of the cashiers. In fact this was not necessary. As the months passed after the Heritage Centre had been opened it became increasingly apparent that lunchtime cover would be needed at the tills. From midday until two in the afternoon only one cashier was on duty while one took an hour's lunch break. Rather than recruit a part-time cashier, the assistant manager started covering at the tills. The manager, who was an excellent organizer of events and people, had very little experience of finance. The assistant manager explained that the cost of hiring extra cover would be out of all proportion to the extra revenue and this would probably be criticized by the auditor (which may well have been true). He substituted photocopies for some of the original stock and pocketed any money taken for copied items at his till. Few if any customers bothered to ask for a till receipt, and he made a point of not emphasizing to cashiers that the receipts should always be torn off and handed to the customer. Even when they did and he needed to enter the sale of items on the till he could usually remember the small number of £1.00s he needed to leave in the till or rely on the fact that he reconciled his own printout to the bankings so that no one else was likely to spot that the equal totals were not actually derived from equal castings. Provided he always sold his 'own stock' no stock check would indicate takings were unreasonably low for the items sold. The auditors might occasionally have checked till rolls against bankings but any discrepancy would be small, and in any case he was always careful to ensure 'his' till rolls were difficult to find. He could expect to sell about 300 guides a week during his shifts, particularly as he tended to make sure that the stock held by the other cashier was likely to run out about midday. At £1.00 each this was a clear profit of up to £300 a week. He had no material costs as the paper and the copying facilities were under his direct control. A few other easily copied items sold for a small fee but his main money spinner was the official Oldtown guide.

CASE STUDY 7.1 *concluded*

The manager's suspicions were aroused when the assistant manager was hospitalized following a car accident. Each week the manager received income summaries from the accounts branch at head office showing income against each main product or service. The income against guides and maps rose substantially during the six weeks his assistant was on sick leave. Looking back over earlier records, he noticed smaller and shorter peaks during the weeks the assistant manager was on annual leave.

This aroused his curiosity, though his initial reaction was to assume that his assistant manager's absences had coincided with major events. His diary soon refuted this theory. Perhaps his assistant manager was forgetting to stock up on the guide? So, on his return, the manager asked him how sales and stock were.

'Always a poor line – lots of stock left over,' was the reply. 'Except when you're not here,' thought the manager, his suspicions now aroused. The manager called in the internal auditor. Together they checked the detail of the tally rolls from the tills against the reconciliations of the assistant manager and found some discrepancies relating to times when till slips had been requested, or possibly when other staff had been close by the assistant manager when he was serving a customer and would have noticed if he had not issued a receipt. They counted the stock of guides on several occasions prior to the lunch break shift of the assistant manager and the manager made rough estimates of the number of customers who appeared to be purchasing them. The auditor asked the assistant manager how sales of various items, including guides, were going. The guides, he was told by the assistant manager, averaged only a few per hour. Together the auditor and manager searched the assistant manager's office while he was still on till duty and found a cupboard full of guides, all reasonably good colour photocopies but on close examination not produced by the printers. The staples were out of alignment and the edges contained a narrow black rim where the originals did not quite correspond to the size of the standard A4 paper used.

The assistant manager was disciplined and dismissed.

The main weakness that led to this case was the lack of separation of duties over cash accounting and the failure to issue receipts. The manager, or even perhaps one of the cashiers, should have counted the takings (entering the totals on the bank paying-in slip) and checked these to the printout and the summary, for example:

Tally roll total + oat = total cash in till
= bankings plus oat.

All three totals should have been entered on the reconciliation sheets with checkable explanations of any adjustments.

Even if this had been done the assistant manager might actually have been able to pocket cash before his shift ended, though with another cashier present at cashing-up this would have been difficult to achieve on a large scale.

For discrete items coded to a separate income code auditors often check stock movement against income. Basically the sum of opening stock (number) plus additional item purchases less the closing stock multiplied by the selling price should equal income. In this case this method would have been ineffective as the assistant manager supplied his own stocks.

CASE STUDY 7.2

THE CRÈCHE GRANT SCHEME

There are a great many government grants and rebates available that are administered by various departments of state, for a wide variety of purposes. Occasionally these are ad hoc but most are of a recurring nature. They range from fuel duty rebates for bus operators in rural areas to grants to other public bodies for urban renewal. The arrangements, although largely a matter of expenditure consideration (see Chapter 6) rather than income, often involve substantiation of the income of the grant-aided body and direct income due to the department from refunds.

The government has decided that employers who are willing to provide a crèche for working mothers in their employment will be entitled to a grant of 50 per cent towards any capital costs and all direct revenue costs (mainly the costs of a full-time nursery nurse).

Shortly after the scheme was introduced the national economy went into a relatively sudden and unexpected economic slump. The rate of company bankruptcies increased dramatically, including those among companies operating the crèche grant scheme. It had always been anticipated that a small number of companies might start up but not be able to continue a crèche and an executive officer had been designated to chase up any grant monies due to be refunded. The manager responsible for the executive officer collecting the refunds noticed a serious backlog of work was outstanding after only the first two months of the year. He suggested that a further one or two staff be recruited, hopefully on a temporary basis, to help clear the backlog. To his surprise the Executive Officer told him that the backlog was due mainly to his suffering from an in uenza virus rather than the economic downturn. He assured the manager that with some overtime he should be able to reduce the backlog to a month or so at most. The manager, a little reluctantly, agreed to give the Executive Officer a further three months during which time he, the manager, would keep a close watch on the backlog.

Over the next three months the backlog did indeed appear to be reducing at a substantial rate. Each fortnight the Executive Officer presented the manager with a case-load summary showing fewer and fewer outstanding cases. Most firms who were no longer able to proceed with the crèche scheme appeared willing to refund all, or nearly all, of the grant monies. In many cases there were letters from company officials mentioning cheques enclosed for the relevant amounts. By the end of the three months the manager, who had a great many other problems on his mind, was grateful that one more potential headache had abated.

At this point the Executive Officer announced – much to the manager's disappointment – that he had found another job abroad. He offered to work his full notice but explained that his new employers would be grateful if he could start as soon as possible. Arrangements were made to facilitate his departure a week later.

The crèche scheme refunds were classified as 'appropriation-in-aid'. This means that they could be treated as income by the government department concerned, rather than having to be surrendered to the government's consolidated fund as so-called 'extra receipts'. A few days after the Executive Officer had departed and before his replacement arrived, the manager received a telephone call from a colleague in the accounts branch asking whether much income had been received from refunds as they were about half way through the financial year. The original estimate mentioned approximately £50 000 may be due. (The colleague had no obvious way of deducing that the rise in companies'

CASE STUDY 7.2 *continued*

financial problems would mean that many more than anticipated would back out of the scheme and therefore be required to make a refund.)

After some searching the manager could find no record of banking the sums listed as received. In fact the list of receipts itself seemed incomplete and he then recalled that the only detailed records shown to him were breakdowns of case-loads. He hurriedly scanned through the Executive Officer's desk instructions and noted that an under-copy receipt should have been filed on each case file. After fumbling further through the contents of the former Executive Officer's desk he found the key to a large filing cabinet containing the case files, about 900 in all. He undid the lock, the double doors of the cabinet sprang apart and the manager was swamped with files – all of which contained a duly signed and authorized copy receipt.

His initial relief soon dissipated when he compared the amounts receipted to the amounts granted according to the earlier documents on each file, usually less than half, sometimes much less. Worse still each receipt has been made out 'in full and final settlement of any claim'.

The internal audit section, with the help of the manager, pieced together the following scenario and promptly called in the police.

The Executive Officer after starting off quite honestly begins to 'go bent', perhaps after receiving bribes from desperate businessmen trying to avoid bankruptcy. He knows that the accounts branch are not expecting any substantial monies to be paid over 'in the books', at least for a few more months. Occasionally he accepts and pays over to the accounts branch receipts for those companies who have paid the whole amount on a genuine basis.

Most companies are eager to accept a generously lower settlement than the total grant due to be refunded, especially if the revenue element is quite large. They did not (or did not want to) question the Executive Officer's authority – he was a genuine officer and the receipt was an official and binding one. Many firms were happy to pay cash.

The Executive Officer had, quite properly, opened a bank account in the name of his employers. He was required to make visits to attempt recovery of the monies and this account was intended to cover his expenses and any urgent temporary bankings. The bank had a letter from the manager authorizing the account to be operated by the Executive Officer. But this letter mentioned a credit ceiling and required monthly statements to be sent to the accounts office. The Executive Officer had simply photocopied a similar letter with the manager's signature; altered the banking details and the details of the accounts office to his own office; recopied the altered letter so that no erasing marks were evident and inked over the signature so that it appeared to be an original. He used this forgery to open another account into which he paid the money, and withdrew any cheques.

The main factors facilitating this fraud were (not necessarily in order of importance) the following:

1 No one had budgeted for large sums to be recovered and the accountants monitoring the income were not expecting substantial (if any) sums.
2 The Executive Officer was left largely unsupervised despite the fact that the manager expected him to be overworked.
3 In particular, no separation of duties existed between the assessment of amounts due and the collection and receipting of monies paid.

During the time the Executive Officer was employed on this work (just over six months) no senior officer, or indeed any peer, reviewed the detailed files or questioned the actual takings.

CASE STUDY 7.2 *concluded*

Eventually the Executive Officer would probably have been found out: the bank's own auditors may have circularized the department to confirm year-end balances; the manager would, eventually, have taken a closer interest in the Executive Officer's work; and the department's own auditors would have asked to see the files.

In the meantime the Executive Officer made off with various proportions of salary, rental, capital, and so on – costs granted to and now refunded by the 900 or so firms. Say 900 firms at an average £5000 – this totals £4.5 million!

Concluding points

For ordinary revenue income the most difficult problem, from the viewpoint of preventing fraud and corruption, is ensuring completeness. The organization may not be aware of all the income due and two key controls are recurrent in helping to prevent this – supervision of activities (including management checks) and separation of duties. In particular no single officer should control debt-generating activities, invoicing and cash receipting.

In the private sector, matters affecting income and cash ow into the organization affect its lifeblood and are generally at the very top of senior management priorities. In the public services macro-level considerations of income, especially taxation levels, are important but the cash ow aspects are generally secondary matters compared with issues surrounding expenditure. Political debates often revolve around spending plans, less so cash ow projections. Senior managers are frequently involved in implementing changes in expenditure programmes geared to the latest policy objectives but less concerned with monitoring organization/local level revenues. Objectives change continuously without the constancy of market-driven long-term objectives such as profit maximization or market share maximization. Such shifting sands may be inevitable in a free political system but the special risks at the micro-level should not be forgotten.

CHAPTER

8 *Transfer Payments ..Bene ts, Claims, Grants and Rebates*

Introduction

A wide range of grants, benefits, allowances, rebates subsidy payments, and so on, are made to individuals, families and organizations ranging from student grants, housing benefits, new business grants, grants to parish councils and aid to foreign countries. Most of these are subject to some form of means-testing or agreed conditions, whether in the fine detail or as part of more general terms, negotiations and conditions.

This topic is a particularly wide and difficult area in relation to fraud and corruption. The common factor that links the elements together is the fact they all involve some form of 'transfer payment': transferring monies from the tax-funded and government-controlled funds to private citizens, corporate bodies, or other governments. Apart from some cases of collusion, the root of the problem, like that of tax evasion (see Chapter 7) lies outside the public services itself. In this case it is to do with the honesty of individual citizens or organizations acting as 'claimants'.

False claims for grants and benefits, caused either directly or by omitting to notify a public body of a relevant change in circumstances, are almost encouraged by some conditions and are, it is generally accepted, not cost-effective to prevent altogether. In spite of this pessimistic perception it is both possible and cost-effective to put into operation a number of key controls and to channel resources (usually labour) to both detective and preventative work in areas where they are likely to provide good value for money.

Redistribution

The overall purpose of most transfer payments is redistribution of national or local resources. Most governments have adopted policies of redistribution of income or wealth for varying political reasons, some of which were mentioned in Chapter 2. The funding of popular social and philanthropic causes tends to be expected by voters whether they themselves are beneficiaries, think they may be possible beneficiaries at some future date, or simply consider the causes to be justifiable and worth paying for. Although not all redistributed benefits are means-tested the risk of widespread fraud and corruption for, say, the universally provided child benefit are minimal compared to means-tested housing benefits. For the former one has only to prove the existence of a dependent child; for the latter a relatively large number of conditions regarding rents or mortgages paid, tenancy, residence, income, savings, and so on, have to be disclosed and verified. It is therefore the aim of this chapter to concentrate wholly on means-tested benefits, though much of what is written applies to both types.

The mechanics of redistribution are invariably controlled by the state. This is likely to remain true even when public agencies and private firms are asked to compete for contracts to provide or manage the distribution of transfer payments. Such situations run up against the problems of self-interest and the basis of rewarding such an agency or firm (see Chapter 2), as a con ict of interest is likely to arise. For example, if a standard rate is paid for processing a claim, what would be the incentive to check the validity of the claim in detail? A government inspectorate or similar independent persons such as private management consultants or auditors could be asked to audit and certify the records of the agency; but would the cost of this be outweighed by the benefits of competition? The answer may depend very much on what other work was undertaken by the agency or by the consultants or auditors. So far limited contracts have been issued, mainly for local government housing and council tax benefits, and the results have been rather mixed. In any event, the act of compulsory redistribution, whoever performs it, may be considered the role of the state in a modern society and as such may be divided into the categories displayed in Figure 8.1.

Only a few examples are shown, though in Britain and most other developed countries these are subject to virtually continuous legislative change. Benefits and grants come and go as parties, policies and economic conditions change. A complex and confusing set of terminology and regulations is continually revised, amended, reinterpreted (often by the courts or any one of a number of tribunals) and subject to varying definitions of means. For example, age is sometimes taken as synonymous with need as with winter heating awards for pensioners, or some grants such as discretionary tree planting grants, are awarded on the basis of benefits to others who remain undefined or to the environment, that is, the community in general.

Any attempt to consider all the detailed regulatory aspects of benefits and grants on an individual basis would need to be voluminous, to say the least.

Recipient	*Examples of benefits and grants*
Individual	Income support, community charge benefit, various disablement allowances
Family	Housing benefit, benefits in respect of children
Commercial organizations	Research grants, rural development grants
Political unit	Selective aid programmes to developing countries, grants from local government to parishes
Owners or 'custodians' of property	Renovation grants
Non-political not-for-profit organizations	Grants to voluntary bodies

Note: some overlap in definition is inevitable in what is invariably a fluid situation

Figure 8.1 Compulsory redistribution of local or national resources

Certainly such detailed consideration is beyond the scope of this work. Fortunately sufficient important procedures and key controls are repeated to make a generalized summary worthwhile.

Key risks and controls – transfer payments

RISKS

Most of the risks relating to transfer payments involve some level of overpayment. In this sense they have a lot in common with expenditure risks outlined in Chapter 6:

1 The key overall risk is one of totally invalid payment, because the payment is not really due or in accordance with stipulated conditions.
2 There is also the risk of overpayment of a basically valid claim, because of accidental or deliberate miscalculation.
3 There is of course the risk of non-payment or underpayment of a valid claim, though this is only of concern in relation to fraud and corruption if the amount is diverted by a fraudster. A genuine non- or underpayment error of any significance is likely to be queried by the claimant.

TYPICAL CONTROLS TO COUNTER THE RISKS

In what follows a distinction has been drawn between what may conveniently be called 'organizational' and what may be called 'case management' controls. Although the dividing line is sometimes blurred, the former relate to the wider arrangements for processing payments whereas the latter relate more to controls that need to be active at the level of each individual payment.

ORGANIZATIONAL CONTROLS

1 *All claims relating to each individual claimant or grant receiving body should be led together (or clearly cross-referenced).* Quite often information supplied by the claimant or verified by a case officer in relation to one claim will, in cases of fraud, contradict or call into question that of another claim. Also, particularly with individual claimants, if one claim is found to be fraudulent in a hitherto unsuspected manner it is quite likely that some other similar claims will also be affected. Likely cases may involve housing benefits, income support or community charge benefit, for example. Sometimes, as with income support and housing benefit, these benefits are administered by different public bodies. While close liaison between officers and prompt notifications of changes in circumstances may be possible, the files and data will be kept separately and are, of course, subject to the provisions of the Data Protection Act (see Chapter 5).

2 *Separation of duties: no single of cial should be involved in processing and authorizing a complete claim.* As with most separation of duties this can be difficult to achieve in situations of very limited resources. However, most benefits are processed by departments with numerous staff dedicated to processing claims on the basis of area, alphabetic order, or a similar broad division. It is usually feasible for the work to be separated into:

(a) initial review of claim and so on, documentation and enquiries;
(b) location, site or home visit; and
(c) final review and authorization of entitlement letter, exchange of agreement, and so on.

It is usually cost-effective for the final authorization and any site visit to be carried out by officers not involved in the initial receipt and vetting of the claim. Often complications arise and costly or disputed items have to be referred to a senior officer for clarification which is a natural separation feature. Ideally the powers of junior staff and circumstances requiring the attention of senior officers should be clearly documented and explained to new recruits (see point 9).

3 *Cases should be checked by management,* particularly where numerous cases are being processed daily (and especially if a separation of duties is difficult to maintain). Selection should ensure a range and frequency of cases sufficient to form a reliable opinion on the remainder. It may well be worthwhile in practice to choose a small statistical sample or use a combination of randomly selected statistical samples and a judgemental selection from high risk types.

This control is often combined with the extraction of a sample of encashed cheques to check the bank account into which they have been paid (given by the bank's stamp on the face of the cheque). Some payments depend upon the recipient having declared their bank details, sometimes the recipient may have been forced to hand over the cheque to a third party (not so common with payee-only cheques but still sometimes possible).

4 *Claim reference numbers should be issued in sequence as soon as a claim is received or generated.* Claims that are, or become, invalid or refused should be retained for the relevant statutory period or audit-required period, whichever is the greater. Any delay in the allocation of a number while the claim is being handled and perhaps given its initial vetting adds to the risk of loss, misfiling and, most importantly from our viewpoint, the risk of false creation or amendment of the claim itself, or any subsequent suppression, cancelling or amending of documents received during these initial stages. Sometimes an excuse is made along the lines of 'a number can not be allocated until the claim has been entered on the computer, or after it has been checked'. This usually means that it does not get numbered until everything has been cleared up and it can be processed without a hitch. In most cases this involves a significant time, for example, more than an hour or so. In the days of batch processing some credence may have been attached to such an excuse; rarely so today. If a claim must be delayed before numbering, it should be given a short-term reference which should usually be incorporated in its final reference number.

5 *Adequate staff/supervisory ratios must be maintained*: like most controls this is simply good management practice. It is not difficult to see that in an environment where rules are changing, revised rates are being introduced intermittently and staff turnover rates are often fairly high, the work needs to be closely supervised. Most means-tested benefits are such that the creation of false case files or amended files could produce a lucrative temptation for what are, almost inevitably, fairly low paid clerks. Case study 3.1 provided an example of this type of fraud based on false payroll files.

6 *Investigation of cers*: most claims/benefit and so on, administrating organizations maintain some form of investigatory arm, usually under the control of senior management, though

at times internal audit or even external audit may be called upon to advise. It is crucial in preventing fraud and corruption that neither the investigating officers themselves, nor the officers processing the claims, are able to have complete control over which cases are investigated or the level of investigation involved. Senior management should set down strict guidelines on the conduct of investigations and should ultimately determine which cases are allocated to the investigating official(s). If it is not practically feasible for managers at an independent level to be involved in determining the choice of each case, strict guidelines should be set down for the selection procedures and the actual selection should be subject to periodic management review. The purpose of such provision is to encourage and maintain impartiality and accountability. Fortunately, in most circumstances, these objectives coincide with good management objectives. A manager may consider it important that all investigation officers get a fair share of difficult cases, or deal with cases most suited to their particular specialist skills, or whatever criteria he or she requires. Provided these are objectively-set criteria designed to meet corporate objectives, and the manager issues appropriate instructions and takes steps to ensure these are followed, the risk of partiality and any consequent corruption is likely to be minimized.

Much investigatory work involves pre-award as well as post-award situations. It is important that if both pre- and post-award work is undertaken this is cross-referred and also considered in the light of any other case management controls, particularly over post-award assessment – see points 12 and 13 below.

CHEQUES

7 *Cheque/BACS control*: any direct cheque/ BACS payments should not be routed back via the officers responsible for processing. This is a standard key control for all payments systems (see also Chapter 6) helping particularly to prevent the creation of false cases.

Any cheques returned because of non-delivery, recipient 'gone away', wrong address, and so on, should, as with cheques posted out and for the same reasons, not be routed directly to the officers responsible for processing.

All cheques should be crossed 'Not transferable – A/C payee only'. See also point 3 above.

8 *Analytical (trend) reviews*: sometimes the wood can be missed for the trees, especially when staff are under pressure from the short-term requirements of individual case-loads and regular management reports. Analytical review considers the broad picture shown by trends over time and comparisons to other related data. This can be as simple or as complicated as the individual manager thinks is merited (or has the time for). From the viewpoint of fraud the comparisons offer a chance to consider why changes in one variable, say, a disability allowance have not brought about the expected changes in a related variable, say, demand for home helps for the disabled. The use of an analytical review tends to be rather limited either as a preventative or a detective aid in combating individual cases of fraud and corruption but it can be effective when considering the likelihood of widespread malpractice, particularly when one variable measures a means and the other measures the cost of a benefit. For further references on analytical review see the Bibliography, for example, Jones and Bates (1994).

CASE MANAGEMENT CONTROLS

9 *Operating instructions/manuals that are understood, relevant and up to date*: see Chapter 1 for more on this. The key point of control is that staff acknowledge, in writing, that they have received, understood and updated these. In fact this is often seen as an organizational control but it is more on the borderline here as such instructions will usually explain how to deal with both the routine and the exceptional situations and when to refer to higher authority. It may well be that staff will need to use operational instructions and manuals of various descriptions on each individual case.

10 *Good quality case papers*: criticism is sometimes levelled at the poor standard of working papers associated with grants and means-tested benefits. Exceptions can and do occur. But, given their importance to the claimant and the risk of subsequent court or tribunal proceedings, it is surprising if due care and attention is not paid to the quality of case papers. Pressure to attain a quick turnaround of case-load, or low staff morale, or the fact that the officer first dealing with the case is unlikely to deal personally with any appeal or court action, may be among the causes. Whatever the cause, untidy and disorganized case papers provide ready camou age for fraud. Errors and uncertainty will become acceptable, first upon a small scale, later becoming more widespread. Fraud perpetrated externally by the claimant will become less easily spotted. Confirmations of income, rents, acreage, damage, dependants or whatever will become delayed, then missing until after the case has been decided, and then in some cases it may not be sought at all. The author has come across situations where 'error correction teams' or 'control sections' have been set up within the benefit or grants administering bodies. This step may at first have some deterrent effect, though in practice it is more likely to be a negative in uence and lead to dependence upon the error correction team to act as a safety net, so encouraging even more lax attitudes to the quality of work. In most normal circumstances errors should be very infrequent or well within the capability of motivated staff and diligent supervision or management to reduce to acceptable levels. Quite the opposite effect to that of error correction teams can be obtained if the emphasis is placed upon quality control or quality enhancement. This may be achieved by existing officials or may, in some organizations, be best achieved by seconding officials from other departments to work for specified periods as part of a separate quality control team. The critical difference, from the viewpoint of both errors and deliberate fraud, is that every set of case papers or at least examples of the work of every officer (including computer-held records) should be assessed from a quality viewpoint whether it contains errors or not. Officials should be made aware of high standards, not merely poor performance. Obviously both management and unions may be able to use such findings to reward or seek rewards for enhanced performance or productivity. Error correction safety nets, if they are in place, should be replaced as soon as possible by quality motivations designed to reverse any trend towards poor quality case papers.

Some of the more usually important types of working papers and documented control features are indicated in the checklist in Appendix 11.

11 *Noti cation of awards should be fully recorded and independent of processing*: this is already implied above in point 2, but it is worthy of emphasis. The notification of the final award is usually a crucial stage. This may refer to a single grant payment or to an ongoing weekly benefit or some combination of intermittent payments. Ideally, a senior manager,

or panel of adjudicators, or some other person(s) outside the receiving and checking of the claim should give the final approval, albeit that this is done on the advice and calculations of the officials involved in processing the claim. The person(s) involved in finally approving the amount and conditions, if any, attached to the award constitute a separation of duties that provides one further safeguard against the improper or irregular claim. Such persons usually develop a feeling for what is acceptable in various circumstances particularly if, as is usually the case, they have themselves been involved in processing similar claims or grants in the past and have over the years come to experience a wide variety of circumstances and processing procedures. As with cheque payments, discussed below, the final notification should not be handed back to the officer involved in processing the claim but should be posted out to the claimant.

12 *Changes in circumstances*: the system should have key controls that draw attention to changes in circumstances. These are with a few exceptions more appropriate to ongoing benefit than to single payment grant claims. Such controls might involve periodic reassessments of circumstances, such as reassessment of entitlement to housing benefit. Another example might be comparisons between council rent or tax accounts and benefit claims, or even inter-body comparisons involving employers and the Inland Revenue. Inter-body comparisons would of course need to be carefully considered in the light of the Data Protection Act and if appropriate the current Official Secrets regulations. See also point 14 below.

13 *Follow-up visits*: for grants and benefits follow-up visits are often standard practice, as part of the post-assessment of work done or in order to confirm changes in circumstances. Often these visits may act as a deterrent to fraud and generally should be performed by officials not previously involved in the case. Apart from reducing the risk of collusion, this separation of duties offers the chance for a second professional opinion and for the beneficiary to voice any concerns to a new face. Except in the most complicated of cases these advantages usually offset any additional costs of familiarization required of a new officer.

14 *Termination procedures*: the need for these is very similar to the need for such controls in a payroll system – to avoid ghosts – though controls are usually more problematical. The claimant, landlord, and so on, will not be physically absent from among other officials and no real equivalent of a staff-in-post to payroll comparison can be readily made between claimants and claim files. Typical controls include 'do not forward, to be opened only by addressee' type notices on envelopes, regular review actions (such as confirmation letters or age reviews) by management (as with point 12 above), regular comparison of claimants files to other data such as electoral roles, employment data and so on – once again subject to the Data Protection Act, and possibly hand delivery of payment cheques.

Figure 8.2 links the above risks and controls in a grid format, similar to Figure 6.2. It attempts to link the key control(s) that relate to each risk, though once again in practice other controls may help reduce the level of risk, and in many practical situations managers may bolster up the effectiveness of particular controls or use other controls not listed here that work effectively in their situations. Also in the case of transfer payments each control is likely to affect more than one risk, indeed many affect all three. Some would see this widespread applicability of controls as indicating that perhaps fewer are needed in total. However, the sad truth is usually that the lapse of one or two controls simply increases the risks, mainly because in transfer payment situations the inherent complexity of the system and its changing regulatory and policy framework usually leaves greater scope for the error and confusion so easily exploited by fraudsters.

Control→	1	2	3	4	5	6	7	8	9	10	11	12	13	14
Risk↓														
1 (invalid)	o	o	o	o	o	o	o	o	o	o	o	o	o	o
2 (overpay)	o	o	o		o	o		o	o	o			o	o
3 (diverted)	o	o	o		o	o	o		o	o	o	o	o	o

Figure 8.2 Risk/control grid for transfer payments

Causes taken from various real cases of means-tested fraud

Rather than provide the reader with a few case studies relating to at most one or two types of means-tested benefit, the variety of fraud occurring in this area can best be appreciated by considering the numerous cases reported. Examples are published in the 'Fraud' pages of *Audit Viewpoint*, published by CIPFA, or the Audit Commission's information circulars. A brief synopsis of some of the main causes is given below:

1 Lack of separation of duties in the claim processing departments leading to:
   (a) fictitious cases;
   (b) deliberate overpayments;
   (c) deliberate non-actioning of cancellation orders; and
   (d) deliberate failure to notify other agencies.
2 Lack of resources or poorly targeted resources leading to:
   (a) inability to deter or detect claimant dishonesty; and
   (b) lack of separation of duties as in 1 above.
3 Routing of outgoing cheques, confirmation letters, enquiry letters, and so on, back through the hands of the officials processing the claim rather than posting out through the normal postal arrangements leading to:
   (a) interception of payment for fictitious or deliberately overpaid cases; and
   (b) maintenance of a fictitious case of the deliberate failure to action cancellations orders.
4 Collusion between:
   (a) the claimant and officials (especially where officials deal with the cases of family or friends);
   (b) the claimant and a third party such as an estate agent, solicitor, landlord or employer; and
   (c) officer and officer, for example, processing clerk and investigation officer.

5 Lack of evidence of the operation of internal control, particularly of authorizations. Such causes include:
   (a) lack of an adequate audit trail particularly during computer updating; and
   (b) failure to obtain first-hand evidence of circumstances from bank accounts, rent books, home visits, and so on.
6 Lack of regular liaison between different government agencies leading to:
   (a) incomplete information passed from, say, the Department of Social Security to local authorities;
   (b) incomplete cross-checking of common data such as address, income, needs assessments, and so on; and
   (c) fraud being detected by one agency but not being notified to another affected body.

Experienced managers and experts will no doubt be able to envisage other causes. The list is virtually endless given the changing regulatory position. Clearly the above should also be read in conjunction with Appendix 11.

Summary

Transfer payments are always open to abuse, as there is an inherent risk that the claimant or other recipient will by their nature have an incentive to act dishonestly. Recent Audit Commission surveys indicate this is by far the largest category of fraud, though largely perpetrated by outsiders rather than insiders. This area has a lot in common with expenditure generally – see Chapter 6 – yet they are invariably a result of direct political policy and as such require close scrutiny by officials to ensure that often detailed regulations are followed. There are also issues of vulnerability and fairness to be taken into account as well as the usual considerations of honesty and legality. All these factors tend to cloud and complicate the application of controls. The key controls considered in this chapter are often the very minimum required. Quite often officials involved in this area can counter fraud by thinking imaginatively and gaining a high level of familiarity with their clients and the environments in which fraud is committed. This is often at least as important as the careful application of key controls.

CASE STUDY

Only one detailed case study is given and this is provided mainly to provoke the reader's thoughts on the variety of topics that this one area can encompass. As explained earlier, the diversity of fraud related to means-tested benefits and grants warrants regular updating from published sources.

CASE STUDY 8.1

GRANTS FOR IRRIGATION PROJECTS

Under a multilateral aid agreement between the United Kingdom and several African countries severely affected by drought, grants are provided for irrigation schemes. This is done on the basis of a formula that takes into account national per capita income, the proportion of the schemes' cost raised by the recipients of the grant (including other donations) and the cost of purchases (capital and first year revenue) made from companies designated as UK owned for the purposes of this particular agreement. The formula determines the proportion each of the recipient and donor nations contributes towards the estimated total costs of each scheme.

The national per capita incomes of the various recipient countries are taken from published sources and are in any case estimated figures. However, the total estimated project cost, the proportions of this total funded by the UK, other donors or the recipient nation, and the costs of purchases from UK companies can all, in theory, be manipulated to favour the UK, other donors (if any) or the recipient. Approximately £20 million has been allocated to this type of aid.

Each scheme prepares separate 'stage claims' which are sent to the sponsoring government department as the scheme progresses. The total value of the grant has been worked out on the basis of estimated figures. At the start of the scheme stage claims should contain a certified account that the scheme has been completed to an agreed stage and funding is on target. Variations in cost (usually overruns) are considered by the sponsoring department for additional funding in accordance with the formula. The certification of the stage claims is usually undertaken by the government auditors of the recipient nation.

At first sight these arrangements may seem quite adequate to ensure an optimum distribution of limited resources between the UK, other donors and the recipient, always provided the formula is agreed by all to be fair. The main risk with such intergovernmental arrangements is that while they may be well suited to one nation with the ethos and usually the controlling in uence of a single government they may be totally unsuited to another, say the recipient nation. Here are some examples:

1 The external audit of the UK government by the NAO is generally considered to have a high degree of independence. This may not be the case in other countries where audit may simply be seen as checking undertaken by the government into its own financial affairs to ensure they are conducted in its (the government's) best interest. This is quite different from audit by an independent body not under government control.
2 How are costs to be measured? Stock valuations are notoriously difficult as are valuations of work in progress. The problems of cost measurement are difficult enough in the UK; in an international context where each party has differing accounting conventions and financial incentives to interpret terms in its favour these problems are likely to be multiplied. To some extent cost ceilings can be imposed by the donor, but if this leads to a partly finished project then all the sums spent so far might have been wasted and it is usually more acceptable politically to make an increased contribution.
3 Irrespective of problems of interpretation of terms such as costs, values, profits, and so on (a degree of which can be catered for by strict wording and agreed arbitration procedures), further problems

CASE STUDY 8.1 *continued*

of information-gathering are likely to arise. Information originally envisaged may be impractical to obtain in the field situation. Foreign companies may not keep the types of records envisaged or may not supply them on time. Records may change in translation, or over time as new companies and managers arrive to take part in, or take over, the projects.

4 Any audit visits on behalf of the donor will of necessity have to be agreed well in advance and unless the auditors are familiar with the language and custom of the host nations they are likely to be of limited value compared to home audits. Permanent representation on the project is likely to be required if any reasonable measure of control or effective monitoring is thought necessary.

All these problems and the myriad of complications implied in any individual case apply when all parties are assumed to be honest. In this case study two major areas of dishonesty arise and will be examined.

The most obvious and frequent area of corruption was the simple siphoning off of funds. The sheer lack of reliable records and the inability of the UK government representatives to value goods and services at the going (that is, local) rate enabled as much as 60 per cent of some payments to be used to line the pockets of middlemen and others. In fact, it is open to question as to whether or not corruption, in the deliberate and malicious sense of the word, actually occurred.

Officials more familiar with some of the local schemes pointed out that to some of those involved it might seem that the UK authorities interpreted valid cost in terms of their own legal systems and peculiar national, even Christian, values. Such an approach merely served to omit some quite normal costs associated with widely accepted behaviour – including bribery – in the recipient nation.

It is certainly true that a corrupt or fraudulent action in one nation's cultural and perhaps legal environment may be quite acceptable in another. This much leeway in interpretation any multinational organization or international trading company might acknowledge. Aid, however, does not, it might be argued, fall into the same category as just any other international transaction.

The donor might well feel entitled to assume that the conditions of the aid will be interpreted in a manner that meets the donor's rather than the recipient's expectations. The donor is after all acting in a largely voluntary capacity, unlike a multinational company. The donor, it might be argued by those who hold this view, should at the very least be made aware in advance of the donation of the likely unanticipated (on the donor's part) uses to which these funds will be put.

The second major area of corruption concerned the listing of UK firms. A listing which, one is bound to admit, begins to call into question the donor's disinterested altruism in funding the aid. Giving some form of favourable advantage to companies from donor nations is not an unusual convention, and the listing of approved UK firms means that while a recipient country could order equipment that they could not themselves supply from any foreign supplier by using a UK supplier, the UK government would be prepared to increase its funding to the relevant scheme. The risk of corruption in this case was caused by an inadequate definition of a UK firm. In practice there was nothing to prevent a non-UK company setting up a UK subsidiary, or using one already in existence, to channel goods and services to the recipient nation; goods that were in effect produced and marketed by non-UK companies. The UK subsidiary company merely acted as a front when

CASE STUDY 8.1 *concluded*

applying to sell the goods or services to the managers in charge of the scheme.

SUMMARY OF CASE STUDY

In the first area of corruption, the siphoning off of funds, lack of management control in general and timely and accurate cost data in particular are largely to blame. However, it is difficult to see, certainly once a project is up and running, how such management information can be imposed upon existing arrangements without significant extra costs and possibly serious delays. In practice the feasibility and desirability of obtaining the information required would depend largely upon the scale and duration of the project. The larger (in cost terms) and longer the project the more desirable and feasible it is likely to be to obtain the required information. The second area of corruption, the definition of a UK firm, is much less of an ongoing problem than the first. It is basically a matter of closing a loophole, though it is unlikely that any extra funding provided before the loophole is closed can be justifiably reclaimed. Ideally an independent financial assessment from a financial enquiry agency could be obtained. Alternatively the companies bidding successfully for work on a scheme could be contacted directly to provide proof of their controlling interests.

In both areas of corruption the problems encountered by the donor stem from a lack of clear understanding of the culture and attitudes of the recipient and the firms involved, due, possibly, to the lack of experience or precedents in similar situations.

Concluding points

Relatively few frauds in this area are perpetrated entirely within an organization by its own employees. Most involve claimant/beneficiary dishonesty. Very little can be done by an organization to alter the standards of honesty of their clients in this respect, but given that many claimants succumb to dishonesty partly at least because the systems involved are easy to manipulate or are managed and controlled in a lax or inconsistent manner, much can be done to prevent temptation arising and to deter future cases once a fraud is discovered.

In particular a chain of responsibility should involve more than one officer from initial claim assessment to payment (or initiation of a regular stream of payments). This responsibility should be clearly evidenced as should any checks undertaken by investigating officials, management or supervisors. What, after all, is the point of carrying out constructive and often diligent work if nothing of it remains from which to gain recognition or judge the need for change or future efforts?

CHAPTER

9 The Main Accounting and Reporting Function

Introduction

Accounts include many and diverse financial statements, from the main financial accounts for the organization published after the year end, annual budgets and long-term financial projections, to the regular, usually monthly, management accounts (out-turn statements as they are sometimes called).

A set of accounts being, essentially, a financial picture of an organization's efforts and achievements to date or projected into the future, cannot in themselves either cause or prevent fraud and corruption, any more than can a photograph of a government building. The accountant's decisions of what to include in the picture and, sometimes, to whom the picture should be shown are of course quite a different matter. For the time being we shall assume, with some unavoidable rashness, the accountant to be a completely honest and professional figure. As far as possible the reader will be spared the intricacies of accounting techniques and arguments over what form the accounts should take and how the figures should be described, measured, presented and used. Rather we will concentrate on the basic mechanics of public services accounting and draw attention to typical areas of risk and control that would enable such an honest and professional accountant to make a very significant contribution to preventing fraud and corruption. Anything more would require a separate book to do justice to public services accounting (see the Bibliography for further reading).

The purpose and objectives of the main accounting and reporting function

Despite what has been said about keeping to the basic mechanics of public services accounting, we cannot avoid considering a fundamental question of theory: what purpose do the accounts serve? The accounts must have a purpose, which must be appreciated, at least at a basic level, if the mechanics themselves are to be understood. The general purpose of an organization's published accounts is undoubtedly one of public accountability – to inform the reader of its financial affairs. Beyond this other aims of accounts become somewhat hazy, not least when a major fraud is uncovered. Theoretical questions arise, such as to whom should the accounts be directed? What information should they portray? To what level of detail? On what basis should this or that particular figure be calculated? There are probably as many answers to theoretical questions such as these as there are accountants. Professional bodies give guidance that should be followed, especially in respect of what figures should be included and the basis of their calculation. But even this leaves much to be interpreted and debated.

SYSTEM OBJECTIVES

For convenience let us imagine that acceptable theoretical answers can be found to the above questions. This still leaves the more practical question to be answered (on which hopefully agreement is easier to reach): what are the system-level objectives of the main accounting system?

Let us first consider what is meant by the main accounting system. This usually refers to the final arrangements for collating and accumulating the figures produced by other feeder systems into the annual published accounts and estimates and any intermediate financial or management accounts relating to the organization as a whole, or at least a fairly substantial part of it. This may be a simple matter of listing the total figures produced by the payroll, debtors, creditors, and other feeder systems (computerized or manual) and entering them up once a month into a personal computer or ordinary bound ledger. More often in the public services and any sizeable organization, both the feeder systems and the main accounting system are computerized and different balances are transferred at different periods from immediate online update, to weekly, monthly or annual transfers.

Figure 9.1 outlines a typical large main accounting system obtaining information from a number of feeder systems and producing trial balances, management accounts and estimates and year-end accounts.

In practical terms, the system needs to produce accurate, complete and valid accounts (in accordance with agreed or assumed answers to the more theoretical questions asked above) by ensuring the following three system-level objectives:

1 Transfer – all feeder account transactions (individually or bulk figures) are transferred to the main system;
2 Bookkeeping – all transactions transferred (including brought forward and carried forward figures) are correctly and completely updated in the relevant ledger accounts; and
3 Reporting – all figures extracted from the ledgers are correctly entered into the published or management reports and accounts (balance sheet, revenue accounts, budgets, and so on).

Key risks and controls – main accounting function

RISKS

At a detailed level the risks to the completeness accuracy and validity of the processing and output of any accounting system are many and diverse: miscoding, computation errors, compensating errors, omissions of initial input, and so on. Such risks are the rationale behind the work of external audit. But overall the risks can be summarized as the converse of the three objectives set out above:

1 Incomplete data capture/transfer to the main accounting system.
2 Inaccurate bookkeeping treatment.
3 Incomplete, inaccurate or otherwise misleading reporting in/transfer to the published or management accounts.

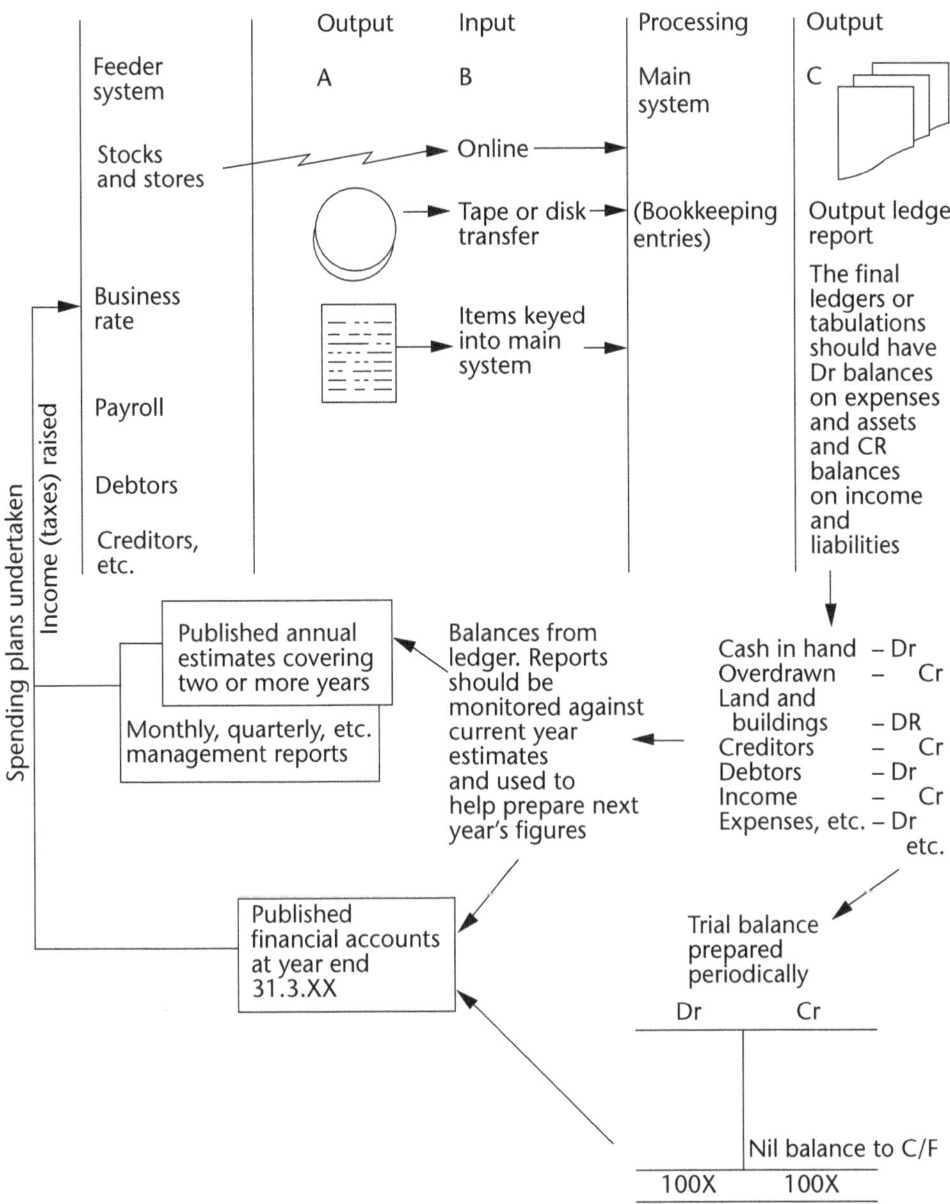

Figure 9.1 Accounting system in outline

TYPICAL CONTROLS TO COUNTER THE RISKS

In the context of major financial accounting systems that vary greatly between different public bodies and different reporting requirements, individual controls are often best summarized into control types. This means that the control headings outlined below will have slightly varying mechanisms and procedures in different organizations.

1 *Reconciliations of feeder to main accounting systems* For all the feeder systems, manual or computerized, it is essential that line managers are able to ensure their data, that is, instructions to the main system, are correctly and completely received and input to the main system, that is, A to B in Figure 9.1. It is usually just as important to ensure that the input thus provided has been used correctly to update the appropriate accounts and so it should also be possible to reconcile from B to C or A to C. Such reconciliation can take various forms, sometimes manual, sometimes involving data vetting and processing controls programmed into the accounting system software. The security of the initial data inputting is often a key countermeasure to combat fraud – see also Chapter 5.

2 *Reliable double entry bookkeeping* In the (usually dim and distant) past, accountants and auditors spent considerable efforts in manually checking and following through bookkeeping from initial journal entries to the final published or management accounts. The whole system of double entry acts as a control feature, and the risk of it being misapplied or breaking down and the consequent re-entering of transactions and journal transferring of entries to correct the system meant that time spent checking entries and generally keeping an eye on the balances in the accounts was merited. This is done far less so today, because normally one can rely on a well-tried and reasonably securely operated computer system to process the same type of transaction as accurately and completely each time. But fraudsters do not act normally, and such 'taking-for-granted' attitudes can even aid the perpetration of a fraud. This control depends upon three elements:

2.1 The design of the bookkeeping itself: can a computerized system cope with every conceivable transaction faced by the particular organization? In manual systems this issue can be readdressed as unexpected entries arise, in computerized software a poorly designed system will often encourage or even force the bookkeepers to misuse particular entries. Nowadays the standard of bookkeeping in most accounting software is perhaps better than in the early days and the design factor is often less of a problem.

2.2 The attitude of the accounting staff to using the system: shortcuts or poor training can weaken the control factor in double entry. Double entry means that each transaction must be entered twice, a debit and a credit. This is repeated each time the amount is transferred between accounts or coalesced into larger totals which will themselves be debited and credited and so on. If the double entry principle is followed and applied consistently to assets, liabilities, income and expenses then a fraudster will have to plan and carry out or control a larger number of entries than would otherwise be the case. This in itself is a countermeasure in many circumstances and quite often a fraudulent entry will show up as a debit that cannot be easily traced to a credit or vica versa, or simply an unbalanced set of accounts (see below under trial balance). However, this control feature of double entry will only work if staff use the control features and diligently follow up any apparent discrepancies. If odd entries and discrepancies are a usual feature of the system then it is human nature not to take these seriously, or to accept almost any old excuse – an ideal environment for a fraudster!

2.3 The regular operation of and attention to control key features: particularly, the production of trial balances and the reconciliation of control accounts. In practice each software package or in-house development usually has its own set of such features; random selections of transactions for audit testing is popular. This element is merely an extension of the second element mentioned above, except that it is usually more experienced or senior staff who are responsible for operating such control features. For such control features to be effective they must be used on a frequent basis so that staff get used to the trends and the patterns and can spot unusual items; even so it is often difficult to spot small irregularities. Trial balances will usually reveal any obvious breakdowns in the double entry, but more sophisticated errors or frauds may not show up in a trial balance; for example, compensating errors or false entries, say, the understatement of an asset (a lower debit entry or a credit entry to the asset account) to balance off the fraudulent overstatement, debit, of an expense account. Control accounts are used to reconcile large numbers of entries in individual debtor or creditor accounts to the control account entries but again, fraudulent entries will often involve false individual debtor or creditor accounts which the control account itself will not reveal.

3 *Monitoring of out-turn statements against budgets and providing political accountability* Nearly all public services bodies are accountable to elected, political members or political appointees, though the link may, at times, be indirect as with health service boards or the accountability of individual state schools to local authority education committees and, ultimately, to an education minister. At the strategic political level the budget, its comparison to last year's approved spending and most importantly the implications for the next (possible election) year's spending is of prime importance. At times this focus on the relatively short-term spending and taxation requirements may seem short-sighted from a long-term planning viewpoint. Nevertheless detailed scrutiny of budgetary performance and future taxation focuses attention and demands political accountability in a way that is alien to most commercial accounts. Open political – and hence public – scrutiny generally acts to deter fraud and corruption. In most public bodies politicians will require verbal or written explanations of the main variations of out-turn expenditure against budgeted estimates at least once a year if not more frequently. Individual budget headings and subheadings will catch the attention of opposition members, the press and public and require delving into by politicians and subsequent investigation by senior finance staff. Such explanation may well be reported widely in the press. Ideally, finance officials should monitor expenditure of various related budget headings and provide management with regular performance accounts and statistics as well as providing the political explanation. This environment encourages open accountability and discourages secretive and corrupt practices, though not of course completely.

These safeguards against fraud and corruption tend to operate to a greater or lesser extent in most public bodies, depending upon the accounting requirements of the body concerned. They are, or should be, first and foremost macro controls to ensure sound financial and management accounting and hopefully adherence to policy objectives and good financial management. Nevertheless the importance of such controls in limiting fraud and corruption to a level generally recognized to be far lower than for private sector bodies should not be underestimated.

4 *Control over output gures* Controls in this area have been discussed in Chapter 5. Most output is likely to be from computerized systems. It is important to maintain security of output not so much to avoid sensitive or personal data falling into the wrong hands, as is often the case with individual records, but to ensure that summarized totals and key

performance data actually reach the relevant managers or other senior officials. A separation of input and output duties is often difficult if not impossible to maintain on a cost-effective basis. Also, any overspend or diversion of funds, while it may be possible to conceal on the micro-level by omitting particular line items from accounts will, on any serious scale, often show up as a variation on a budget head. Such a variation will require an explanation to senior management and quite likely politicians too, as described in the preceding section.

5 *Bank reconciliation* This is no more than a particular reconciliation of the types already mentioned. However, it is of such fundamental importance as to warrant individual attention. In particular it is important to ensure that all bank accounts are reconciled. Most bodies will have separate accounts for income and expenditure and any balance should be transferred to an interest-bearing account at the end of the day's trading. Separate accounts may be kept for capital expenditure and investments and short-term borrowings depending upon the nature of the body. Any cash in transit or in the hands of officials (such as expenses imprests) should be verified on reconciliation.

6 *Suspense accounts* All the ledger accounts merit attention and a set of manual or computerized ledgers kept to a high standard undoubtedly assists in deterring or revealing any fraud. But among all the accounts suspense accounts are particularly important and vulnerable. Any misappropriated shortages or gain that have to be held for a while will attract attention if transferred to a designated account and, even if they remain unnoticed for a short time, they will probably be picked up by a control account not balancing to zero at the end of the month or week. But a suspense account is often treated more favourably (from the fraudster's viewpoint). Many organizations will only clear out their suspense accounts once a year towards the year end. Until then unexplained balances of quite a genuine and innocent nature such as unexplained receipts or badly coded expenditure items will, for a time, help to conceal any fraudulent transaction. The specific circumstances under which suspense accounts can be used should be clearly set down and the movements into and out of suspense accounts should be independently authorized at a senior level if control is to be effective.

7 *Transfers and virement* Journal transfers are widely used for many reasons, to move amounts between accounts. These present similar risks to suspense accounts, particularly for local government, partly due to their year-end accounting procedures (see below) and partly due to their proliferation of budget codes. Virement (the swapping of politically approved expenditure between budget headings) can take place in any public services body. Both these procedures tend to add to the general complexity and reduce the open political accountability of the bodies' main accounts. Controls in this area may be lax if relatively junior staff, or a large number of senior officials can, with little need to explain or obtain independent authorization, transfer funds or budgets between coded headings. In this way monitoring (see above) and accountability can be seriously weakened. If lax control over transfers is combined with lax control over suspense accounts the combined risk may be even more serious. Once again, senior and independent authorization should be recorded so that a trail of accountability is clear.

Value for money, management performance, fraud and corruption

Good value for money and achieving a low risk of fraud and corruption are mutually supportive objectives. In the short term and on a small scale a situation might arise where an organization is forced to choose between the cost of internal control, say, employing extra staff in order to maintain separation of duties, and a saving on wages otherwise achieved. In the long run, if any organization is to be controlled by and accountable to its sponsors, their directors/strategic managers, or service level managers, it must have systems that are either self-checking – which implies adequate internal control – or that are sufficiently simple so as to be directly verifiable by senior management (a rare situation in modern, complex organizations).

In the example of a choice between maintaining separation of duties and saving wages costs, senior management must be certain that the cost of wages saved is not being, or likely to be, offset by fraud or the need to deal with increased errors. This implies they can demonstrate that all is well in respect to the transactions or values affected by the systems no longer subject to the separation of duties. For example, modern computerized payroll systems can often be operated by one or two officers whereas in the past many may have been required. A single officer might perhaps calculate and produce the payroll, and collect and disburse any cash wages. Clearly the scope for fraud is increased compared with a situation where each of these stages would probably involve separate officers with one effectively checking the work of another. To compensate for this lack of control, the management may need such additional controls as regular independent checks on the work of the payroll officer, or reviewing the overall level of payments on a regular basis taking account of uctuations caused by pay rises, overtime requirements, and so on. Sometimes computerization enables a natural separation between systems, such as payroll and time recording or payroll and personnel duties, to be conveniently utilized and the records to each to be reconciled in total.

Whatever the individual circumstances, the operation of the public services organizations as a whole is utterly dependent upon an honest and largely fraud-free working environment if it is to offer anything approaching good value for money. The effective monopoly or near-monopoly situations of some bodies and the inevitable discretionary powers of most, mean that any corrupt management (usually without any risk of bankrupting the body) can eece the taxpayer no matter how they may appear at first to encourage competition, thrift and efficiency. It is always worth bearing in mind that for many public bodies the very compilation and dissemination of information used to provide measures of value for money are, to all intents and purposes, under the control of their management.

If value for money is to be bettered by adopting suitable commercial and other performance indicators, the body concerned must be placed in a genuinely commercial environment and be able and expected to compete with similar organizations in a workable free-market situation. But this is not always possible or practical as Chapter 2 discussed. Some reported fraud cases and cases of serious mismanagement have highlighted examples of public services bodies adopting the trappings of big business and a new commercial style of management when their underlying operational circumstances have remained largely unchanged. The ethos of open accountability had been shelved (temporarily at least) in favour of commercial confidence and achieving financial targets in what was still essentially a publicly funded, near-monopoly situation. It may be argued that for a large public services body, a transitional or semi-commercial situation is required while, say, it adjusts to a market environment in sectors where competition is being encouraged. If this is indeed the case then such a transitional situation should be particularly well controlled and monitored. For example, the use of price-setting arrangements or industry regulators must be open to public scrutiny. Much of the foregoing is subject to intense political debate and the author, without wishing to offend any particular viewpoint, seeks only to stress the importance of maintaining the openness and accountability of public services bodies at a time of intense and often confusing changes in organizational structures and management attitudes.

Summary

This is a critical area often staffed by people who have a relatively high degree of autonomy and lack supervision, such as head teachers, chief accountants, finance directors and others whose detailed work is often hidden from open scrutiny by others. It is therefore vital that the risks and controls are carefully reviewed from time to time by auditors and others. Yet auditors have a poor record historically of uncovering fraud in this and other areas. Quite often, as some of the real life cases in Appendix 14 show, auditors have been unable and at times unwilling to dig too deeply or display the details of fraud to public scrutiny. In the long run, sound corporate ethos, close scrutiny by top managers and public accountability offer more hope of preventing fraud in main financial systems than the relatively eeting attention of auditors.

CASE STUDY

Any case study produced in relation to this chapter would be likely to have more than the usual air of contrivance about it. Essentially, events causing fraud and corruption will almost inevitably relate less to the main accounting system than to the feeder systems that produce the accounting information and to which (including the political decision-makers and other outside parties) this information is distributed. Usually any fraud conceived by staff involved solely in the main accounting function will require collusion with others, though the case below examines a possible exception: the internal transfer of funds and falsification of related accounts.

CASE STUDY 9.1

THE TRAINING AND REHABILITATION ORGANIZATION

The Training and Rehabilitation Organization (TRO) is sponsored by several government departments. It provides vocational skills and education to those who have been held for prolonged periods in institutions, such as prisons or mental hospitals, but are now considered fit for life in the general community. Approximately 50 approved training centres are in operation at any one time, in local colleges, schools (evenings), skill centres, and so on, providing courses funded and approved by the TRO.

Each month income and expenditure statements are forwarded from each training centre to TRO headquarters, showing actual

CASE STUDY 9.1 *continued*

figures and progress against annual budget. Statements of student numbers are also sent at the start and end of each term.

At TRO HQ the income and expenditure (net) figures are input to the main accounting system to produce a subsidy total to draw against their grant-in-aid, a grant funded by central government. This is undertaken by the Chief Accountant at TRO HQ. Once the monthly subsidy figure has been calculated he fills this in on a return form to the relevant government department.

The chief accountant is also responsible for preparing the annual report and accounts of TRO and the monthly management reports. These are sent to the chief financial officer (CFO) and various line managers respectively. Occasionally the CFO requests various management accounts and the auditors (internal and external) may require copies of all sets of accounts on demand. The subsidy claim is also sent to the external auditors who may make a separate visit, independent of their audit of the annual accounts, to audit this claim. This is a short audit and basically involves agreeing the net total of each claim to the total of the subsidy. The auditor may also select about four or five of the claims for detailed checking and possibly undertake site visits to the approved training centres if any of the claim figures appear doubtful.

Throughout the year and particularly at the year end the chief accountant prepares journal transfers. These are brief documents authorizing and recording the transfer of monies from one account to another. Transfers between accounts may, for example, be justified towards the year end if one is underspent and another would risk going over budget. This type of transfer is required to be approved by the CFO in order to avoid misrepresenting the validity of the initial budgets by virement between totally unrelated accounts. Another example is the requirement to correct errors and mispostings. This type of transfer is authorized entirely by the chief accountant, usually as a result of matters raised by one of his staff or one of the audit staff.

Given these procedures it was a relatively simple matter for the chief accountant to transfer funds between claims for training centres and the HQ budgets. Figure 9.2 suggests a possible method. This state of affairs might have continued indefinitely had not an internal audit value-for-money study involved a comparison of subsidy payments made to training centres to records of student numbers and noticed that very high payments appeared for several centres with very low student numbers. Further enquiries of the centres revealed the falsified claims held by the chief accountant.

Even in this example, systems outside the main accounting function have played a small part. This is almost inevitable if value is to be transferred to one of the staff involved in the accounts. Nevertheless Figure 9.2 illustrates the crucial controlling role of the chief accountant.

In this case the main accounting system failed because:

1 Journal transfers were not always countersigned, or at the very least made up by a junior accountant and authorized by the chief accountant.
2 There was a general lack of separation of duties involving the chief accountant. For example, the payments (or at least copy 1 of the claim) could have been sent directly to the training centres (and verification of the total sent to the chief accountant) from the government department.
3 The external auditor might have noticed the fraud if he had checked copy 3 of the claim (the accountant's copy made available to him during his visit) to copy 4, or copy 1 after this had been returned to the training centre. But very few visits

CASE STUDY 9.1 *continued*

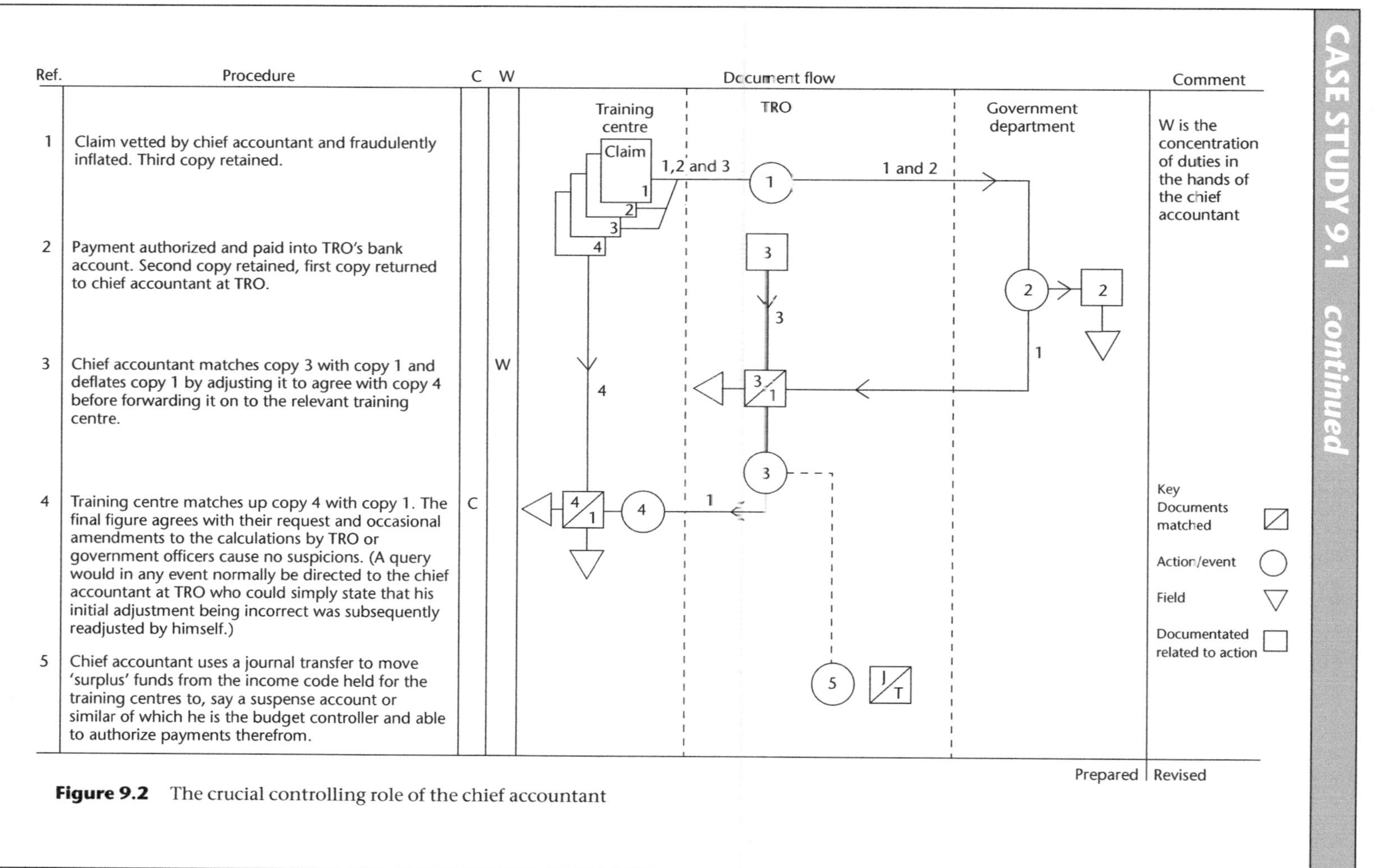

Figure 9.2 The crucial controlling role of the chief accountant

CASE STUDY 9.1 *concluded*

were made to training centres and so the risk of detection was very low. The internal auditor had no effective right of access to the training centres and (as the money was repaid by central government) subsidy claims were considered low-priority internal audit work.

4 Routine audit attention given to suspense accounts was generally low as these were usually small in value in relation to the organization's income or expenditure, though not of course in relation to the chief accountant's personal income or expenditure.

Concluding points

This short chapter has singled out for particular attention an area of key control that applies to all financial and related systems where risks of fraud and corruption occur. As such it is a fitting penultimate chapter of this book, which has attempted to encompass a wide range of managerial and financial functions that occur in most organizations throughout the public services. The main accounting system should act as the final safety net after all others have played their part. It is very rare for a fraud to be conceived and executed entirely within the accounting function, if only because cash or value must ow to a third party for the fraud to occur. In the private sector the directors of a company may falsify the accounts to attract investments which they may squander in their own interest, or milk dry the reserves of the company. Even this will usually involve mechanisms within the feeder systems, such as payments for dubious reasons to outside companies or additional unwarranted payments to directors. The mechanisms for senior public services managers at director level to act in the same manner, though they exist, are usually present to a lesser degree.

It is vitally important for the public services accountant never to lose sight of the purposes, especially the broadly political purposes, of the accounts. He or she should strive to maintain openness and accountability; to monitor and present the accounts in ways that best reveal the effects of policy and the performance of the management in meeting the policy objectives of the body.

The greater accountability of public services accounts facilitates value for money. Achieving good value for money and low risk of fraud and corruption is, at least in the long run, a mutually supportive exercise.

Appendices

APPENDIX 1

Selected Statutes, Regulations and Key Extracts

Note: these regulations are not an exhaustive list, rather they are among those currently thought to be most commonly relevant. Entries in bold type are those thought likely to have widest application in the public sector.

Fraud

Not strictly defined but including theft, false accounting, embezzlement, and so on.

Prevention of Fraud (Investments) Act 1958 especially S13.
Theft Act 1968, especially S15–19 re misappropriating property, deception, false accounting, and so on., also see 1978 Theft Act re obtaining services, evading liability
Criminal Law Acts 1967, 1977
Criminal Damage Act 1971
Criminal Attempts Act 1981
Insider Dealing Act 1995 and 1998
Social Security (Fraud) Acts 1997–2001

Fraud investigation/case handling/regulation of behaviour

Local Government Act 1972 especially S95, S117, re disclosure of interests
Police and Criminal Evidence Act (PACE) 1984
Companies Act 1985 especially S235–237 re auditors duty and S447–452 re company investigations
Company Directors Disqualification Act 1986
Insolvency Act 1986 – S212 – misapplication of assets and so on may be subject of court order to restore or compensate
Companies Act 1989 especially S28 re offence to continue an ineligible appointment
National Code of Local Government Conduct, for example, DoE Circ. 8/90
Social Security Act 1992, especially S109–110 re certificated investigation officers
Criminal Justice Act 1993
Accounts and Audit Regulations 1996
Financial Services Act 1986
Criminal Procedure and Investigation Act 1996
Social Security Administration (Fraud) Act 1997 re cooperation between agencies
Police Act 1997 especially S52 re certificate of unspent convictions
Human Rights Act 1998
Crime and Disorder Act 1998 especially S115 re disclosure of information to authorities
Public Interest Disclosure Act 1998
Regulation of Investigatory Powers Act (RIPA) 2000
Financial Services and Markets Act 2000 re the FSA
Freedom of Information Act 2000
Proceeds of Crime Act 2002

Corruption

Public Bodies Corrupt Practices Act 1889
Prevention of Corruption Acts (for example, 1906, 1916, 1972)
Competition Act 1998 re cartels and so on
Money Laundering Regulations 2003
Developments following on from Nolan enquiry (Committee on Standards in Public Life)
Audit Commission standards for registration of interests of Council Members and Officers. Your own organisation's Code of Conduct, Honesty Policy, Standing Orders, and so on.

Forgery

Forgery Act 1913
Criminal Law Act 1977
Forgery and Counterfeiting Act 1981

Computer Crime

Data Protection Act 1998
Copyright, Designs and Patents Act 1988
Computer Misuse Act 1990

We will now set out in more detail key extracts from some of the above, except for the RIPA which, given its complexity, is considered separately in the next appendix.

Key extracts from statutes

Theft Act 1968

This is a basic piece of legislation with some very important definitions. A full reading of the act is recommended to obtain any significant legal appreciation of the definitions extracted.

Theft
S1 'A person is guilty of theft if he dishonestly appropriates property belonging to another with the intention of permanently depriving another of it '
The act carries on to define 'dishonest', 'appropriate' and 'property'.

S11 is often of particular interest to public sector organizations which contain areas open without restriction to attract members of the public free of charge such as museums, galleries, council meetings or parks.
S11 ' any person who without lawful authority removes from the building or its grounds the whole or part of any article displayed or kept for display to the public shall be guilty of an offence.'

Under fraud and blackmail the act defines the following:

Obtaining property by deception
S15 'A person who by any deception dishonestly detains the property belonging to another with the intention of permanently depriving the other of it, shall be liable to imprisonment for a term not exceeding ten years.'

Obtaining pecuniary advantage by deception
S16(i) 'A person who by any deception dishonestly obtains for himself or another any pecuniary advantage shall be liable to imprisonment for a term not exceeding five years.'

The act defines pecuniary advantage as an evasion of or a reduction in debt, being allowed to borrow or take out insurance or annuity or being allowed to earn remuneration or greater remuneration or to win money by betting.

False accounting
S17 'Where a person dishonestly, with a view to gain for himself or another or with intent to cause loss to another,

(a) destroys, defaces, conceals or falsifies any account or any record or document made or required for any accounting purpose or;
(b) in furnishing information for any purpose produces or makes use of any accounts, or any such record or document as aforesaid, which to his knowledge is or may be misleading, false or deceptive in a material particular; he shall be liable to imprisonment for a term not exceeding seven years.'

Similar provisions cover suppression of documents under S20, also for a term of seven years.

Blackmail
S22 'A person is guilty of blackmail if, with a view to gain for himself or another or with intent to cause loss to another, he makes any unwarranted demand with menaces; '

The act then goes on to define 'unwarranted', and the maximum term of imprisonment is fourteen years.

Theft Act 1978

This effectively replaces S16(2) of the Theft Act 1968.

Obtaining services by deception
S1(i) 'A person who by any deception dishonestly obtains services from another shall be guilty of an offence.'

Prevention of Corruption Act 1916

Presumption of corruption in certain cases (that is, in public bodies)
S2 'Where in any proceedings against a person for an offence under the Prevention of Corruption Act 1906, or the Public Bodies Corrupt Practices Act 1889, it is proved that any money, gift, or other consideration has been paid or given to or received by a person in the employment of His Majesty or any Government Department or a public body by or from a person, or a guest of a person, holding or seeking to obtain a contract from His Majesty or any Government Department or public body, the money, gift, or consideration shall be deemed to have been paid or given and received corruptly as such inducement or reward as is mentioned in such Act unless the contrary is proved.'

The 1906 Prevention of Corruption Act S1 and the 1889 Public Bodies Corrupt Practices Act S1 and S2

These outline corruption and corrupt transactions in quite comprehensive detail which for the sake of reasonable brevity is not reproduced in full in this appendix.

The 1981 Forgery and Counterfeiting Act

Forgery

S1 'A person is guilty of forgery if he makes a false statement with the intention that he or another shall use it to induce somebody to accept it as genuine, and by reason of so accepting it to do or not to do some act to his own or to any other person's prejudice.'

Copying a false instrument

'It is an offence for a person to make a copy of an instrument which is and which he knows or believes to be, a false instrument ' The act includes further detailed definition of the intention and offences relating to using false instruments and particular details relating to money orders, passports, share certificates, and so on.

Local Government Act 1972

Disclosure of of cers interests

S117 'If it comes to the knowledge of any officer employed by a local authority that a contract in which he has any pecuniary intent, whether direct or indirect has been, or is proposed to be, entered into by the authority or any committee thereof, he shall as soon as practicable give notice in writing to the authority of the fact that he is interested therein.'

Disclosure of political members interests

S94 ' if a member of a local authority has any pecuniary interest, direct or indirect, in any contract, proposed contract or other matter, and is present at a meeting of the local authority at which the contract or other matter is the subject of consideration he shall at the meeting and as soon as practicable after its commencement disclose the fact and shall not take part in the consideration or discussion of the contract or any other matter or vote on any question with respect to it.'

The act goes on to define pecuniary interests in some detail. Those provisions are given added weight by the Local Government and Housing Act 1989, S19, which gives the Secretary of State powers to require members to give information about their pecuniary interests.

APPENDIX

2 Regulation of Investigatory Powers Act 2000 (RIPA)

This appendix selects aspects of RIPA aimed more at public servants likely to be undertaking a limited range of non-intrusive but covert surveillance. (Copies of the full Act, of related Statutory Instruments (SIs) such as SI 2417/2000, and of the Code of Practice can be obtained via HMSO or viewed on the Home Office website www.homeoffice.gov.uk)

Aims

> Regulation of Investigatory Powers Act will ensure that individuals rights are protected while also ensuring that the UK's law enforcement and security agencies have the powers they need to do their job effectively.
> Home Office Minister Charles Clark

INVESTIGATORY POWERS

What does RIPA mean by 'investigatory powers'?

RIPA covers a wide range of investigations where an organization is granted powers to:

accept and/or acquire communications;
undertake surveillance;
gather human intelligence; and
decode and analyse encrypted data.

The implicit concern here is that surveillance will be covert, that is, 'surveillance which is carried out in a manner calculated to ensure that the persons subject to the surveillance are unaware that it is or may be taking place;' Draft Code of Practice 2001.

The Act is set out broadly under five main themes, called parts.

i Interception of communications and the acquisition and disclosure of communications data
ii Surveillance and covert human intelligence
iii Investigation of electronic data protected by encryption
iv Scrutiny of investigatory powers and the functions of intelligence services
v Miscellaneous and supplemental (a diverse range of topics from regulation of wireless telegraphy to criminal liability of directors)

The Act also contains five schedules, the first three list relevant public authorities.

Looking a little more deeply into the second of the above themes, at surveillance:

COVERT SURVEILLANCE

Two types

Directed	*Intrusive*
Relates to a specific investigation	Relates to a specific investigation
Likely to obtain private information	Likely to obtain private information
Not an immediate response to events that is, a planned response situation	
Includes intercepted communications where sender or receiver agree	
	Intrudes into residential property or private vehicle using a person or device located on or in these, or if outside is such that equivalent detail would be obtained

The above are very broad distinctions between the two types of covert surveillance and they should be read in conjunction with the Home Office Code of Practice.

JUSTIFICATION FOR SURVEILLANCE

Directed surveillance needs to be controlled and accountable and at the start investigating managers need to be clear about the justification for the covert surveillance. Basically justification tends to fall into the following categories:

In the interests of national security
For the purpose of preventing and detecting crime or of preventing disorder
In the interests of the economic well-being of the UK
In the interests of public safety
For the purpose of protecting public health
For the purpose of assessing or collecting any tax duty levy or other imposition, contribution or charge payable to a government department
For any other purpose prescribed in an order of the Secretary of State.

IMPORTANT BASIC QUESTIONS SURROUNDING THE AUTHORIZATION OF DIRECTED SURVEILLANCE

Is the surveillance proportionate to what it seeks to achieve? If not then there may be no justification in the first place.
Is your organization in one of the categories listed in Schedule 1 of RIPA?
If not, have you adopted a policy to comply with the Act to avoid any challenge/ impediment to prosecution under the Human Rights Act 1998?
Have appropriate senior managers/officers been designated and trained to undertake authorization? SI 2417 of 2000 lists appropriate grades.

KEY MANAGEMENT ARRANGEMENTS FOR DIRECTED SURVEILLANCE

A policy on surveillance approved at director level. This may well be part of a wider policy on combating fraud and corruption
Operational guidelines/instructions
Designated and trained staff with clearly delimited powers and responsibilities
External links from senior audit/investigation staff to the Police, HM Customs and so on, arranged in advance for their cooperation, for example, re intrusive surveillance, prosecution, intercepting encrypted communications, and so on
Internal links from senior audit/investigation staff to related functions, for example, finance, personnel, legal, data protection, and so on
Oversight and coordination records of the number, progress and staffing, and so on, of investigations.

DETAILED OPERATIONAL PROCEDURES RE DIRECTED SURVEILLANCE

At this point it is useful to consider a wide range of implications, links to other regulations, for example, Data Protection, and possible organizational arrangements. We will simply give a minimal outline of key common procedures which must be well documented.

Authorization in writing on a standard application form to the authorising officer/ manager
Description and title/reference of case to be investigated
Officers involved
Identities of subjects
Grounds on which surveillance is justified
Assurance re proportionality of surveillance
Explanation of likely desired product/ information (it may help to indicate why this will meet the objectives of the investigation)
Any potential for collateral intrusion
Likelihood of acquiring any confidential, confessional, and so on, information
Record of when and by whom authority was given or refused
Record of when the authority expires (3 months)
Record of any urgent authorization (72-hour expiry)
Record of any renewals
Record of cancellation.

APPENDIX

3 General (non-surveillance) Considerations in Fraud Investigations

Corporate level awareness

AWARENESS OF CULTURE

Awareness of a corporate culture is often very difficult to achieve. If you are part of the organization you may simply be told to accept various norms and become too close to events to view them objectively. If you are outside the organization it is very difficult to get close to people and events and most insiders will want you to accept the publicly stated ethos of the organization. In the long run there is no easy substitute for patience and time. But in the short run asking some basic questions can help indicate cultural norms that may have a bearing on fraud and corruption.

Is your corporate culture one that cares about fraud?

Are travel and subsistence payments really checked?
Are member's allowances claims ever questioned?
Are receipts always required?
Are corporate assets treated as private?
Are malefactors always disciplined/dismissed?
Do (can?) you involve the police?

Is there a corporate fraud policy?

Recent?
Circulated and explained to people?

Is recruitment undertaken independently and professionally?

Are recruiting managers aware of what to look for?
Employment gaps, uncheckable periods, poor references, honesty, inaccurate statements, reasons for leaving all previous jobs and so on. Things that should be clear unless there is something to hide.
Is a probationary period clearly assessed?

Are managers aware of fraud-type risks?

Do they actually do anything to counter fraud before it comes to light?
Is protection/anonymity provided to whistle-blowers?
Is guidance offered/counselling provided for staff put at risk?
Are managers able to understand the relationship between risk and control?
Do managers ensure effective controls are in place?

Tell-tale signs

Factors that should be considered as potential warning signs throughout an organization include:

climate of stress/fear
unquestioning acceptance of superiors
unquestioning acceptance of 'practice and custom'
unreasonable 'perks'
lack of recording
immoral/unethical work practices
open tolerance of petty crime.

These are by no means exhaustive, but they are intended to alert an investigator or manager to the presence of an environment conducive to fraud.

Signs in the workplace

The previous section considered some wider corporate indications, but what about situations in the workplace, for example at a systems or function level? Again, the following are not exhaustive and some examples may be acceptable. But if several occur during the same audit visit, or while standing in for someone else – concern may be justified.

Is something being hidden?

Inability to obtain access to key staff, arrange meetings, see minutes of meetings and so on
Secret files (manual and computer)
Missing files or documents
Unexplained alterations
Long-standing suspense items and uncleared accounts
Reluctance to take leave
Frequent computer system failure, particularly during audit or management checks
Diversionary allegations/red herrings

Are appearances odd?

Insupportable lifestyle
Offers of exceptional hospitality
Unexplained, frequent, or unusual visits to or from contractors, suppliers, landlords and so on
Unusual work undertaken by senior managers? For example, taking control of incoming mail, unusual suspense accounts, and so on

Are key control arrangements worse than you might expect?

Exclusive or unexplained use of a single contractor or small group of contractors for a particular type of work
Lack of separation of duties; particularly custody (receiving)/authorization of payment/recording, or a single person dealing with design and commissioning, or an independent reconciliation of bankings, income, payment, cash to bank account-type functions
No clear responsibility for authorizations and/or management checks (see quote)
Only one person present during key checks, for example, counting of takings, post opening, and so on

Chapter 3 looks in more detail at key control arrangements.

At what point should I be concerned?

You should always be concerned and open to awareness of fraud. However, taking the three questions in italics from the previous section:

If you begin to get the feeling that things are being hidden from you and
appearances are unusual and
controls are poor,
you probably need to dig deeper.

I knew from my experience that when it came down to detail, no senior manager actually wanted to get their hands dirty and investigate the numbers. They always felt they were above that.

Nick Leeson

What if the evidence begins to mount up?

Get your own records and evidence in good order.
Seek advice if there is time and you can do so without endangering your investigation, (consult your Head of Audit). If possible call in the police at this stage.
Prepare for any formal interview checking regulatory requirements and any internal procedures.

Let us look in further detail at these three vital points.

GET YOUR OWN RECORDS AND EVIDENCE IN GOOD ORDER

This is often one of the weak points in any investigation and it usually deserves particular attention. All papers and computer documents should be retained, initialled or password-protected and dated. Sources of evidence should be clearly stated even if this is an anonymous tip-off.

Obtain *written con rmations* of verbal facts and opinions, for example:
- balances owed
- instructions issued
- warnings given
- work undertaken
- dates, times

and other detail that might have been given in the ordinary course of events but without its significance being realized at the time. This may need to be done discreetly if the other party is not to be made aware of your suspicions. Such phrases as

'So that I can put something on my file'
'Just to confirm things in writing'
'For the record'
'Could you send me the details in writing'

can be useful if used with tact.

Take possession of all relevant documents, hard copy printout and so on. You can usually leave behind photocopies, though it may be vital to ensure the originals are dated and even timed.
If possible take photographs of damaged or substituted goods. You can obtain cameras with a built-in time display.
Update and cross-reference all your working papers and evidence. This must be of a standard sufficient not just for another auditor to follow but for a lay person to follow under pressure. For example, a police officer or disciplinary officer who is not familiar with financial and systems documents, possibly while under cross-examination.
All papers should have a file and page reference and be listed in the file index.
All cross references on a page should be easy to spot, for example, circled or red ink.
If possible, take immediate steps to *prevent any suspect transactions* proceeding. If it is too late or you do not yet have sufficient grounds, then take full details of all parties involved. Try to obtain telephone confirmation of authenticity from outside organizations provided this will not jeopardize subsequent action.

SEEK ADVICE AND/OR CALL IN THE POLICE

Keep the Head of Internal Audit or equivalent, or Finance Director in the picture, though in some urgent cases this may not involve a detailed review of your findings at this stage.
Make sure you are following any *relevant guidelines* in your own audit/security manual and standing orders.
Most police forces have a special fraud unit – find out the telephone number. They are much more experienced at interviewing suspects than most internal auditors but they like all your evidence clearly presented, preferably before any suspects have been placed in a position where they should be cautioned.
Note: Your insurance requirements may stipulate that the police be notified/consulted.

If you cannot involve the police but still need a formal interview

Follow the provisions of the Police and Criminal Evidence Act 1984 (note caution amendment 1995) and the Criminal Procedure and Investigations Act 1996.
Make no inducements or promises or threats. Avoid phrases such as 'we will go easier on you if you confess' or 'everything will be all right if you '
Caution suspects along the lines of:

You do not have to say anything. But it may harm your defence if you do not mention when questioned something which you later rely on in court. Anything you say may be given in evidence.

Note: You should seek advice from your own legal staff about the precise wording to be used in your organization as opinions can vary.

Caution the suspect at the start and the end of an interview.
The suspect must be told that he or she is not under arrest, or obliged to remain and that they may obtain legal advice (or Trade Union or other representation). It is a good idea to ask them if they want anyone else to be present as soon as you feel you should caution them, but get the other person to come to you.
It is also a good idea to *have another interviewer/auditor/independent person present if possible* so that your version of events can be confirmed.
Take written notes of start time, any breaks, finish time, exact location, who is present and the main points.
Allow the suspect to read the notes and make any comments he or she wishes to be included.
Make sure the suspect gets a copy of the notes.
You may prefer to let the suspect make or dictate his or her own statement. Make sure he or she signs and dates it and says at the start:

I make this statement of my own free will. I understand that I need not say anything unless I wish to do so and that what I say may be given in evidence.

As with the wording of the caution, it is a good idea to get your own lawyers to agree this wording in advance.
As a general rule it is best to avoid the formal interview if you can get the police to take on the investigation at an early point.

APPENDIX

4 *WACI . . A Documented Audit*

This appendix gives the reader, in the form of a case study, an insight into how a fairly typical internal audit file might be compiled. It is simply for illustration and intended to be of benefit to anyone not particularly familiar with internal audit.

Western Association of Combined Institutions

This case study is about the internal audit of the weekly paid wages of WACI, a large organization employing many hourly paid and contract staff. A typical audit file has been used to describe the system. Our apologies to those unfamiliar with this approach to documentation, though in reality it is not all that far removed from many other forms of professional documentation by systems analysts, project managers, administrators, and the like.

Feel free to make any reasonable assumptions about the working situation, though for the purposes of this case the system at WACI is deliberately fault-ridden.

SCENARIO

The wages system at WACI is audited separately from salaries because a large number of hourly paid temporary workers are employed at all main sites, often being hired and laid off seasonally and at short notice. They are paid a week in arrears in cash, unlike permanent staff who are always paid monthly by BACS.

An auditor, I. Canny, has just audited the weekly wages and the working papers are being reviewed by B. Bloggs, audit manager.

Suggested tasks

PART 1 OF CASE

1 Read through the case, as far as page 203 to familiarize yourself with the audit taking place and the progress as far as the first 3 stages of a SBA outlined on page 45.

2 As you read through try to summarize the main points in terms of systems risks and existing controls and, in view of the weaknesses in control, ask yourself what additional controls you might design into the system. Hint: First try to summarize the objectives of the system, then consider the potential risks and finally ask what procedures, arrangements and events currently are, or could be put, in place to counter such risks – these are the controls.

3 Compare the weaknesses and controls from 2 to the comments on page 204.

PART 2 OF CASE

4 Read through the rest of the case, which outlines the results of compliance and substantive testing and the final end of audit meeting, corresponding to the remaining stages of the SBA.

5 To finish the case you may find it helpful to draft a list of points to be raised at the end-of-audit meeting (neither the example given nor the example of points actually raised at the end-of-audit meeting is intended to be perfect).

There is no perfect solution to this case; it simply aims to give you a avour of how a typical SBA might be conducted.

Audit	Weekly paid wages

Audit le ref.	AUD/123

FILE INDEX

DOC.	WP No.

CLIENT/DEPT Payroll	**File ref.** AUD 123 **Doc. ref.**
SYSTEM Weekly cash wages	**Prepared by** IC **Date** **Reviewed by** **Date**

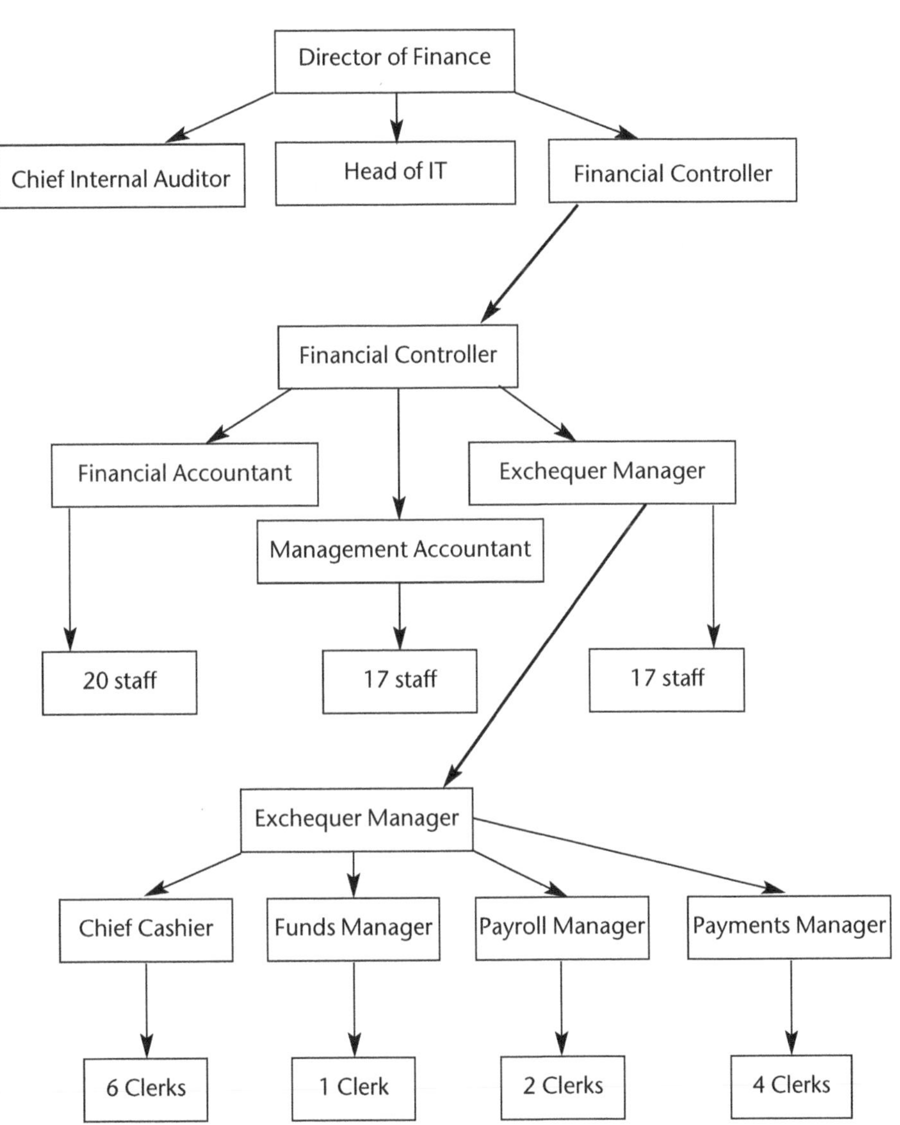

WACI

MEMORANDUM

DATE: 6 October

TO: G. Green

FROM: I. Canny

SUBJECT: Forthcoming audit of wages

Thank you for agreeing to meet me on 12th this month when I plan to commence our scheduled audit of the wages system. Our memo to the Chief Accountant Ref AUD345/69 of 1 October refers.

I understand from our earlier telephone conversation that the same system is in place that was initially set up some years ago and no changes have occurred since our last visit nearly a year and a half ago. You mentioned that one of your staff is on long-term sick leave, so I can understand the pressure you must be under and will try to keep my visit as short as I can.

You also mentioned that you were not employed by us prior to the start of this financial year so I shall look forward to meeting you in your current post for the first time.

IC

CLIENT/DEPT Payroll	**File ref.** AUD 123 **Doc. ref.**
SYSTEM Weekly cash wages	**Prepared by** IC **Date** 12/10 **Reviewed by** **Date**

Meeting with Mrs G. Green, payroll manager, 12 October, visit started 9.30 a.m.

Starters: The first they get to know about weekly wages due is the PN6 form from personnel with details of a new starter.

Processing: This is followed by the receipt of a time sheet (P3) from the line department, these are checked for name, payroll number, rate and hours to ensure the correct total has been entered, Green or her assistant Tim Brown sign the section 3. (Mostly done by Brown as Green is too busy with salaries work and answering phone queries.)

A list of authorized supervisors who can countersign the time sheets is held but mostly the signatures are easily recognized by Green or Brown who do this work, any unfamiliar ones are checked to a list which is updated each month by Green as she is given written details of any salaries changes (promotions, demotions or leavers).

Time sheets are batched and the total number of sheets and hours are entered on the batch header slip.

Each batch is keyed into the computer by Brown. Time sheet batches are filed by Brown in batch no. order, which is also week order.

Payroll Z program is run to calculate amounts including deductions from information previously keyed in from PN6. Brown gets the following printouts:

Payroll listings: two copies, one with spaces for signatures next to each line showing name, pay number and amount. One copy is filed after agreeing it (see file note of walk-through test below), the other is used to take signatures of workers when they arrive on Thursday p.m. or Friday am to collect their pay packets.

CLIENT/DEPT Payroll	**File ref.** AUD 123 **Doc. ref.**
SYSTEM Weekly cash wages	**Prepared by** IC **Date** 12/10 **Reviewed by** **Date**

Complete payslips: one for each person. Brown (and if available Green) make up the pay packets; tearing off and inserting the slips, and cash, into each, then checking it before sealing. I was told that originally Brown made up the packets and Green checked them but nowadays Green does not have time to check them all, so they both make up the packets and check a few of each others. No record of this check is kept.

Wages are usually ready by 4.00 p.m. Thursday, but Brown and Green stay late Thursday night (7 p.m.) to cater for latecomers. Any remaining packets are locked in cupboard overnight (Green has key) and handed out Friday. Green says that as a matter of custom and goodwill they deliver some packets to one remote site Friday afternoon, though this is not in their job descriptions or set out in the work manual.

Other points
No one seems to check the job codes on time sheets to work rosters, supervisor's shift and so on.

No one seems to have thought of locking wages overnight in Cash Office safe – Green says usually only a few hundred pounds' worth is left over.

Despite requirements for passwords to be changed, Green is still using the old password from her predecessor. Green seemed embarrassed about this. She said she had mentioned it briefly to someone in the IT department in her first week at work and was told it was just a temporary measure, her previous employer never required staff to change passwords, so she had not queried it further. She agreed to change her password immediately.

Decided to do some walk-through tests in company of Brown.

WACI

FORM P3

TIME SHEET – WEEKLY PAID STAFF

Section 1 to be completed by weekly paid employee.

Week No. ...... Name...................................... Pay No. .... Dept. ....

I claim the following hours for this week Signed .... Date...........

DAY	JOB CODE(S)	START TIME	FINISH TIME	TOTAL
MON				
TUES				
WED				
THURS				
FRI				
SAT				
SUN				
TOTAL HOURS CLAIMED				

Section 2 to be completed by supervisor

Checked and Authorized by .... Date

Section 3 to be completed by payroll clerk
Checked and details input to payroll on .... by ....
Batch No. [__]

WACI

PERSONNEL DEPARTMENT FORM PN6

TO BE COMPLETED FOR ALL NEW WEEKLY PAID EMPLOYEES PRIOR TO COMMENCEMENT OF EMPLOYMENT

NAME [ ]

TAX CODE [ ]

EMPLOYEE /PAYROLL No. [ ]

ADDRESS [...

....]

POST CODE [ ]

START DATE [ ]

GRADE [ ]

RATE [ ]

DETAILS OF SPECIAL CONDITIONS/ BONUS/ CHANGES

___

___

___

COMPLETED BY (Inls) ....DATE ....../..../....

WHITE COPY TO FILE, YELLOW COPY TO PAYROLL SECTION

CLIENT/DEPT Payroll	**File ref.** AUD 123 **Doc. ref.**
SYSTEM Weekly cash wages	**Prepared by** IC **Date** 12/10 **Reviewed by** **Date**

FILE NOTE

Walk-through test
Undertaken while in company of Brown – see interview note.

Traced 3 payroll records to yellow copies of start form, agreed procedures as stated by Green: keyed in on first day of employment, details on payroll agreed to form.

Traced 3 undercopy payslips to payroll listing signed by workers to confirm receipt, to time sheets P3.

Wage packets appear suitable and clear-faced to enable checking before opening.

Agreed 3 form CO12 from payroll file to copies held by cashier, one not signed by Brown, says he forgot.

Brown confirms he carries out the following checks which I followed through for last week's payroll:

Agreed form CO12 to printout of payroll, total £ value.

Agreed payroll printout to batch header slip, total number of payslips and hours worked.

CLIENT/DEPT	**File ref.** **Doc. ref.**	
SYSTEM	**Prepared by** **Reviewed by**	**Date** 12/10 **Date**

Interview with R. Brown payroll clerk

Following the brief walk-through testing I decided to interview Brown further.

Brown collects cash from Cash Office first thing Thursday morning, no particular procedure mentioned in operating manual. It seems that Brown telephones the amount to the Cash Office on Wednesday, there is usually enough cash in the safe but if they are short a cashier is sent to the bank just round the corner. The wages are waiting for Brown in a sealed bag together with form CO12.

Brown breaks open the seal back in the Payroll Section and they both count it into the packets. CO12 top copy kept in Cash Office, bottom copy filed away by Brown. This has a space for overs and unders, printed details of total and breakdown and boxes for cashiers and wages' clerks signatures.

Brown can not recall ever having any unders or overs. Occasional unclaimed wages are held indefinitely in locked cupboard until collected, only one packet held at time of visit – payee called in sick.

When asked about leavers Brown simply said that if no time sheet is filled in for a few weeks they assume the person has left but keep the details on computer because usually they will come back six to twelve months later.

I noticed a lot of nil payment payslips were automatically printed off at the start of each run.

CLIENT/DEPT Payroll	**File ref.** AUD 123 **Doc. ref.**
SYSTEM Weekly cash wages	**Prepared by** IC **Date** 14/10 **Reviewed by** **Date**

Note for file – telephone call to W.E. Snagum, Personnel Dept

RECRUITMENT PROCEDURE

Line manager telephones personnel department who keep the list of temps, usually manager has a name in mind, personnel telephone temp and make arrangements to start. If no one suitable they may advertise or go through staff agencies but not usually for less than four or five people. Snagum says the last time this happened was about three years ago but they have added a few names to the list of people who know there are temp. jobs going at WACI – students mostly.

Personnel only complete a new starter form PN6 the first time someone is employed, or to notify payroll section of changes to name, address rate and so on. Personnel key in the details to the personnel system, sign and date the form and the undercopy is sent to payroll section who update payroll system.

Snagum also mentioned that the personnel and payroll sections both take sandwich course students for a few months each year in common with other parts of WACI, though at the present none were employed. The work they undertake is at the discretion of the manager or supervisor.

Systems Flowchart	**System:** *Payroll*	
Client/Department *Finance*		
Subject *Wages*		

Procedure	**C=Control W=Weakness**	
Payroll processing	*C*	*W*
1. *Time sheets (TS) completed on site: signed, checked and counter-signed by supervisor. Sent to payroll section.*		
2. *Payroll clerk (C) checks details and total hours, but not job code, and signs. List of authorized supervisors kept and updated by senior clerk (SC) but not usually needed.*		
3. *C batches and keys-in TS, Batch Header Slip (BHS) showing no. of TS and Total hours prepared (but not signed).*		
4. *C runs payroll program Z on PC. Calculates all amounts, deductions and produces payroll prints 1+2 and payslips.*		
5. *C agrees BHS to print 1 (Tot. hrs + payees) and to no. of payslips (not recorded). Batches filed in batch order = week order.*		
6. *C telephones £ amount and b/down to cashier, Wed. Money and form CO12 (shows £ amount and b/down) prepared in cash office and held overnight in safe in a sealed bag. Bag collected Thurs a.m. by C. Cashier + C sign CO12 to confirm transfer only. C takes undercopy, top copy filed by cashier.*		
7. *C agrees CO12 £ amount to print 1 (not recorded), breaks seal and together with SC makes up wage packets + cash + wage slips. Any overs/unders entered on CO12. (Unrecorded sample check of each other's work.)*		
8. *Pockets sealed + disbursed Thurs p.m. – evening + Fri. Recipients sign to confirm amount on print 2.*		
9. *Wages held overnight to Fri and longer if unclaimed in locked cupboard, key held by SC. Unofficial wages round to remote site Fri p.m. Print 2 signed on site.*		
10. *Unclaimed wages held indefinitely in cupboard until ownership verified. No details recorded.*		

Figure A4.1 WACI systems owchart – payroll

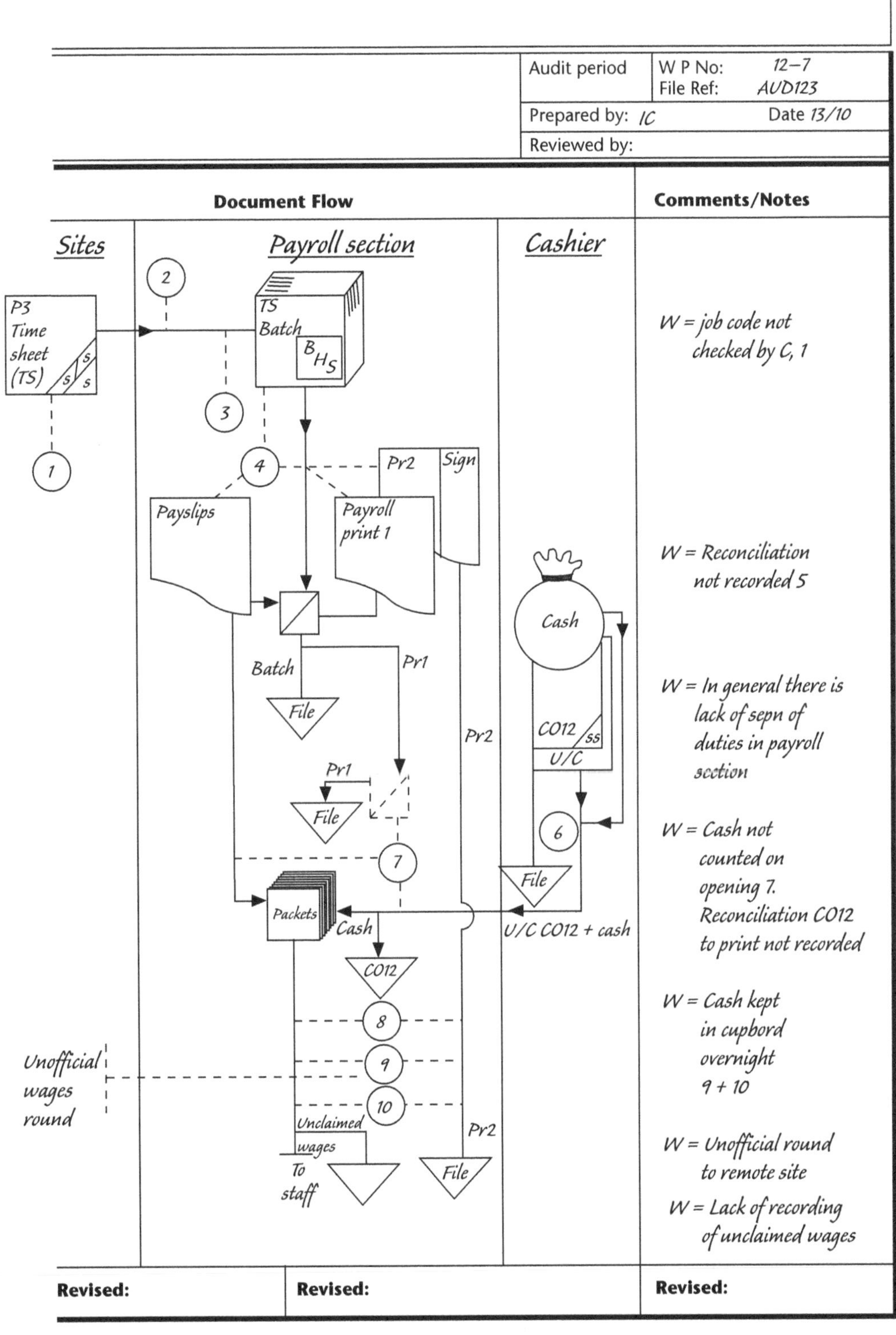
Audit period
W P No: 12–7
File Ref: AUD123
Prepared by: IC
Date 13/10
Reviewed by:
Document Flow
Comments/Notes
Sites
Payroll section
Cashier
P3 Time sheet (TS)
TS Batch
Payslips
Payroll print 1
Pr2
Sign
Batch
File
Pr1
Pr2
Cash
CO12
U/C
Packets
Cash
U/C CO12 + cash
Unofficial wages round
Unclaimed wages
To staff
W = job code not checked by C, 1
W = Reconciliation not recorded 5
W = In general there is lack of sepn of duties in payroll section
W = Cash not counted on opening 7. Reconciliation CO12 to print not recorded
W = Cash kept in cupbord overnight 9 + 10
W = Unofficial round to remote site
W = Lack of recording of unclaimed wages
Revised:
Revised:
Revised:

WACI

BRIEF NOTES ON WEAKNESSES IN CONTROL

Starters and leavers – hiring and firing is rather lax and possibly subject to the whim of individual managers.

The tendency to keep defunct details on the payroll and produce nil payslips presents risks of 'ghosts', as does the lack of a signature and sequential numbering of forms PN6, that is, the risk of a false payslip and perhaps a false time sheet for someone who has left or never existed in the first place. Not difficult for perpetrator to sign false name on the print 2, especially if many people are turning up for their packets at once. Risk that Brown or Green will contrive the ghost and signature. Need definite procedure for managers or supervisors to notify personnel when staff leave, and production of payslip suppressed.

Cash handling – very weak. No unders or overs is unusual but possible. How large and complex is the wages payroll?

Cash office seems lax in obtaining cash from bank; perhaps the payroll section could arrange for a direct security delivery every Thursday and phone through the amount to the bank rather than the cash office - why do cash office hold such large volumes of cash anyway? Difficult to reconcile the impression that only a few hundred pounds worth of wages is held over to Friday to be taken direct to site with the need to do this in the first place.

If the payroll staff were perpetrating a ghost then direct-to-site wages round would provide a good opportunity to conceal this. Also, unclaimed wages are not listed; one would need to search through the copies of print 2 to see if any were not claimed. Need to be listed and action annotated.

Lack of some obvious separation of duties – there is a general lack of separation of duties in payroll due to limited staff numbers. This could be mitigated by dividing duties between Green and Brown, e.g. Green could open and count the cash (noting any overs/unders) and even check a larger sample of Brown's work without involving herself in initial making up of pay packets – but there may be insufficient time. In any event the extent of their sample checking of each other's work should be clearly documented.

Although there is a separation between personnel and payroll functions the payroll staff do not sign under-copies of the PN6.

Useful control actions not evidenced – for example, no evidence of who input PN6 details in payroll section. Also, suggest signing reconciliations of print 1 to CO12 and batch header slips. Thus for negligible extra effort more reliance could be achieved from controls and staff would be able to show a trail of accountability.

Forms – auditors need to obtain copies of printouts and CO12 form and to suggest the need to have sequential numbering, especially for PN6 which would be better signed than initialled. This should be done by the personnel officer and there should be a separate signature by payroll staff when they have checked and input their copy to update the system. It could be very difficult to prove who had generated and/or input any incorrect or false details at present.

Computer controls – such as passwords regularly renewed (confidential passwords are a must). Also there do not seem to be any computer reconciliation or reporting facilities, such as for separate listing of new staff, reconciliation of staff in post to payroll, exception reporting of amounts over £X, and so on. Although weekly paid and temporary staff are often paid in cash the auditors may want to raise the possibility of BACS payment. Auditor would need to ask more on this area but things are not looking too hopeful.

Use of safe – for overnight cash holdings and any unclaimed wages.

Unof cial wages round to remote sites – need to be clarified and sanctioned if needed.

Additional checks by payroll staff – for example, job codes, work shift rosta, and so on, provided time is available.

Operations manual: clearly needs updating.

Do not be overly concerned if you have included differently worded points. This is only a suggestion, reconsider your points in the light of your assumptions.

Part 2 of case

You will have already needed to use your imagination to fill in the detailed picture of what is going on in this audit in Part 1, you will need even more imagination in Part 2. All audits offer no more than a eeting impression of what is actually happening in the client's systems and a sample of tests that may or may not give rise to a true impression of the strengths and weaknesses. Here you will be expected to imagine most of the actual records examined and details of the testing – there is simply not room to reproduce a full audit file. But it is hoped that you will get a fair impression of what a full audit of this system could involve. We have included two test programmes and a summary of the results.

You are encouraged to think through how you would draft a list of points to raise at the end-of-audit meeting. The draft given is not perfect but simply aims to re ect what might be forthcoming at the end of a busy audit and prior to the drafting of a more detailed internal audit report. You will notice that all the papers have been prepared by a relatively junior auditor but have not yet been reviewed by a more senior member of the audit team. In practice several reviews might be expected, so that the work of relatively inexperienced staff is maintained at a high standard and the opportunity for a second opinion presents itself. In fact the review process is one of the key learning and quality control features of an audit, though once again space does not permit this level of detail to be given here.

Compliance Test Programme 4

Client/Department	Finance	Audit Period	W P No: 14 File Ref: AUD 123
Subject	Wages	Prepared by: IC	Date: 13/10
		Reviewed by:	Date:

System/Audit Area:

Control Objective Ref.	Control Ref.	TEST	Control Working? No. Tested	No. Working	WP Ref.
VALID STAFF/ CHANGES	1.	For sample of new staff and changed details on payroll system trace to PN6 and check authorisation by personnel officer. Sign and date.	60	60	SEE ATTACHED
	2.	For sample of weekly paid time sheets, form PN6, check sign/date of:			
		i Operative	60	60	
		ii Authorizing supervisor	60	60	
		iii Inputting payroll clerk.	60	60	
	3.	For samples of CO12 cash transfer forms check cashier and payroll clerks have signed/dated to agree transfer.	20	20	
	4.	For samples of print 2 check signatures of operatives to confirm receipt of payment wage packet.	350 (1 week)	348	1 – absent 1 – unsigned but issued – see attached WP

Figure A4.2 WACI compliance test programme – wages

Substantive Test Programme *4*

Client/Department	*Finance*	Audit Period	W P No: *15* File Ref: *AUD 123*
Subject	*Wages*	Prepared by: *IC*	Date: *14/10*
		Reviewed by:	Date:

System/Audit Area:

SAMPLING METHOD: *Judgemental* **WP REFERENCE:**

SYSTEM CONTROL AND TEST OBJECTIVE SUMMARY SHEET REF.:

Ref. Test Objective	Test Programme	WP Ref.	Initials:
Accurate, complete and valid payment of weekly wages. ① – ④	*FOR A SAMPLE OF WEEKLY PAYSLIPS FROM PRINT 1 =*		
	① *AGREE* *Payee to personnel file + PN6* *Name,* *Grade* *Department.*	*ST1*	*IC*
	② *AGREE* *Any allowances, + deductions to personnel records + tax code to PN6.*	*ST1*	*IC*
	③ *RECAST* *Time sheet (hrs + rate).*	*ST2*	*IC*
	④ *AGREE* ③ *To gross pay on payslip.*	*ST2*	*IC*
Accurate, complete and valid use and recording of weekly cash wages.	*FOR 1 WEEK =*		
	⑤ *Remain present throughout the collection/transfer of wages between cashier and payroll to review safe custody/receipt as per doc of system.*	*ST3*	*IC*
	⑥ *Remain present throughout the making up of weekly wage packets to review overs/unders as per system doc.*	*ST4*	*IC*
	⑦ *Review hand-over for collection of wages and safe custody + recording of unclaimed packets.*	*ST4*	*IC*

Figure A4.3 WACI substantive test programme – wages

CLIENT/DEPT	**File ref.** AUD 123 **Doc. ref.**
SYSTEM	**Prepared by** IC **Date** 15/10 **Reviewed by** **Date**

SUMMARY OF TESTING RESULTS

COMPLIANCE TESTS

Tests 1 to 4 of CT programme were undertaken. Detailed results are on attached A3 sheet. Only one control was not properly applied resulting in non-compliance re test 4. Explanation given was that J. Bloggs had simply hurried away without signing. I telephoned him and confirmed that everything was in order.

SUBSTANTIVE TESTS

See substantive test programme and attached A3 sheet of detailed result. No errors re tests 1, 2 and 4 to 7. One error re test 3, one time sheet for P. Jones had been miscast by £7.50 over, copy attached. Adjustment agreed by Green who will action it on next week's pay run.

CONCLUSIONS FROM TESTING

The limited internal controls that are in place appear to be operating.

There is no indication of any material substantive error.

Conclusion to be summarized in the points for end-of-audit meeting and draft report.

CLIENT/DEPT	**File ref.** AUD 123 **Doc. ref.**
SYSTEM	**Prepared by** IC **Date** 15/10 **Reviewed by** **Date**

ASSIGNMENT SUMMARY SHEET — *WP ref*

AUDIT PLANNING AND OBJECTIVES

Refer to background information and planning document on client file — *Aud 122*
Objectives: evaluate system controls and accuracy and validity of wages.

AUDIT APPROACH

Systems-based (risk evaluation on planning file) including C Test and — *WP 14*
S Test programmes on this file — *WP 15*

SUMMARY OF FINDINGS

Only limited reliance can be placed on internal controls, weaknesses are documented on this file — *Flow chart*

Rpt paras

CT – of relatively limited internal control, for results see — *WP 16*
ST – extensive ST undertaken for results see — *WP 17*
May need to do more ST

CONCLUSIONS
Significant systems weaknesses and potential risk high control/issues raised regarding starters, changes and leavers, cash handling, computer password, evidencing of existing control procedures

Rpt Paras

Off-site actions, need for operating instructions and other minor points

CLIENT RESPONSE

RECOMMENDATIONS

These are the draft report points prepared by IC, some are better than others.

You might compare the draft paragraphs you have prepared to those below or simply try improving these examples.

WACI

MEMORANDUM

DATE: 16 October

TO: G. Green

FROM: I. Canny

SUBJECT: Draft points for end-of-audit meeting

Page 1 of 2

KEYING-IN OF THE PN6 FORMS

Points from ndings

These forms should be sequentially pre-numbered – as a control to reveal if any go missing.

The personnel department should sign these forms rather than simply initial them as more than one person could have the same initials and, in any case, initials can easily be forged and are also often illegible.

It was noticed that no one in the payroll department annotates these forms in any way to evidence that they too have processed them.

Recommendation

As per each of the above points.

PASSWORD CONTROL

Findings

It is recognized good practice to issue individual passwords to each member of staff. and for these to be kept in strictest confidence. A clear breach of this practice was noted: the payroll manager has retained the use of her predecessor's password. We understand that a new password has been issued.

Recommendations

As per point above. We also recommend that passwords are automatically deleted from the system if not changed within a period of three months, this can be arranged via the IT centre manager.

CASH HELD OVERNIGHT

Findings

Wages not issued at the end of Thursday and small amounts not claimed are held in a locked drawer. This is a venerable location and one not covered by our insurance policy. The wage packets could be easily opened and the contents taken or used for teaming and lading.

WACI

MEMORANDUM

DATE: 16 October

TO: G. Green

FROM: I. Canny

SUBJECT: Draft points for end-of-audit meeting

Page 2 of 2

Recommendation

It is recommended that any undelivered or unclaimed wages are locked outside working hours in the cash office safe. The print 2 should be noted accordingly and a separate record of all amounts, payees and action taken should be maintained by the payroll manager.

DELIVERY OF WAGES TO SITE

Findings

It is unclear why this is done, it is not sanctioned in operational manuals or any instructions. This practice simply re ects the custom of the payroll staff to be helpful to site manager requests.

Recommendation

It is recommended that these cease while the senior finance and site management review the need for this practice to be sanctioned.

CESSATION

Finding

Payroll staff rely on line managers to inform them when staff leave. This information is unreliable.

Recommendation

It is recommended that payroll staff seek telephone confirmation from managers for any staff who have failed to submit a time sheet. Any leavers should be immediately deleted from the payroll and their details confirmed in writing from/to the line manager and the personnel department. A suggested form to be used for this purpose is attached.

CLIENT/DEPT Payroll	**File ref.** AUD 123 **Doc. ref.**
SYSTEM Weekly cash wages	**Prepared by** IC **Date** 20/10 **Reviewed by** **Date**

NOTE RE POINTS ARISING FROM END OF AUDIT MEETING, 20/10

Present:
BB and IC (audit), DS (chief accountant), GG and TB (payroll section).

1 *BB talked through the main systems findings and compliance test results. IC handed out draft paras for report. No objections were raised and only minor amendments were made to the draft paras. All audit-recommended systems improvements were verbally accepted, including proposals and timing of management action.*

2 *The results of substantive testing were agreed but AS expressed concern about the overpayment error on ST 3, given the small sample size of 12 he felt that any errors were worrying. BB agreed and suggested HG carry out some further checking of the castings. HG agreed but pointed out that P Jones' time sheet might well have been cast by the sandwich course student who had now left. As this student had only been allowed to check the forms for the last week of the placement she and TB would just recheck that week's sheets.*

3 *TB had recalled a similar incident about three years ago and mentioned that the DSO general manager (for whom P. Jones and most of the weekly paid staff worked), had expressed strong concern that a poorly paid worker was to suffer given that the error had been missed by both his own supervisor and the wages section, he had felt that no action should be taken.*

4 *BB agreed to let them have a draft report in four working days after it had been agreed with the Head of Audit.*

APPENDIX

5 Objectives and Controls Grids

It is neither practical nor desirable to provide a list of objectives or controls that purported to be exhaustive. Apart from becoming obsolete as soon as new developments arose, what forms an adequate control in one situation may be totally irrelevant in another apparently similar one. Changing objectives present new risks and new or revised controls must be put in place to counter these. In any case, good managers have a tendency to 'invent' new controls to suit their particular responsibilities and resources rather than rely on published advice or past best practice.

Despite this caution, a summary of possible key controls in relation to likely objectives may have its uses, particularly as a starting point for design or review of a system. To this end the contents of this appendix should be seen only as possible examples, and most importantly, examples relating to maintenance-type systems.

First, the following grids set out a range of possible corporate-wide maintenance objectives (column 1). These have been worded in fairly widely applicable terms to provide a relevant context for many different organizations.

Second, a more detailed range of possible system level objectives, each broadly in line with one or more of the high level corporate objectives, has been selected (column 2).

Third, the same range of corporate and system objectives could be restated in terms of risks. However this is not done on these grids, as this would simply involve rewording the objective in a negative way, for example the objective 'All capital expenditure is genuinely required' would become the risk that 'not all capital expenditure is genuinely required'. Similarly, the objective that 'investment policy is always followed' would become 'investment policy is not always followed', and so on.

Fourth, at right angles, that is, vertically, down the side of each appendix are example system controls for a selection of systems. These are matched to the appropriate objective, in this case by 'x's on the grid.

The use of a standard corporate-wide template, although each organization should of course tailor the one used in this appendix to meet its own needs, has two advantages.

First, it gives a useful overview of the whole organization, its objectives, risks and controls and highlights any objectives that appear out of line or any areas with inadequate controls.

Second, it allows an audit or similar committee to see a global picture of all systems controls and link these more easily to the audit work. This should give assurance and help in forming their conclusions about the adequacy of internal controls throughout the organization for their annual report thereon.

																																								All incurred. Production is required	
																																								Only authorized production is incurred	
																																								All production stages/processes are authorized	Production to point of delivery is in line with corporate policy
																																								All liabilities are authorized	
																																								All liabilities are unavoidable	
																																								Physical assets are complete and evidenced	
																																								All staff are fitted for work	
																																								Organizational structure is sound	
																																								Objectives at each level of body are synchronized	Operations meet corporate objectives
																																								Planned output measures are achieved	
																																								Quality failure is minimized	Quality assurance is optimized
																																								External (customer) quality standards are achieved	
																																								Internal quality standards are achieved	
																																								All standards are updated	Standards are in line with policy aims
																																								Quality assurance standards followed	
																																								Safety at work code followed	
																																								Conditions of service followed	
																																								Organization's internal regulations and codes are observed	All activities are legal
																																								All staff are adequately trained	
																																								All payroll payments are due	

Human resources are optimized			Financial resources are adequate but not excessive	Investment policy is followed		Accounts are complete, accurate and valid					Budgets are met			Budgets are met		⇦ STRATEGIC OBJECTIVES
All posts are required and valid	Only genuine employee (pensions) are paid	Over/under spends are acceptable	Budgets are monitored and variations explained	Investments are accurate and valid	Capital expenditure is genuinely required	All payments assets and liabilities are accounted for	Payments made are for genuine invoices	Goods/services invoiced were ordered and accepted	Payments are due accurate and valid	Only goods/services orders are accepted	All orders are genuinely required	Income received is due	Income received is brought to account	Income due is received	All assets and liabilities are accurately measured	SYSTEM LEVEL ⇦ OBJECTIVES / KEY CONTROLS IN PURCHASE SYSTEM ⇩
		X	X			X	X	X	X	X	X					1. A separation of duties exists between
																(a) ordering/requistioning/custody
																(b) negotiation/purchasing
																(c) bill payments and accounting
																(d) budget monitoring/variation
																analysis.
								X	X							2. All invoices payable are
																first checked to official
																orders and evidenced. (For example,
																by initialling and dating or entering
																a password-controlled code onto a
																tamper-proof field on a computer.)
								X		X						3. All invoices are evidenced to
																show satisfactory receipt of
																goods/service prior to payment.
							X									4. All orders are evidenced to
																show goods received and
																invoice processed to avoid
																duplicate payment.
											X					5. An independent purchasing manager
																negotiates and effects all
																purchases on behalf of
																budget holders/ordering staff
																checking also that internal
																regulations have been followed.
			X						X		X					6. Internal regulations
																set expenditure limits
																against each budget
																holder/ordering staff
																who evidence compliance with
																these on each order.
									X	X	X					7. Internal regulations require all
																purchases to be made under official
																purchase order (or sealed contracts).

Figure A5.1 Example objectives and controls grid for sundry purchases

																																								All incurred. Production is required	
																																								Only authorized production is incurred	
																																								All production stages/processes are authorized	Production to point of delivery is in line with corporate policy
																								X					X										All liabilities are authorized	
																				X									X										All liabilities are unavoidable	
																																							X	Physical assets are complete and evidenced	
																																								All staff are fitted for work	
																																								Organizational structure is sound	
																																								Objectives at each level of body are synchronized	Operations meet corporate objectives
																																								Planned output measures are achieved	
																																								Quality failure is minimized	Quality assurance is optimized
																																								External (customer) quality standards are achieved	
																																								Internal quality standards are achieved	
																																								All standards are updated	Standards are in line with policy aims
																																								Quality assurance standards followed	
																																								Safety at work code followed	
																																								Conditions of service followed	
																																								Organization's internal regulations and codes are observed	All activities are legal
																																								All staff are adequately trained	
																																								All payroll payments are due	

⇦ STRATEGIC OBJECTIVES	Human resources are optimized			Financial resources are adequate but not excessive	Investment policy is followed		Accounts are complete, accurate and valid					Budgets are met			Budgets are met	
SYSTEM LEVEL OBJECTIVES ⇦ / KEY CONTROLS TREASURY CAPITAL MANAGEMENT ⇩	All posts are required and valid	Only genuine employee (pensions) are paid	Over/under spends are acceptable	Budgets are monitored and variations explained	Investments are accurate and valid	Capital expenditure is genuinely required	All payments assets and liabilities are accounted for	Payments made are for genuine invoices	Goods/services invoiced were ordered and accepted	Payments are due accurate and valid	Only goods/services orders are accepted	All orders are genuinely required	Income received is due	Income received is brought to account	Income due is received	All assets and liabilities are accurately measured
1. Equipment and asset registers independently reconciled (monthly/quarterly/annually and so on) to sales, purchases, depreciation and so on.							X									X
2. Directors/valuers certify valuation at least annually.					X		X									X
3. All capital expenditure loans and investments over a de-minimus value to be authorized by finance director, board and so on as appropriate.					X	X				X		X				
4. Bankers to be provided with specimen signatures for all commitment BACS accounts, cheque payments and so on.					X					X						
5. All contractual obligations over a de-minimus level (set to exclude sundry purchases) are under a sealed official contract.																
6. All dealing/arranging to be undertaken by staff not involved in accounts settlements.					X		X					X			X	
7. Bank reconciliation (monthly, daily and so on) includes all loan and adjustment transactions* and is undertaken by staff not involved in lending or dealing.							X							X	X	
* including interest and repayments																

Figure A5.2 Example objectives and controls grid for capital expenditures, loans and investment

		Production to point of delivery is in line with corporate policy						Operations meet corporate objectives		Quality assurance is optimized			Standards are in line with policy aims				All activities are legal		
All incurred. Production is required	Only authorized production is incurred	All production stages/processes are authorized	All liabilities are authorized	All liabilities are unavoidable	Physical assets are complete and evidenced	All staff are fitted for work	Organizational structure is sound	Objectives at each level of body are synchronized	Planned output measures are achieved	Quality failure is minimized	External (customer) quality standards are achieved	Internal quality standards are achieved	All standards are updated	Quality assurance standards followed	Safety at work code followed	Conditions of service followed	Organization's internal regulations and codes are observed	All staff are adequately trained	All payroll payments are due
																			X
																			X
																			X
																			X
																			X
																			X

Human resources are optimized			Financial resources are adequate but not excessive	Investment policy is followed		Accounts are complete, accurate and valid					Budgets are met			Budgets are met		⇦ STRATEGIC OBJECTIVES
All posts are required and valid	Only genuine employee (pensions) are paid	Over/under spends are acceptable	Budgets are monitored and variations explained	Investments are accurate and valid	Capital expenditure is genuinely required	All payments assets and liabilities are accounted for	Payments made are for genuine invoices	Goods/services invoiced were ordered and accepted	Payments are due accurate and valid	Only goods/services orders are accepted	All orders are genuinely required	Income received is due	Income received is brought to account	Income due is received	All assets and liabilities are accurately measured	SYSTEM LEVEL OBJECTIVES ⇧ / KEY CONTROLS IN PAYROLL SYSTEM ⇩
	X														X	1. A separation between: (a) compilation/processing payroll (b) initiating/changing key information such as starters, leavers, promotions and so on.
X	X															2. Independent reconciliation of payroll to staff employed ('Ghost check') (including temporary staff).
																3. Computerized reconciliation (as appropriate) of: (a) Input to payroll generation (b) Output of computerized or manual systemized to produce (a) (c) Values and nos/grade of payslips produced.
X	X															4. Clear evidence of authorization from letter of appointment to details on payroll, for example, rank, salary, special allows, deductions and so on from non-payroll managers and payers for deductions.
																5. All timesheets of non-salary staff to be authorized by supervisor.
X	X															6. All payroll changing stationery (starters, promotions and so on) to be sequentially pre-numbered and accounted for.
X	X															7. Computerized 'data-vet' checks of – payments over £x – more than one payment to: (a) same name (b) same bank account (c) same post/account employee references (nt. job-share posts).

Figure A5.3 Example objectives and controls grid for payroll

All incurred. Production is required	
Only authorized production is incurred	
All production stages/processes are authorized	Production to point of delivery is in line with corporate policy
All liabilities are authorized	
All liabilities are unavoidable	
Physical assets are complete and evidenced	
All staff are fitted for work	
Organizational structure is sound	
Objectives at each level of body are synchronized	Operations meet corporate objectives
Planned output measures are achieved	
Quality failure is minimized	Quality assurance is optimized
External (customer) quality standards are achieved	
Internal quality standards are achieved	
All standards are updated	Standards are in line with policy aims
Quality assurance standards followed	
Safety at work code followed	
Conditions of service followed	
Organization's internal regulations and codes are observed	All activities are legal
All staff are adequately trained	
All payroll payments are due	

Human resources are optimized			Financial resources are adequate but not excessive	Investment policy is followed		Accounts are complete, accurate and valid					Budgets are met			Budgets are met		⇦ STRATEGIC OBJECTIVES
All posts are required and valid	Only genuine employee (pensions) are paid	Over/under spends are acceptable	Budgets are monitored and variations explained	Investments are accurate and valid	Capital expenditure is genuinely required	All payments assets and liabilities are accounted for	Payments made are for genuine invoices	Goods/services invoiced were ordered and accepted	Payments are due accurate and valid	Only goods/services orders are accepted	All orders are genuinely required	Income received is due	Income received is brought to account	Income due is received	All assets and liabilities are accurately measured	SYSTEM LEVEL OBJECTIVES ⇦ / KEY CONTROLS IN INCOME SYSTEM ⇩
														X		1. Income levels per outlet/source are independently monitored (daily, weekly, monthly and so on), all peaks/troughs are explained.
														X		2. Sales margins per product/services are independently monitored (daily, weekly, monthly and so on) all unexpected variations are explained.
														X		3. Independent stock checks reconciled to sales less returns plus stock in hands of sales staff.
													X			4. Separation between: (a) cash takings (b) banking (c) accounting (including bank reconciliation).
													X			5. Takings agreed to bank paying in slip and agreement evidenced by *both* sales/cashier *and* person responsible for making up bankings.
												X	X	X		6. Separation between: – credit sales staff – accounting for debtors.
												X		X		7. All sales must be evidenced by: – cash receipt – sales invoice – legally enforceable contract as appropriate.
													X	X		8. Telephone sales are logged or recorded and followed up/invoiced by non-sales staff.

Figure A5.4 Example objectives and controls grid for sales/income collection

			X				X						X														X																	X	Production is efficient	
			X				X						X					X									X					X					X							X	Products/services meet customer demands (ineffective)	
																							X				X					X					X							X	All incurred. Production is required	
																							X				X																	X	Only authorized production is incurred	
																							X				X																	X	All production stages/processes are authorized	Production to point of delivery is in line with corporate policy
																																												X	All liabilities are authorized	
																																													All liabilities are unavoidable	
																																													Physical assets are complete and evidenced	
																																													All staff are fitted for work	
																																													Organizational structure is sound	
																																X												X	Objectives at each level of body are synchronized	Operations meet corporate objectives
			X										X														X					X												X	Planned output measures are achieved	
			X										X														X					X												X	Quality failure is minimized	Quality assurance is optimized
			X															X									X					X					X							X	External (customer) quality standards are achieved	
			X																								X					X												X	Internal quality standards are achieved	
							X																				X					X												X	All standards are updated	Standards are in line with policy aims
			X																								X					X													Quality assurance standards followed	
																																													Safety at work code followed	
																																													Conditions of service followed	
																																													Organization's internal regulations and codes are observed	All activities are legal
																																													All staff are adequately trained	
																																													All payroll payments are due	

Human resources are optimized			Financial resources are adequate but not excessive	Investment policy is followed		Accounts are complete, accurate and valid					Budgets are met			Budgets are met		⇦ STRATEGIC OBJECTIVES
All posts are required and valid	Only genuine employee (pensions) are paid	Over/under spends are acceptable	Budgets are monitored and variations explained	Investments are accurate and valid	Capital expenditure is genuinely required	All payments assets and liabilities are accounted for	Payments made are for genuine invoices	Goods/services invoiced were ordered and accepted	Payments are due accurate and valid	Only goods/services orders are accepted	All orders are genuinely required	Income received is due	Income received is brought to account	Income due is received	All assets and liabilities are accurately measured	SYSTEM LEVEL OBJECTIVES ⇦ / KEY CONTROLS FOR QUALITY ASSURANCE ⇩
																1. Internal instructions and guidelines cover at least:
																(a) production procedures
																(b) distribution/delivery
																(c) maintenance/follow-up
																and are kept up to date.
																2. Compliance with customer/client specification is evidenced by:
																(a) confirmation from customer/client
																(b) internal quality audits.
																3. 'Quality audits' are conducted independently of line management, that is, testing the quality assurance system controls.
																4. Recognized external quality assurance certification is in force, for example BS ENISO 9000 (formerly BS 5750).
																5. All budgeted production/service provision is agreed at board level, and authorized by production manager for each run, batch and so on.
																6. Customer/client specification is confirmed in written contract. Signed, sealed and delivered, including any subsequent changes.
																7. Rejects/returns/complaints are recorded independently, kept isolated from stock and actioned by senior managers including necessary quality control improvements.
																8. Quality improvement is formarly reviewed and suggestions initiatives recorded.
																9. The effects on the quality control system of all proposed changes is documented and evaluated (prior and post).

Figure A5.5 Example objectives and controls grid for quality assurance

																																								All incurred. Production is required	
																																								Only authorized production is incurred	
																																								All production stages/processes are authorized	Production to point of delivery is in line with corporate policy
																																								All liabilities are authorized	
																																								All liabilities are unavoidable	
																																								Physical assets are complete and evidenced	
																																								All staff are fitted for work	
																																								Organizational structure is sound	
																																								Objectives at each level of body are synchronized	Operations meet corporate objectives
																																								Planned output measures are achieved	
																																								Quality failure is minimized	Quality assurance is optimized
																																								External (customer) quality standards are achieved	
																																								Internal quality standards are achieved	
																																								All standards are updated	Standards are in line with policy aims
																																								Quality assurance standards followed	
																													X											Safety at work code followed	
																													X											Conditions of service followed	
																		X											X											Organization's internal regulations and codes are observed	All activities are legal
																						X							X											All staff are adequately trained	
																																								All payroll payments are due	

Key controls for stocks and stores	All posts are required and valid	Only genuine employee (pensions) are paid	Over/under spends are acceptable	Budgets are monitored and variations explained	Investments are accurate and valid	Capital expenditure is genuinely required	All payments assets and liabilities are accounted for	Payments made are for genuine invoices	Goods/services invoiced were ordered and accepted	Payments are due accurate and valid	Only goods/services orders are accepted	All orders are genuinely required	Income received is due	Income received is brought to account	Income due is received	All assets and liabilities are accurately measured
STRATEGIC OBJECTIVES	Human resources are optimized			Financial resources are adequate but not excessive	Investment policy is followed		Accounts are complete, accurate and valid					Budgets are met			Budgets are met	
1. All stocks and WIP are subject of regular (at least year end) reconciliation to stock/WIP records and valuation.																X
2. All issues, receipts into damages and returns to store are accurately and completely recorded and signed for by storekeeper/site foreman and the recipient of issues.																X
3. All staff undergo induction and refresher training re: – safety – data protection – other legal reports – of work place.																
4. All staff have a training needs assessment at appropriate frequency and at least annually																
5. Required policy and procedures are agreed at board level and written guidance is provided and kept up to date.	X															
6. All staff provided with a handbook which is updated clearly and recorded covering their responsibilities in respect of conditions of service, safety and so on.																

Figure A5.6 Example objectives and controls grid for stocks and stores

All incurred. Production is required	
Only authorized production is incurred	
All production stages/processes are authorized	Production to point of delivery is in line with corpcrate policy
All liabilities are authorized	
All liabilities are unavoidable	
Physical assets are complete and evidenced	
All staff are fitted for work	
Organizational structure is sound	
Objective ats each level of body are synchronized	Operations meet corporate objectives
Planned output measures are achieved	
Quality failure is minimized	Quality assurance is optimized
External (customer) quality standards are achieved	
Internal quality standards are achieved	
All standards are updated	Standards are in line with policy aims
Quality assurance standards followed	
Safety at work code followed	
Conditions of service followed	
Organization's internal regulations and codes are observed	All activities are legal
All staff are adequately trained	
All payroll payments are due	

STRATEGIC OBJECTIVES	SYSTEM LEVEL OBJECTIVES	KEY CONTROLS																																							
Human resources are optimized	All posts are required and valid																																								
	Only genuine employee (pensions) are paid																																								
	Over/under spends are acceptable																																								
Financial resources are adequate but not excessive	Budgets are monitored and variations explained																																								
Investment policy is followed	Investments are accurate and valid																																								
	Capital expenditure is genuinely required																																								
Accounts are complete, accurate and valid	All payments assets and liabilities are accounted for																																								
	Payments made are for genuine invoices																																								
	Goods/services invoiced were ordered and accepted																																								
	Payments are due accurate and valid																																								
	Only goods/services orders are accepted																																								
Budgets are met	All orders are genuinely required																																								
	Income received is due																																								
	Income received is brought to account																																								
Budgets are met	Income due is received																																								
	All assets and liabilities are accurately measured																																								

Figure A5.7 Example general template of objectives

APPENDIX

6 Capital Works Contract Checklist

Tender conditions

1 Is tender:
  (a) in standard form? (for example, ICE, JCT.) If not describe basis of tender and attach copy.
  (b) priced?
  (c) unpriced?
  (d) lowest submitted? (Copy file papers to Audit file.)
  (e) correct or has an error been detected in the tender submission? If yes, has it been dealt with in accordance with the Code of Practice for Single Stage Selective Tendering or any internal regulations?
  (f) signed by contractor and dated?
2 Is a filed record of tender bids signed by an Opening Committee?
3 Have letters been sent to all contractors who were unsuccessful/failed to tender, detailing the amounts bid? Note: letters need not usually be sent to tenderers who have written notifying of their inability to tender.
4 Are there any late amendments to the conditions of contract? If yes, give details and note any amendments to be signed by both parties.
5 Are there specific provisions for:
  (a) health and safety at work;
  (b) overtime working;
  (c) audit of final accounts and supporting documents/books/accounts of contractor;
  (d) site access and conditions;
  (e) contractor's area, noise, hours of work, and so on;
  (f) works sanitation and accommodation;
  (g) supply of water, electricity and telephones;
  (h) precautions against damage to roads, trees, utilities supply, and so on;
  (i) gifts and unfair inducements;
  (j) monthly accounts;
  (k) new rates (star rates);
  (l) daywork;
  (m) records (site and other);
  (n) sequence, schedules, programme of works;
  (o) repair and construction details;
  (p) materials details;
  (q) accurate identification of sites, buildings, land, plots, and so on;
  (r) checking details against property register if appropriate, for example, housing maintenance; and
  (s) other main provisions – give details.

Review and, if appropriate, comment on each.

Bill of quantities (or schedule of rates)

1 Preamble/Preliminaries should cover:
  (a) cost of site services;
  (b) cost of temporary works;
  (c) cost of testing of materials or ground/site investigation;
  (d) any other costs that are not proportional to works done;
  (e) charging methods; and
  (f) method related charges.
2 Review bill of quantities: compare to standard conditions: note any omissions or additions. Consider general reasonableness of quantities and rates.

Final account/final audit

1 Obtain copies of any interim (current) audit work and include with this file.
2 Record date of receipt of final account and any subsequent related information. Record date of commencement of final audit.
3 Check that a certification of practical/substantial completion has been issued and signed by the quantity surveyor (QS), architect or engineer.
4 *Arithmetical checks (see also Appendix 7)*
  Check off final account details and arithmetical calculations against amounts, rates, and so on, in bill of quantities. Note:
  (a) errors;

(b) large variations from the bill; and
(c) whether star rates (if any) have been agreed.

The following (5–19) should be covered as appropriate.

5 *Prime costs*
Check that any prime costs of works, materials, and so on, agree to values and any percentage of costs agreed in the bill of quantities (the bill).

6 *Provisional sums*
Check that any provisional sums have been accurately transferred to the final account from the bill of quantities. Check that any adjustments (omissions or additions) are fully supported.

7 *Variation orders* (refer to interim audit working papers where applicable)
Check that any variations are supported by orders signed and dated by architect/engineer/QS. Variations should apply to the requirements of the contract rather than to simple increases/decreases in the measurements laid down in the bill of quantities. Significant increases/decreases should be fully documented. Variations should be costed if significant.

Note: variation may be subject to different methods of measurement from the main contract bill of quantities. Any variation relating to prime costs should be fully supported by subcontractors' invoices.

8 *Dayworks* (refer to interim audit working papers where applicable)
Dayworks should be agreed to a national schedule, for example, as agreed by a professional institute or to a rate set down in the bill of quantities; for example, the Federation of Civil Engineering Contractors' Schedules of Daywork carried out incidental to contract work (issued 23.8.88).

Check all daywork sheets are certified.

9 *Approved contingencies*
To be treated in the same manner as a provisional sum. These should have been catered for by a fixed sum or an agreed percentage of the tender sum. Check any such percentage if figures are available. Bring to the attention of audit management any contingency items not included at tender stage.

10 *Liquidated damages* (refer to interim audit working papers where applicable)
Commencement date .... Period ......
Anticipated completion .... + extensions.

Agree to rate × week or part week. Rate should be set down in bill of quantities.

Note: liquidated damages are a compensation rather than a penalty.

11 *Retention*
Check calculation of retention (usually a percentage of the value of the work) as specified in the contract, for exmple JCT 5 per cent practical completion; 2.5 per cent to final completion; ICE 5 per cent for contracts up to £50 000 to a maximum retention of £1500; 3 per cent for contracts more than £50 000; 1.5 per cent after a certificate of completion has been issued and up to the issue of a maintenance certificate.

Check that no retention monies have been released without the QS, architect or engineer having signed a certificate of completion, or a maintenance certificate.

12 *Tax*
This should normally be excluded from contract prices but check that any tax charges for VAT, fuel tax, and so on:
(a) are correctly calculated and applied; and
(b) relate only to certified works.

On completion of the works, adjustments may be made for changing tax rates. These should be agreed to legislation.

13 *Price uctuations* (normally only large contracts over more than one year)
Check that the contract is not a fixed price contract. Otherwise a price uctuation to allow for in ation can be expected. If a price index formula has been agreed recalculate the agreed addition or subtraction checking that the correct values have been used.

14 *Interim certi cate* (refer to any interim audit working papers where applicable)
Check that all interim payments are fully supported by certificates signed by the QS, architect or engineer. Check that items included in the certificate are also included in the bill of quantities and/or agreed variations. (See also item 7 above.)

15 *Claims for unforeseen circumstances*
These should be agreed by the architect/engineer/QS and after checking any supporting documents and calculation they should be brought to the attention of the audit management.

16 *Ex gratia claims* (including claims for compensation)
These should be brought to the attention of the audit management.

17 *Direct payments to un-nominated subcontractors or other third parties*
These should be brought to the attention of the audit management.

18 *Payments to nominated subcontractors*
These should be checked to the original tender/bill of quantities as for normal payments.

19 *Payments for betterment*
These are received from third parties for betterment of their existing assets or other conditions, for example, rail bridges.

20 Date final account audited...........................
Balance due .... to contractor.
Balance owed .... by contractor.

21 Final certificate or expiration of period of maintenance for completion and release of retention monies checked arithmetically and agreed to terms in contract.

APPENDIX 7

Final Contractor s Account Audit ..Arithmetical Checks

1 Trace all item descriptions and rates from the original bills of quantities to the final account.
2 Check build-up of all item rates where shown.
3 Check all extensions (quantities × rates) including any supporting sheets.
4 Cast extensions to compare with page totals (ensuring that credits where appropriate are deducted).
5 Ensure correct page totals are carried to the section bill summaries.
6 Trace correct section bill summaries to final account summary and cast.
7 Ensure that the correct total figure is the one certified by the engineer/architect.
8 Agree total payments to date to capital ledger/record of capital payments.
9 Check interim payments listed on ledger to interim certificates issued. Certificates should be signed by the engineer, QS or architect.
10 Any separate invoice for consultants' fees should be agreed to the rate (usually a percentage of the contract value) and the type of work specified in an exchange of letters or contract. (An additional audit programme may be used for consultants.)

APPENDIX

8 Key Contract Counter-fraud and System Evaluation Issues

Management and audit issues

Insist on a high standard of documentation. This may be a war of attrition but it is vital that you win, with tact and good humour.

Never rely solely on an arithmetical check of final accounts.

Even if you can not afford a lot of current contract audit you can still check evidence of most of the currency of the contract at the time of the final account – better late than never!

Review which contractors get chosen regularly? And which ones rarely get picked?

How are select lists of contractors compiled, reviewed, used?

Specification and design – who decides? How does the user benefit? (The new IT system – wanted or imposed?)

Look closely at the opening procedures, are they well controlled?

Are negotiating rules fair and actually followed?

For each contract

Always ask why was it needed?

How was it awarded/tendered?

The reasons for over/underspends?

Have any lessons been learnt?

What do the final users think?

Negotiations

For any negotiations check:

Why was negotiation needed? What was the core issue(s)?

Was the core issue really clarified and resolved? A fudge?

Where? Formal? Informal?

How? Face-to-face telephone, letters, all means possible?

By whom? One-to one? One to several? Recorded?

Same information and access given to all tender firms?

Committee/board involvement?

How were discordant voices dealt with?

APPENDIX 9

Extracts from the Data Protection Act 1998

Extracts from the Data Protection Act 1998

THE DATA PROTECTION PRINCIPLES

1 Personal data shall be processed fairly and lawfully and, in particular, shall not be processed unless –
   (a) at least one of the conditions in Schedule 2 is met, and
   (b) in the case of sensitive personal data, at least one of the conditions in Schedule 3 is also met.
2 Personal data shall be obtained only for one or more specified and lawful purposes, and shall not be further processed in any manner incompatible with that purpose or those purposes.
3 Personal data shall be adequate, relevant and not excessive in relation to the purpose or purposes for which they are processed.
4 Personal data shall be accurate and, where necessary, kept up to date.
5 Personal data processed for any purpose or purposes shall not be kept for longer than is necessary for that purpose or those purposes.
6 Personal data shall be processed in accordance with the rights of data subjects under this Act.
7 Appropriate technical and organizational measures shall be taken against unauthorized or unlwaful processing of personal data and against accidental loss or destruction of, or damage to, personal data.
8 Personal data shall not be transferred to a country or territory outside the European Economic Area unless that country or territory ensures an adequate level of protection for the rights and freedoms of data subjects in relation to the processing of personal data.

APPENDIX 10

Outline Structure for a Corporate IT Security and Data Protection Policy

Physical security of operations

Damage
Theft
Accountability and trace ability of assets
Environmental security

Disaster recovery

Planning
Testing
Business continuity

Legality of operations

Compliance with:

(a) Data Protection Act
(b) Computer Misuse Act
(c) Copyright, Designs and Patents Act

Confidentiality of data

Access
Updating and changing
Disclosure
Distribution
Destruction

Integrity of data

Access control
Accuracy
Completeness
Validity
Authorization
Relevance
Loss and contamination

Management of operations

Monitoring performance
Availability of vital systems
Suitability
Training
Personnel screening and development

APPENDIX **11**

Checklist of Key Case Papers and Control Features for Means-tested Bene ts and Grants

Organization

1 Are all claims relating to a single individual or organization filed together?
2 Are all types of claim dealt with by the same group of officers? If not, on what basis do they specialize?
3 Are reference numbers promptly issued in strict sequence to each initial claim?
4 Consider the organization's family tree: do staff-to-supervisor ratios appear adequate?

Case papers

5 Are all claims, including notifications of changes in circumstances, on a standard official form?
6 Are forms pre-numbered?
7 Are all forms given the sequential claim number immediately on receipt (see 3)?
8 Are all claims signed and dated by the claimant or by a recognized official on behalf of the claiming body?
9 Are all the relevant documents that are transferred between organizations, including cancellations of entitlement by one body, stamped or signed or otherwise authenticated by an identifiable officer before posting out to another body?
10 Is a log kept or a date stamp used for all incoming claims, showing date received, department, and so on?
11 Is any manually performed benefit calculation clearly laid out?
12 Are the computer input values (for example, 'applicable amounts' relating to housing renovation grants and housing benefit) clearly set down when the calculation is done by computer?
13 Can the officer performing a calculation or inputting data to a computer be easily identified?
14 Is any computer program adequate in respect of 'data vet' checks (for example, reasonableness or ceilings for income)?
15 Are any manual calculations checked by a second officer?
16 Are input details checked by a second officer?
17 What evidence (including photocopies) is retained on file for such factors as:
(a) rents, for example, rent book or lease?
(b) capital, for example, Building Society/Bank statement?
(c) income, for example, wage slip?
(d) status, for example, student?
(e) family circumstances (if applicable)?
(f) ownership of land or property, for example, deeds?
18 Are copies of all correspondence (outgoing) traceable to the originating officer, for example, by reference?
19 Are key original and copy documents, for example, letters confirming awards or letters of agreement, signed?
20 Is a complete list made of all incoming actionable documents, for example, housing benefit cancellation certificates sent to local authorities from the Department of Social Security?
21 What evidence is filed to show the extent of any supervisor or management checking?
22 Is a diary or list of home visits or site inspections kept? (Visiting officers' notes should indicate the name of the officer, the time and date, and the conclusions reached including supporting document references.)
23 Are such visits (as at 22 above) undertaken by an officer not otherwise involved in the case?

24 Is it possible to confirm that cheques are not returned to the hands of the claim-processing or visiting officers after payment has been initiated?
25 Are all cheques crossed 'A/C payee only not transferable'?
26 Are any cheques intercepted for last minute alteration or cancellation fully recorded and properly authorized?
27 Are any control totals affected by 26 above promptly amended?
28 Are all cheques that have been returned to the funding organization, and the explanation, recorded in an independently kept register?
29 Are all spoilt cheques checked and authorized by an officer not responsible for generating the replacement?
30 Is there any mechanism for ensuring that all suitable cases, for example, recovery of overpayment cases, are handed to independent investigating officers?

APPENDIX **12** *Some Basic Comparisons Between Private and Public Sector Accounts*

Absence of shareholders

In the private sectors all or some of the capital to fund the business is provided by investors who buy shares whereas in the public services, where the taxpayers are the ultimate 'owners', a variety of statutes provide for accumulated funds, consolidated funds or public dividend capital.

Entity accounting versus fund accounting

In the private sector the accounts are prepared for specific entities, that is, a private limited company, a plc, a bank and so on. In the public services, while accounts are still prepared for individual entities they are often also prepared for 'funds' with those entities. Each fund will have a specific purpose(s) and within the wider entity there are severe restrictions on moving monies between funds. In local authorities for example there are several funds that are reported in the accounts together with a consolidated balance sheet for the entity as a whole.

Cash and accruals accounting

In the private sector published financial reports and accounts are invariably prepared on an accruals basis where transactions are matched or accrued to the period in which the income was earned or the expenditure incurred irrespective of the date the cash was received or paid out. In the public services such accruals accounts are often supplemented with cash-based accounts that also show the transactions on the basis of when the cash actually moves into or out of accounts.

The variation from common reporting formats

In the private sector the profit and loss accounts and balance sheets are the main published accounting statements that enable a high degree of understanding and common comparisons to be drawn between many commercial organizations. Even though these statements are supplemented by cash ow statements and notes that give further insight into the accounts, there is little doubt that the common formats of profit and loss accounts and balance sheets greatly aid intercompany comparisons and provide a well established basis from which to start further financial analysis. In the public services a wide range of accounting statements with differing formats applies. Many public bodies do indeed provide balance sheets, though the balances are not always prepared on the same bases as most commercial organizations, and many provide income and expenditure accounts that are roughly analogous to profit and loss accounts – these statements are generally on an accruals basis. Beyond this, though, numerous other accounts are published on various accounting bases, such as the Appropriation Accounts of central government on a cash basis, or the Housing Revenue Accounts of local authorities, which are a particular type of income and expenditure account prepared on a fund basis.

Capital accounting

This is always a complex area and no less so in the public services. The key is to realize that capital charging and the commonly held concept of depreciation in the private sector as a measure of the gradual using up of an assets worth, while still often applying to the public services, needs special care and attention. For example, many assets are not used for commercial or commercial-like purposes and their values and basis of depreciation may seem somewhat contrived. Donated assets, heritage assets and infrastructure assets are examples that have extra considerations.

There are a great many more contrasts and comparisons that could be drawn between the public and private sectors and between different sectors within each but the vital point for the fraud prevention manager, auditor or fraud investigator is the need to spend time becoming familiar with or seeking expert advice about the public body he or she is considering.

The Bibliography lists works that give a suitable introduction to public services accounting.

APPENDIX

13 Financial and Accounting Glossary

This appendix includes a wide range of accounting and financial terms most of which apply to commercial situations, but a larger than usual proportion of entries relate to public services terms which are often missing from many published listings aimed at commercial readers. The entries are not intended to provide dictionary-style definitions but plain descriptions in accessible language that explain the ordinary use of the term.

Absorption – usually refers to methods of charging overhead costs to output, for example, once the *direct costs* of labour and materials, licence fees and so on have been calculated for producing each product or service, an absorption formula or rate will be agreed for ensuring each unit is charged its 'fair share' or proportion of costs such as administration, personnel, financial and other *indirect costs*. See also break-even point.

Account – record(s) of business transactions both personal – relating to debtors and creditors (see below) – and impersonal – relating either to assets (see below) or to 'nominal' gains and losses. See also ledger.

Accounting period – the calendar year, financial year (April to March) or other period covered by the accounts.

Accrual accounting – the matching of revenues and costs to the period, usually the accounting year, in which they were earned or incurred. Usually the sales invoice date and the expense order date will be used, though precise situations and agreements may cause this to vary. For example, the total value of sales invoices sent out just before the end of the financial year in late March yr.0 would be accrued as income to the yr.0/yr.1 financial year even though the income would not be received until say, late April in the financial year yr.1/yr.2. Similarly most income and expenses for the previous April Year 1 would be accrued back to the previous financial year. Accruals systems contrast to cash accounting where all revenues and expenses are matched to the year in which the money was received or paid, or some commitments systems where amounts are matched to the formal decision to incur expenses (which may be an internal requisition or the minutes of a meeting rather than the order date) though it is unusual to take income as committed before issuing a sales invoice.

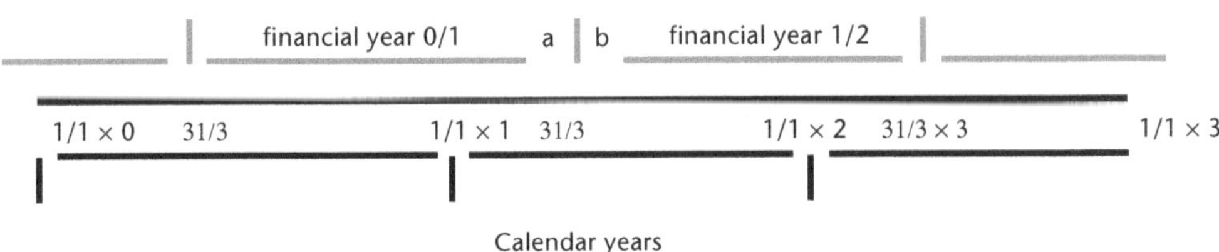

Thus, in the diagram above, a sales invoice sent at 'a' and paid at 'b' would be accrued to financial year 0/1 even though it was paid in financial year 1/2.

ACT – Advance corporation tax. The basic rate of tax, paid on dividends to shareholders. It counts as part of the firms' mainstream corporation tax.

Advice note – usually a delivery note, or goods received note accompanying and listing the contents of a shipment received from a supplier.

Allocation – usually the direct sharing out of costs in relation to their generation, for example, material costs of a product may be allocated to each production centre according to the number of units produced.

Amortization – see depreciation.

Annuity – right to receive or obligation to pay a series or regular annual amounts.

Apportionment – the indirect sharing out of costs according to a formula or agreed method, for example, the cost of a subsidized canteen may be apportioned according to the number of employees per department even though in practice some never use it.

Asset – property, machines, goods, and so on owned and used by the business. *Fixed:* capital assets, lasting in the business for over a year, the buildings, machines and so on, usually recorded individually in an *asset register*. *Current:* short term or working capital assets, intended to be used up or sold on within a year, stocks, cash in current account and so on. Some very low value assets that will be used for over a year, for example, office calculators, may be treated as current assets simply to avoid excessive bookkeeping (see below). In total, the assets of the business equal its liabilities (see below).

Audit – a professional evaluation and opinion forming process relating to the published accounts of an organization (*external audit*) and/or the systems and procedures put in place by the organization's managers to meet its objectives and ensure its efficient and effective operation (*internal audit*). An auditor works on an independent basis from the client's and management responsibilities being audited. See also testing.

Audit Commission – a public audit body charged with appointing and overseeing the auditors of local and health authorities. See also National Audit Office.

Balance – the difference between debit (Dr) and credit (Cr) totals in an account. Also used loosely to mean the amount of money shown on almost any computer printout, report, or summary, for example, the 'end of run balance, end of day balance', and so on. *Trial balance:* summary of all the account balances at a point in time, it should contain equal totals or Drs and Crs. See also debit and credit. A typical trial balance format is:

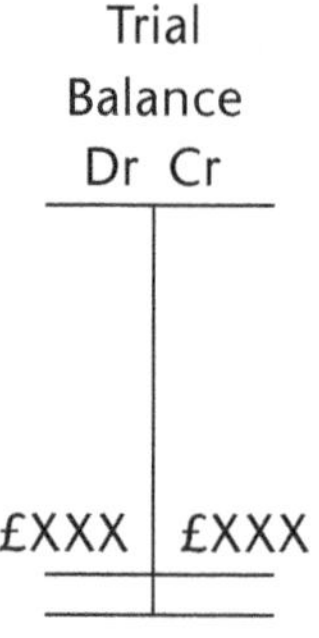

Balance sheet – statement of all the assets (usually Dr balances) and liabilities (usually Cr balances) at a point in time. Note that when drawing up a balance sheet not all assets and liabilities may be fully and precisely recorded in the accounts and some 'estimation' may be required. A balance sheet is usually drawn up in one of the following two broad formats to show that all the assets are balanced by (that is, equal) all the liabilities. (Variations can occur particularly by netting off the current liabilities against current assets on the assets side.)

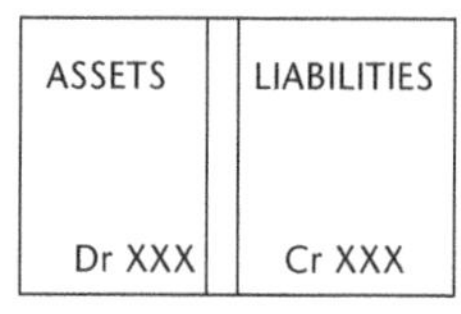

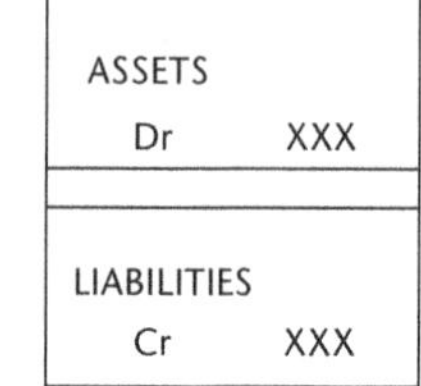

Bank reconciliation – comparing the balances in your cash book/records to the balance shown on your bank account and adjusting for any cheques or deposits not yet recorded by the bank.

Bear – a stock market investor who thinks that share prices will fall.

Bid – refers to the price at which shares are bought, the bid price is less than the selling price of shares which is called the *offer* and the *bid-offer* spread is the difference. Also used regarding attempt by one company to take over another.

Big Bang – nothing to do here with the origins of the universe! Rather more mundanely it simply refers to the deregulation of the London Stock Exchange.

Blue chip – refers to investments in large and highly secure companies.

Bond – a public issue of small loans or a large loan raised on the City money markets. The bond holder does not have a claim on the assets of the business, unlike a mortgage or debenture holder, but relies on the contractual agreement set out in the bond certificate. A *bearer bond* or *bearer security* refers to one whose ownership depends simply on who has possession of the bond rather than being verifiable by reference to a register of owners.

Bookkeeping – systematic recording of all transactions in the 'books' of account (see double entry).

Book of prime entry – the book in which a transaction is first recorded, for example, a sales day book, cash book and so on.

Bought ledger – the personal accounts of all suppliers/creditors.

Break-even point – break-even is the point at which revenue just covers both fixed and variable costs. Generally speaking rents, business rates, capital charges, salaries and so on are considered *xed* because they do not uctuate in relation to goods produced; whereas direct material costs, hourly paid/temporary labour, transport costs and so on needed for each unit or batch made are usually *variable*. Though the distinctions can become blurred and in the long run all costs are variable. Some people find this easier to understand when shown as a graph:

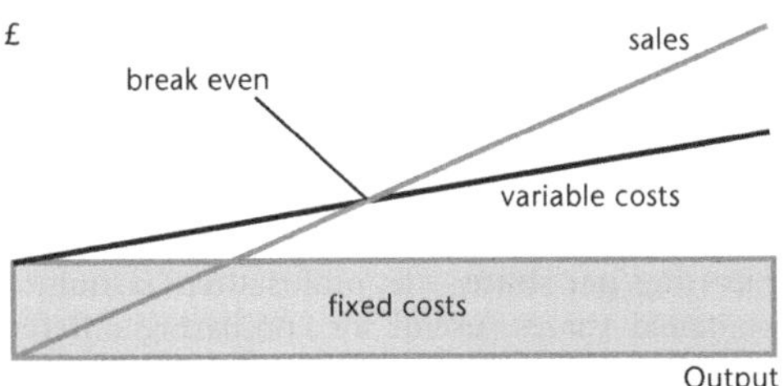

Budget – an estimate of future income and expenses using *standard* costs and prices calculated on the basis of standard rates, hours, volumes and so on that re ect normal operating conditions. Budget is a more precise term than a *forecast* which can be open to any method of calculation or guesswork, or *projections* which are usually based on historical trends.

Bull – a stock market investor who thinks share prices will rise.

Business plan – various meanings but most commonly used to describe a detailed financial plan or proposal showing how your business objectives will be met from the financial and other resources at your disposal. Business plans are often required for example, by banks and other lenders before they will finance a new business, or are prepared by directors and senior managers to help decide upon, and follow the progress of, a new project.

Capital – finance used to get resources for the business. Capital transactions are those that affect the financing and asset base of the organization, compared to *revenue* transactions which refer to ongoing trading events that give rise to the profit and loss account and to current assets and liabilities.

Capital discharged – an accumulated sum of the payments made to pay off debt on the capital assets or *other long-term outlay (OLTO)* usually of a public authority.

Cast – simply to add up: usually a vertical line of figures from top to bottom. The term *cross-cast* is also used to refer to adding a horizontal line of figures. Thus a typical table is cast vertically and cross-cast horizontally to arrive at the grand total in the bottom right-hand corner, the second casting providing a check on the first.

Chinese walls – regulations and practices that supposedly prevent con icts of interest arising in securities and professional services markets.

Consolidated accounts – the accounts of a group of companies merged into one set, that is, a single balance sheet, profit and loss account and so on.

Consolidated loans fund – see loans fund.

Contingent liability – a potential liability that has not yet arisen or been acknowledged at the time the balance sheet was drawn up but is sufficiently large to be worth noting in the accounts.

Contra – the opposite Dr entry to a Cr and vice versa.

Control – see internal control.

Control account – a summary type of account of all the items debited or credited to a number of individual accounts, usually used for sales and purchase ledgers. Often a useful control if one person(s) enters up the individual accounts and another the control accounts, reconciling the records periodically. The control account balances can be used to shorten the trial balance procedure.

Cost – in financial terms is open to more interpretations than the simple cost = price scenario of the domestic shopping trip. Here are six fairly frequently used meanings of cost. The first four tend to be linked to management accounting and the last two to financial accounting. See also unit costs.

Activity-based costs – costs that are recorded according to the usage or magnitude or generation of key activities. This classification is usually needed for planning and budgeting purposes.

Current costs – the historic cost updated to take account of price uctuation; usually by formulae that relate to retail price indices or indices for particular materials. Current cost accounting practices also adjust the accounts to re ect changes in value over the accounting period of the cost of sales, working capital and so on.

Full costs – the total costs of an organization are fully absorbed onto the products and services it sells. Typically, the costs are divided into 'fair' amounts for each product or service and the total for each type of cost is divided by the number of units produced to arrive at a full cost per unit, to which is added a profit margin to arrive at the selling price.

Historic costs – the cost recorded in the books at the time a transaction was undertaken. The cost used for most financial accounting.

Marginal costs – the direct costs of producing one extra unit. In the diagram used to explain the break-even point (above) we see how once the fixed costs are covered by the sales income only the direct variable costs are left. Typically, the direct costs of labour and materials will only vary according to how many units are produced and the marginal cost is the amount of labour and material needed to make one more item or batch.

Opportunity costs – the cost of the missed opportunity or alternative production foregone because a particular course of action is taken. More of an economic concept than precise money costs but can often be calculated in terms of lost business or contracts if a particular decision is made.

Unit cost – the cost of each basic measured amount (that is, unit) of production, for example, tons of grain, man (person) hours worked, batches of pens. Although simple in concept, unit costs tend to be complex in practice, much depends on how (and if) you decide to include the costs of overheads.

Credit – entry, traditionally on the right-hand side of a book, to increase a creditor's account or decrease a debtor's account. Also refers to money outstanding, thus a *credit rating* is a measure of the ability of a borrower to repay trade, credit and so on.

Credit note – an amount to offset an overpayment (usually after goods were returned) to a supplier; suppliers are your creditors, but in their books you are a debtor so they credit your overpayment in their books and send you notes of credit.

Cumulative preference shares – see shares.

Debenture – loan secured on the assets of a company.

Debt charges – can refer to the capital repayments and interest owed on debt, usually only the latter is charged to revenue but in some public services bodies such as local authorities both elements may be charged to revenue accounts.

Debit – entry, traditionally on the left-hand side of a book, to increase a debtor account or decrease a creditor account.

Debit note – the reverse of credit note, see above.

Depreciation – a measure of the using up or declining value of an asset. Usually the total value of the asset when purchased less any estimated residual value will be reduced each year. This depreciation 'charge' may be calculated on a *straight line* basis, that is, equal amounts each year of the estimated life; or a *reducing balance* basis using a constant percentage, which is applied each year until the estimated residual balance is reached or the amount left is too small to be of any concern. One of the problems is deciding at what point in the year to base the calculation; year-end values, mid-point, or perhaps an average? Whatever point is chosen it should be applied consistently from year to year. Other methods include linking the amount of the depreciation charge to the use of the asset, for example the number of machine hours or the amount of a mineral resource extracted. The published accounts should enable a reader to see meaningful totals of depreciation for the main types of assets and describe the basis of calculating the depreciation charge. The depreciation charge usually retains money in the business earning a higher rate of return than most normal investments, but sometimes a specific *sinking fund* is set up which may invest outside the company.

Dividend – see shares.

Double entry – bookkeeping method that ensures every transaction is entered twice once as a debit (see above) and once as a credit (see above). Debits increase assets and expenses and decrease income and liabilities, credits do the reverse, in the books of a business (the owner is considered as outside the business).

Earnings per share – net profits after tax/number of issued shares, useful for comparing different companies.

Entry – the formal recording of an amount in the books of account.

Equity – see shares.

Final accounts – the annual (published) accounts of a business. *Contract nal account* refers to the final summary account of capital works undertaken by a contractor.

Finance – the money and related fiscal implications of funding a business. Finance and financial considerations are essentially resource-based and interact with a broad range of information and decision-making, including accounting measurements, economic analysis and business planning.

Fixed assets – see asset.

Futures – agreements to buy or sell standard amounts of commodities such as rubber, wool, and so on or financial investments, at a specific date in the future. Speculative markets in buying and selling these agreements have become well established.

Gearing – (also called *leverage* in the USA) ratio of share holders funds to borrowings (sometimes turnover is used instead of shareholders funds). A highly geared company has a high proportion of borrowings.

Gilts – UK government bonds.

Goodwill – intangible asset arising from reputation and business connections. Estimated rather than measured.

Imprest – a regular 'topping up' of an expense account.

Intangible asset – assets, not fixed or current, that have no precise material dimensions, yet add to the value of the business, for example, goodwill, trademarks, and so on.

Internal control – a procedure or arrangement designed to enhance the self-checking nature of an organization's systems. Internal controls are put in place to guard against the risks to the financial and operational objectives of each system and the body corporate. Examples include separating key functions and duties, computer password procedures, authorization arrangements, financial reconciliation, and so on.

Invoice – formal document setting out amounts to be paid for goods and services, usually with sufficient detail for the payees to agree to their orders and to satisfy VAT requirements.

Journal – usually a simple first book of prime entry completed on a daily basis, also refers to a correcting document used to authorize amending entries in the accounts, for example, year-end journals. A rather loose term.

Leasing – a way of providing capital to finance fixed assets. Basically, the owner of the asset (lessor) is paid in instalments by the user (lessee), either over the period of use or over the estimated life. This gives rise to two broad types of lease:

An operating lease where the asset is rented by the user, usually for more than a year, the owner is usually responsible for its maintenance and intends to re-let the asset again when the current user's lease ends. An operating lease is usually much easier to cancel than . . .

A nance lease where the user is effectively buying the asset in instalments, usually over the estimated life. The leasing agreement transfers virtually all the maintenance and responsibility of ownership (all the risks and rewards) to the lessee. Generally, the asset is not expected to be worth much by the end of the lease period and instalments tend to be higher than for an operational lease. The user will have effectively paid the market value of the asset by the end of the lease.

Although the distinctions between operating and finance leases can be blurred, it is vital to ensure that finance-leased assets are disclosed in the annual accounts in accordance with current best practice. Otherwise it would be possible to hold assets 'off-balance sheet' distorting the values and giving a misleading impression of performance. The chartered accountancy bodies have issued standards to be followed by their members. Sometimes assets can be sold and then leased back by the seller, a *sale and leaseback* agreement. The seller gains a large one-off capital sum from the buyer and the buyer gains ownership of the asset plus regular lease instalments from the seller. This is sometimes called 'hidden borrowing'. If such sale and leaseback gives rise to a finance lease this, including any gains and losses, must also be treated in accordance with best practice. *Lease and leaseback* is a similar arrangement except that the lessor retains the title rather than selling it to a new owner. Leasing agreements can become very complex and new variations are emerging all the time.

Ledger – a collection of accounts, usually classed as for the descriptions of account; see under account above. Usually the main ledger is the nominal ledger showing the gains and lossess on income and expense accounts.

Liabilities – debts owed to suppliers (creditors), shareholders, banks and so on. In total these will equal the assets of the business, see asset.

Liquidity – the short-term excess current assets over current liabilities, also used to describe the ease with which an asset can be converted into cash, for example, stocks are usually less 'liquid' than debtors because it takes longer to sell them off and get the cash.

Loans fund (pool) – a common fund into which all capital borrowings, whatever their repayment terms, are pooled. From this pool advances are made to numerous different projects, programmes and business units, usually at a common/average charging rate, rather than earmarking different borrowings to individual purposes. Sometimes referred to as a *consolidated loans fund (CLF)* particularly in public authorities.

Materiality – the value at which an amount is judged to significantly affect the accuracy and fairness of the accounts of which it forms a part. Thus the value of paper clips is unlikely to have any material effect on the total fixed assets of a company.

Mortgage – a loan secured against property. Note: local authority mortgage borrowing is secured against revenues.

National Audit Of ce (NAO) – a public audit body that audits the accounts of central government departments and other related public bodies, it is headed by the Comptroller and Auditor General – see also Audit Commission.

Net present value (NPV) – a measure of the present value of future in ows and out ows of money. Usually the cash amounts are multiplied by a 'discount rate' of the declining value of money in the period of the ow. In practice the period is usually taken as a year and all in ows and out ows are assumed to occur at the year end. Discount factor tables are widely available. The discount factors for 10 per cent over three years, for example, are 0.909, 0.862, and 0.751. To calculate the present value of any amount simply multiply it by the discount factor for that year. Thus £1000 paid in three years time equates to £751 in today's money assuming 10 per cent is a reasonable discount rate. In practice the number of cash in and out ows that have to be netted off to arrive at the NPV is usually rather large and most accountants use computer software to do the donkey work. A formula for the NPV calculation is:

NPV = The sum of each period's : $ai/(1+r)^i$

Where a is the cash in or out ow
i is the period number r is the discount rate

Other long-term outlay (OLTO) – capital works such as sewers, sea defences and so on usually provided by public authorities that will not normally have a commercial market value.

Payback period – the time taken for income earned to equal money invested. Usually calculated on a simple cash basis ignoring in ation. See also NPV.

Postings – usually the entries transferring amounts between accounts after they have been first recorded in the books of prime entry.

Preference shares – see shares.

Prepayment – a payment in advance part or all of which relates to a future accounting period.

Price-earnings ratio – market share price/net earnings per share (see earnings per share), useful for comparing different shares.

Pro t and loss account – summary of the changes in the revenue accounts over an accounting period. It will show the turnover (see turnover), followed by various deductions to arrive at a final balance as a net profit (gain) or loss, made during the period. The turnover is usually at the top of the profit and loss account followed by various deductions at different stages. Figures are usually shown for the profit remaining at each different stage. For example, *gross pro t* from the sale of basic goods and services, operating profit from ordinary trading activities, any extraordinary profits from unusual activities and the profit before and after tax. A very basic format is shown below.

*Sales turnover			XXXXX
less cost of sales			XX
gross profit			XXX
less expenses:			
admin	X		
heat	X		
salaries	X		
a/cts fees	X		
bank charges	X		
,etc		xx	
net profit			X

* opening stock
\+ purchase
– closing stock

Provisions – amounts deducted from profits to provide for depreciation, renewals, and other specific and predictable future needs.

Public expenditure borrowing requirement (PSBR) – the net public services expenditure requirement after taxation and other income required to be funded by government borrowing.

Public works loan board (PWLB) – a government body that is able to provide long-term loans to public authorities at favourable interest rates because of the size and borrowing power of government.

Reserves – profits and other general retention accumulated in the business for less predictable reasons than provisions (see provisions).

Revenue – see capital.

Rights issue – see shares.

Sale and leaseback – see leasing.

Securities – see shares and gilts.

Shares – most are ordinary shares (also called *equity*) – an entitlement to a share in a company: a share of its profits in the form of a *dividend*, usually so many pence per share, paid out by the directors at annual or similar intervals from the profits left over after tax and transfers to reserves and provisions. Any final profits left after dividends are accumulated in the profit and loss account. Ordinary shares usually entitle the shareholder to vote on matters raised in the shareholders meetings that decide broad company policy and any particularly controversial matters. *Preference shares* – more like a loan to the company in that these pay out a fixed dividend before any entitlement to ordinary shareholders and sometimes carry voting rights too. If dividends were missed one year because of low profits some holders of *cumulative preference shares* will receive their missed fixed dividend before any new dividends are paid out in the next profitable year. *Rights issue* – sometimes when new shares are issued to raise equity capital, existing shareholders are given rights to the new shares in proportion to their current holdings. If new shares are issued freely to existing shareholders this is called a *scrip issue*, it has the effect of cutting the share price.

Sinking fund – see depreciation.

Stag – an investor who thinks a particular new share issue is under-priced and intends to sell them as soon as dealing begins.

Statutory accounts – those required by law, particularly the annual accounts of limited companies that have to be filed with the Registrar of Companies; also the accounts of registered charities, building societies, housing associations, local authorities, government departments and other publicly accountable bodies required to prepare accounts by law.

Stocks – goods held for ordinary trading purposes. Also used to refer to investments such as shares traded on the stock market.

Suspense account – a temporary or *holding* account used for posting items that require further clarification.
Swap – usually refers to different borrowers swapping the interest payments on their loans, for example, if one has a fixed and another a variable interest loan or between interest due in different currencies.
Tangible asset – fixed and current assets that have a measurable, material existence.
Testing – usually in the context of audit testing. The auditor typically undertakes of both tests the operation of internal controls (see internal control) called *compliance tests* and tests to verify directly the accuracy, completeness and validity of individual transactions and account balances; these are called *substantive tests*.
Trial balance – see balance.
Turnover – the value of sales after netting off the value of any goods returned back into the business.
VFM – value for money: commonly used to describe all aspects of economy, efficiency and effectiveness under one heading, for example, 'to carry out a VFM audit'.
Virement – the transfer of under-spends or reallocated amounts from one budget heading to another, often used in publicly accountable bodies such as government departments and local authorities.
Vouch – to check or agree an item recorded in the accounts. *Voucher(s)*; the document(s) referred to when vouching.
Work in progress – work done to date on an uncompleted contract, project or production run.
Write off – in respect of a debt: to reduce in full or part a debt incorrectly entered in the accounts. Write offs usually require some formal approval as part of control over debtors. The term is sometimes used less strictly in respect of entries to accounts other than debts. If a debt is found not to be due it may simply be *cancelled*, usually a less formal procedure.
Yield – usually the return on an investment compared to its current market price, or if measured over the return throughout its life the *yield to maturity*. There are a great many measures of yield used in different investing situations and short- or long-term projects.

APPENDIX

14 *Selected Cases by Theme of Perpetration*

Introduction

Here we have selected some of the more infamous cases and some that are less well known but illustrate perfectly a particular type of case and its basic cause and method of perpetration. Sometimes the best illustrations have been chosen from outside the public services but the basic theme and potential risks still apply to public services organizations. We have divided the cases into eight broad themes in an attempt to show the common characteristics.

Broad risks underlying perpetration:

1 Charismatic override
2 Corporate malaise
3 Expenditure weaknesses
4 Contracts and cartels
5 Corporate wide deception.

Specific public services risks:

6 Housing benefit and related frauds
7 Health frauds
8 Advance fee fraud.

The first five themes have been chosen because they broadly illustrate risks that can be applied across a wide spectrum of organizations while the last three are themes which, while they may have some wider applicability, are relatively specialized. Some of the cases involve huge amounts and some relatively small sums, though it is generally not the amount involved that matters so much as the manner of perpetration. All eight themes illustrate the importance of maintaining effective internal controls as stressed throughout this book.

This division by perpetration links cases and presents a convenient basis for their consideration and analysis but it does have some disadvantages. Most cases involve more than one aspect and cut across more than one theme. The themes are not classified in terms of the foregoing chapters which are designed to aid our understanding of the subject. It must always be remembered that fraudsters do not think in terms of classification and analysis and in this appendix we should not allow such conveniences to hamper our own versatility of thinking.

Some broad types of fraud are not included, for example, e-commerce fraud, complex computer-based fraud, credit card fraud or identity theft. Such classes of fraud may not be particularly prevalent in the public services or may be subsumed for convenience within one of the chosen themes. But space in a short book like this is limited, so we hope readers will find the choice of cases useful and apologize for leaving out any that people may, for whatever reason, feel should have been included.

At the start of each theme the main characteristics of typical cases are summarized. After each theme one or two short cross-references are listed, to readable articles or reports, related to the cases quoted. This is followed by a summary of the possible lessons to be learned.

Theme 1 – charismatic override

Typical identifying characteristics:

Single dominant perpetrator.
Risks not appreciated or addressed by management.
Internal control ineffective or virtually absent
Internally driven fraud.

These frauds are those of the dominant and/or highly trusted personality. Usually the rogue character (or very small close-knit clique), is at the top of the organization, though not always. Almost any area of business or public service can suffer from such people and from a senior position the tentacles of their wrongdoing and poisonous in uence may spread like a cancer, first to their close peers, then throughout the organization. If they are lower down the hierarchy their in uence may with luck be limited to their own 'fiefdom' of responsibility. Many of the controls and countermeasures raised in the previous chapters would be effective at countering such fraudsters – if only such controls were in place or had been operated effectively. But such fraudsters have the charisma, in uence, dominance, or are otherwise able to project the malign trait manifest in their personalities, to prevent or override such controls. Sometimes they are threatening people, able to intimidate their juniors, sometimes they are surrounded by the untrained and naive, sometimes they are highly respected or simply liked and trusted. The effect is the same – it makes their malicious intentions easy both to achieve and conceal.

THE GRAYS BUILDING SOCIETY

Although this case may seem a little dated, as it did not come to light until the late 1970s, it was something of a landmark case and well illustrates a theme 1 case. The Report of the Registrar of Friendly Societies was presented to Parliament by the Chancellor of the Exchequer in May 1979 (Cmnd 7557) and it reads like a novel.

The fraudster was Harold Percy Jaggard, the respected and trusted Chairman and Secretary of the Grays Building Society. It turned out that for many years Mr Jaggard had been eecing the Society, though no one seemed to have realized what was going on. Then one Friday as a routine audit was in progress he left the office and was not seen again until later that evening when he was found dead in his bath. A suicide note left for his wife read:

> Do not go into thc bathroom alone. For forty years I have tried to put somebody else's misdeeds right and I can take no more. Chapman no blame at all. Be good to my relations. Love H.

Mr Jaggard had used various techniques, all of which were aimed at getting his hands on cash and covering his trail. But during that last fateful audit, discrepancies were spotted, the trail had started to unravel and the truth to come out. He must have realized the game was up by the Friday lunchtime. The Chief Cashier recalled:

> He [Jaggard] must have been upstairs with the auditors. He came downstairs. We heard him come down. He has a distinctive walk. He put his hat and coat on and said 'I won't be long. I'll be about twenty minutes'. That was about twenty past twelve, and he never came back.

One of the main techniques used by Mr Jaggard was 'teeming and lading' which is a common risk among smaller establishments where cash is handled, though one might have expected sufficient controls to have been in place in a building society to have prevented this. Basically cash that should be promptly banked is held over and used, perhaps for gambling as with Mr Jaggard, or 'borrowed' and later replaced. In the Grays case the discrepancies, in the cash that should have been banked, were hidden by banking cheques earlier than originally planned. The banking procedures were rather lax and even when Mr Jaggard was away the same procedures were followed – though the cash was not then misused by the staff.

Mr Jaggard also took large value cheques from the post, usually mortgage redemption cheques, when the post was opened and used these in the same way, to cover his theft of cash. The mortgagor would still be sent the deeds on the property and Jaggard would ensure the account was closed, marked redeemed, even though the payment had not been entered up, or had been entered falsely, in the Society books.

Mr Jaggard even stole investor's cheques, issued false passbooks and sought to bleed the Society of cash and falsify its accounts at various points and times throughout his long criminal career. Although these other sources were much riskier for him he was still able to conceal what was happening for many years.

Anyone reading the full report today would ask, surely he would not get away with it nowadays? Sadly subsequent history indicates a modern day Jaggard might well be able to commit a modern version of the Grays scandal. Jaggard had relied on a widespread lack of understanding among his own staff, particularly understanding of financial controls such as separation of duties, accounting reconciliations, sound double-entry bookkeeping practices and so on. Proper internal controls had either never been put in place or had simply been openly overridden by Mr Jaggard.

The Society itself, while not excessively small for the industry at that time (one main branch and at various times one or two sub-branches) was small enough for Mr Jaggard to keep a close eye on almost everything that went on. No one questioned why the man at the top would be present at such everyday functions as post opening or cashing up and take upon himself certain routine financial duties, or that some customers accounts would be handled directly through him.

> He [Jaggard] occupied a central and dominant position. He was the boss. He was able to, and did, interfere persistently and extensively in the Society's accounting procedures. He opened the post; he served at the cashier's counter; he prepared the banking; he posted entries himself in the ledgers and the share summaries; he opened new accounts for customers, heading

> the ledger sheets himself and issuing passbooks in his own hand; and he adjusted the year end summaries after the office staff had reconciled them

Occasionally some of the more experienced or senior staff appeared to have had doubts but Mr Jaggard appears to have been easily able to satisfy these.

> Nobody at the Grays regarded Mr Jaggards behaviour as unusual. The staff were all untrained and none realized the implications of Mr Jaggard's interference or regarded his dominance as undesirable.

The risks, the controls, the lessons to be learned are all readily apparent from a reading of the full report and nowadays there is arguably more widespread appreciation of sound controls and staff training throughout the financial and public services. Yet cases like this continue to occur. It may be easy for senior managers to say nothing like the Grays could happen in their organization, or that the auditors should have spotted what was going on, but in practice what matters is relatively junior staff who understand the importance of controls and are willing and able to question things. Quite often a fraudster like Jaggard will deliberately seek out inexperienced and/or easily in uenced personnel and when public funds are at stake it is often the case that no one, least of all inexperienced juniors, will be personally concerned at apparent misuse. Although a building society would not nowadays be considered as part of the public services, in those days the distinction was often viewed less decisively, as small societies in particular were assumed to be acting in the public interest and virtually dependant on the government allowing them to retain part of the tax on the investors interest.

THE 'LAIRD OF TOMINTOUL'

Like Mr Jaggard in the last case, Anthony Williams held a senior position of trust: he was Deputy Director of Finance at the Metropolitan Police Force in London until 1994. He swindled £5 million over a period of about eight years from special accounts under his direct control but for which no clear authorizing or proper budgeting and reconciliation controls were in place. Like Jaggard, Williams was trusted, respected and able to set up the accounts, overriding what few controls existed. His very senior position seems to have encouraged junior finance staff to accept his verbal explanations and the auditors too seem not to have enquired as far as they might into what was happening or the apparent lack of control. As at the Grays the Met was not, at that time, as well staffed by trained and qualified people as one might have expected; Williams was not a qualified accountant even though this was the norm among staff at this level in other police forces and most public services bodies.

Some of the key factors behind this fraud were reported as being:

- The generally very poor level of internal financial control that was tolerated at the time, not just in systems set up by Williams but widely throughout the Met.
- The operation of secret bank accounts under the control of one person, Williams, with no effective financial accountability to others.
- No discreet scrutiny of Williams' lavish lifestyle, which was far beyond his salary. He owned properties in the South of England, Spain and Tomintoul, a village and extensive estates in the Highlands of Scotland for which he was seen as a wealthy benefactor.
- The reluctance of the external auditor, the NAO, to insist on better financial control and budgetary accountability from an early stage.
- The failure of the Met to respond positively to the limited warnings the NAO had given.
- The recruitment of Williams, with no formal accountancy qualification and little relevant experience, to a senior post where his work went unchallenged and there was no effective mechanism for accountability to 'director' level.

ROBERT MAXWELL AND MIRROR GROUP NEWSPAPERS

Although this is a very complex case from the private rather than the public services, it does give some useful illustrations. Much has been written on this case and it would be impossible for any summary to do justice to all the dishonesty and fraud perpetrated primarily by Mr Maxwell. However certain events and the implication for risk and control apply widely throughout many organizations and sectors.

Robert Maxwell is infamous for his pillage of the pension fund of the Mirror Group Newspapers plc and bringing ruin or near ruin in 1991 to a range of companies including the Maxwell Communication Corporation. Yet twenty years earlier a 1971 report from the Department of Trade and Industry investigation into Pergamon Press Ltd showed he had something of a record of untrustworthiness.

> We regret having to conclude that, notwithstanding Mr Maxwell's acknowledged abilities and energy he is not in our opinion a person who can be relied upon to exercise proper stewardship of a publicly quoted company.

Such evidence of his character went largely unheeded. Mr Maxwell did indeed have business acumen and he managed to turn around the near bankrupt British Printing Corporation, taking control and renaming it Maxwell Communications Corporation. He obscured the ultimate ownership of this and other companies behind various intercompany relationships, secretly controlling them via a Foundation based in Liechtenstein.

Although the private companies, pension funds and listed companies such as the Mirror Group oated in 1991 should have been operated as separate entities, each looked after by their own boards and directors with proper financial controls and measures to ensure corporate governance and accountability, in fact Mr Maxwell was able to treat them all as his personal empire. He was able, despite involving his bankers and the scrutiny of auditors, to move funds and assets between the different entities, devise intercompany loans, collateral and controlled their bank accounts. As the Summary to the Department of Trade and Industry Report says:

> Mr Robert Maxwell ran his companies and the pension funds as if they were one. He moved assets between them as best suited his overall interests. However the complex ownership and financial structure of his empire and the concealment of the use of the pension funds made it difficult for banks to gain a clear picture of the financial strength of his empire. The practice was to be 'economic with the information' supplied to them. Although all the groups of companies and pension funds within Mr Robert Maxwell's empire were audited, they were not audited at a common date. Nor was there any overview of the empire as a whole.

Although, with the benefit of hindsight, bankers and auditors might have been more wary and senior directors and other employees more questioning, Maxwell was a charismatic leader against whom it was often difficult to make a stand.

Suggested references: on the Grays case, the aforementioned report of the Registrar; on the Williams case, an article by Tim Weeks in *Accountancy Age*, 22 June 1995 neatly summarizes the main concerns of this case; on the Maxwell case, see the *Financial Times* online summary of the DTI report, 30 March 2001.

Lessons

More than any other cause the lack of effective, often quite basic, financial controls is at the heart of the problem in cases such as these: separations of duty, reconciliation, levels of authorization and so on are often missing or their significance is not appreciated. Charismatic override is made easy because controls are simply not in place or are very weak at the outset and discarded as the fraudster becomes more and more respected. Ignorance and incompetence too play a part: those around such characters are reluctant to question their authority and are unlikely to have a full grasp of what is happening. Controls implicit in sound corporate governance and recruitment are also essential and often missing from these cases.

Theme 2 – corporate malaise

Typical identifying characteristics:

- Multiple perpetrators, sometimes led from the top.
- Risks generally unappreciated and poorly addressed by management, who may fear 'rocking the boat'.
- Internal control is ineffective, or in some organizations only applied selectively.
- Internally driven fraud though some cases of external collusion/abuse of power.

This theme is essentially about corporate culture and the cancer-like spread of cultural norms that tolerate or even promote fraud and corruption. Although this theme has something in common with the first theme, it is unusual for a single individual or even a small clique to allow others to follow their example to any significant extent and thus weaken their own control or lessen their rake-off. The charismatic fraudster does not like to feel threatened by subordinates and at the same time usually depends on a veneer of respectability that would easily be split wide open by corporate-wide malaise. In the private sector, corporate corruption malaise is usually relatively short-lived; shareholders will desert the company or install a new broom to sweep the stable clean, or the corporation will fall prey to takeover or even bankruptcy. In the public services, such malaise can last much longer, some might say for generations and point to the former communist regimes of the Soviet eastern bloc countries. But for now we will concentrate on the seriously corrupt but not permanent malaise that can still affect Western-style democracies such as our own.

THE DISTRICT AUDITOR'S REPORT TO THE LONDON BOROUGH OF LAMBETH, MAY 1993

The first thing to say about this case is that the District Auditor's report did not find evidence of theft of monies or recommend any prosecutions for fraud or corruption. Though after reading the report one may be tempted to ask, why not?

The sheer scale of the malaise is indicated when the District Auditor says, in a manner that barely manages to conceal what must be a feeling of exasperation:

> For several years the Council has had many and various problems. It has been criticized by me, my predecessors and others. Since 1979 District Auditors have issued 17 separate audit reports in the public interest. These and annual Management Letters have regularly highlighted the need for improvements

Many unresolved issues remained at that time, including unlawful items in the accounts, but the main thrust of the report revolved around the awarding works contracts to the Direct Labour Organization (DLO). Capital contracts, mainly for highways and housing works, should have been awarded on the basis of regulations aimed at encouraging fair competition and best value but procedures were manipulated to favour the DSO and award hefty profit-share bonuses to staff. Many problems lay behind the failures to produce proper accounts including poor internal control and management practices, lack of accountability, self-serving arrangements and massive over-spending on projects, salaries and so on. However the main problem was the spreading cultural malaise that encouraged tolerance of poor performance, deliberate undermining of selected policies, and acceptance of corrupt attitudes.

The general financial management and accounting arrangements also featured prominently in the District Auditor's report, together with substantial overpayment of salaries (mainly to teachers) and poor control over capital investments.

> It is now eight years since the council last published its annual accounts on time Numerous targets have been set deadlines set by the former Chief Executive, the Director of Finance and the Chief Accountant have all been missed It is clear that my audit opinions when they are eventually published are likely to be heavily qualified. The Council's overall financial health is sapped by the substantial arrears of income

To be fair to Lambeth, by the year 2000 the accounts were up to date (the 1993 ones eventually had 42 separate qualifications) and things are much improved, but this is a landmark case of what can, and sadly still does, go wrong in public services.

HULL CITY COUNCIL

Just in case one is tempted to imagine that the Lambeth case is a unique situation, unlikely ever to repeat itself, it is worth noting that similar cases have come to light both before and since. The 2002 Audit Commission's Corporate Governance Inspection Report into Hull was one of several similar investigations into local authorities. In Hull the main problems seem to have centred around the actions of elected councillors embroiled in political infighting and the report tells of widespread mismanagement, a culture of bullying, financial *'meltdown'* and *' improper practice in the award and running of contracts'*.

THE EUROPEAN UNION

There have been very many reported examples of EU fraud, particularly in this category, that one is tempted to suggest dismantling the EU and starting again. The ousting of the infamous president Santer and his Commissioner cronies in 2000 following Paul van Buitenen's allegations of gross fraud and corruption, did for a while make it look like a new start was being made. But compared to any single local authority or other public body the EU is very large and complex and once corporate malaise has taken hold the solution will rarely stop with a few individuals at the top. It was not long before the same sort of allegations began to reappear, followed by the same response of attacking the whistle-blowers, such as chief accountant Marta Andreasen, and indications that nothing had really changed. Subsequent reports plainly indicate this situation and the malaise seems to continue. By August 2002 van Buitenen was still describing the measures that had been put in place by the EU as 'window dressing' and its former chief accountant had already described the budget as 'out of control'. Auditors reports had already drawn attention to around 7 per cent of the EU 60 billion euro budget being wasted via errors and fraud, including the astounding case of € 35m of EU farm subsidy to Greece being diverted into farm workers 'insurance payments' and 'administrative costs' of farmers' unions.

The root of the problem seems to lie in the lack of a culture of sound financial control and accountability. It is difficult to see how such a culture can be instilled when even the Union's own anti-fraud office under Neil Kinnock have been accused of being part of the cover up. Such allegations may of course be said of other organizations that have turned out to be corrupt and some that have not. The problems of corporate malaise are magnified by the tendency of politically-driven bodies to want to spend money – a spending culture. Investigations have highlighted that poor internal controls over spending are behind many of the frauds. One report notes the EU tendency to see spending as an objective, a response to new political initiatives, ' *to help the commission to make a political mark'* as it says. This tendency in an organization already steeped in corporate malaise is like a magnet to fraudsters. Officials are put under pressure to award contracts, there are rapid increases in spending, budgets with little or no commensurate resources put into control, performance being judged by spending that is, inputs rather than more difficult to measure impacts or outputs: such weaknesses are easily recognized by those who deal with public services organizations and by any corrupt officials within. They know no one will be closely watching how much is spent on this or that invoice or contract, or asking why a particular contract was let to a particular outside body, or why something cost more than might have been expected. Even if anyone does raise questions almost any sensible-sounding excuse will suffice. They know too that calls for more internal control can easily be countered by saying that this will simply lead to more red tape, as it well might if red tape means clear trails of accountability and openness to public scrutiny. But in any part of the public services, when being seen to be spending money becomes a political goal, the lack of commercial cost constraints and sound internal controls almost always leads to waste and often to fraud. The EU is like any other public services body in many ways. But because it is so complex and transcends borders it is particularly difficult to control and hold to account. It is not the only large public body to be riddled with political rivalries or lack direct accountability to elected politicians – one might think of the United Nations too. But these problems have been compounded by a long history of politically driven spending objectives and a corporate malaise culture that is prone to fraud; and while it is fair to draw attention to the EU's own recognition of such faults, particularly via the European Court of Auditors and the setting up of its anti-fraud office OLAF, such measures largely address the symptoms, not the root causes.

Suggested references: the aforementioned reports by the Audit Commission and the NAO, an article by Richard Watson in *Public Finance* in 1999 titled 'Europe's Rising Tide of Fraud' and a summary article in January 2001 in the journal *Internal Auditing and Business Risk.*

LESSONS

Corporate malaise is very difficult to uproot in a public services context, particularly in bodies not subject to competition or takeovers. Even Compulsory Competitive Tendering (CCT), loathed in many bureaucratic quarters, merely hived-off some discrete, relatively commercially viable services. Often CCT, while bringing some efficiencies, transferred vulnerable lower grade staff to new employers while leaving the 'fat cat' career bureaucrats behind with more opportunities and temptations via the liaison with outside bodies, contract design, awarding and management of the client side. Yet objective measures of output performance are one of the effective counters to corporate malaise in the public services. In the UK much work has been done to design and implement performance indicators, for example via best value reviews in local government and the use of 'comprehensive performance indicators'. Where such measures do indeed enhance accountability, running from the top to the bottom of an organization and used to compare performance between bodies, they can indeed counter corporate malaise. This is often seen mainly as a value for money (VFM) issue, though it is also important in countering fraud and corruption. Most importantly, it is essential that the measuring and reporting of such performance is channelled via reasonably powerful and independent third parties such as auditors and others that can not be pressured by the bodies themselves.

Once again one of the recurring lessons from this category of fraud cases is the need for sound, effective and accountable internal control. In the public services while all areas of control are important, controls over expenditure (see Chapter 6) and over major contracts (see Chapter 4) are especially vital.

Theme 3 – expenditure weaknesses

Typical identifying characteristics:

Multiple perpetrators.
Risks generally appreciated and addressed by

management but this is an oft-underestimated source of routine, maintenance-type risk.

Internal control is often in place and relatively effective in some organizations but ineffective in others; the effectiveness of control often varies over time.

Externally and internally driven, cases of internal collusion/abuse of power.

This is a very broad theme including mainly sundry payments but it could also be taken to include payment of benefits, refunds and so on and it overlaps to some extent with contract payments. Revenue contract frauds in particular are often more within this theme than contracts and cartels. Surveys generally show this as a high frequency area, where the numbers of individual cases are large though most are for relatively small amounts. The main risk is that a fraudster exploits a fundamental weakness in the system over a long period of time, leading to very large losses in the long run.

This is a theme that affects all areas of the economy, private and public services alike. Although the examples here are taken from the public services, very similar ones could have been taken from almost any area of commerce and industry.

Audit Viewpoint summarizes many of these cases in local authorities, one for example related to a senior accountant in a local authority who created false invoices and processed these through the system, collecting the cheques himself. Clearly cheques should not be routed back through the system, though it is conceivable that a fraudster would use a 'safe' address prepared in advance or used in collusion with someone who opens post at that address.

> A senior accountant in the city engineers department carried out a fraud totalling nearly £265 000 over a few years. He raised fictitious invoices with the same initials as a voluntary body of which he was the treasurer. Cheques made out to these initials were collected by the fraudster and paid into the voluntary body's bank account over which he had complete control, before the amounts were paid into a third account from which he withdrew the monies. (He even audited the voluntary body's accounts and pretended that it had been done independently.)

Another example related to an assistant financial controller in a health authority who cunningly manipulated payments via BACS.

> The assistant financial controller was responsible for the reconciliation of creditor payments to input controls and production of the payment run. He was able to make payments via BACs into his own bank account without source documentation, as fictitious payments to real suppliers. Fraudulent payments totalling £78 000 were made over two years. He had access to the passwords giving controlling access to the BACS transmissions. He subsequently deleted the bank details from the system and removed the print showing the payees bank details from the files. The authority subsequently included better separation of duties and access controls over BACS.

Many, many more examples could be given. Cheques, even blank ones, left unattended and stolen, some with pre-printed signatures! Collusion with suppliers, creation of false suppliers, claimants, and so on details, in ated and false orders, and so on. Sometimes management are tempted to turn a blind eye to petty expenses fraud. This always encourages the problem and simply makes higher levels seem tolerable; sometimes senior management even try to cover up or deny the extent of such fraud simply to minimize bad feelings with their staff. Some of the saddest examples of this involve reluctance to allow full and unimpeded access to auditors. In ated claims for doctors expenses were the subject of a report to the Public Accounts Committee (PAC) of the House of Commons in 1999 following NHS attempts to restrict access by internal audit.

> MPs have issued a formal protest at the way an NHS internal auditor was ordered to stop his investigations   A report by the PAC said the order from the NHS chiefs came after the internal auditor reported that nine GP practices were presenting high patterns of night visit claims. In his report to the audit committee of the agency   the internal auditor identified possible overclaims amounting to £177 000

Top managers, sometimes rightly, feel that however innocent they may be any publicity relating to fraud within their management remit will have serious repercussions for them as well as the fraudsters. It is worth noting that when Carlo Trojan, the European Commission's Secretary General, was interviewed early on about the evidence that eventually forced the resignations of the Commissioners, his response was an angry one: *There is not a fundamental problem with the management of commission programmes ...what are you insinuating?*

Suggested references: most editions of *Audit Viewpoint*, published by the Audit Commission,

Internal Auditing and Business Risk published by the IIA, and to a lesser extent *Accountancy Age* published by VNU Business Publications contain summaries of expenditure fraud cases such as those above.

LESSONS

At first sight expenditure, involving money going out of the organization and invariably subject to recording, presents many opportunities for financial control and accountability, from initial generating of orders, claims and so on to eventual reconciliation of bank accounts. Expenditure fraud should be preventable in large organizations, particularly public bodies. But the reality is often very different. Expenditure systems often exhibit the characteristics of neglected maintenance systems (Chapter 3, page 43). There is nothing glamorous or intellectually stimulating for most finance staff in agreeing invoices to orders, or the numerous authorizations, reconciliations and other financial control features. But beating the system and gaining wealth, well, such a challenge will be beyond resistance for some, particularly the greedy and anyone who is disillusioned with their work. But then, the same could be said of many working environments; are those encompassed within this theme more prone to disillusionment?

Probably not, but expenditure ows always suffer from weak points that simply offer temptations to fraudsters. Most cases involve absence or breakdown in key controls such as those outlined in Chapter 3. The vital lesson is that it is difficult to keep such controls operating at peak effectiveness in systems where high reliance is placed on routine. If the controls are always followed as a matter of strict routine then they have a good chance of being effective. But the temptation is for junior staff not to appreciate the importance of the routine procedures and paper work and for senior staff to feel they are capable of circumventing controls or trusting others, perhaps 'rubber stamping' an authorization. Even when poorly controlled systems are improved, some years later the underlying attitudes can still prevail and the controls need improving again. Insisting on following internal controls such as say separations of duty, can sometimes smack of mistrust and it can be difficult to convince people that such insistence is no re ection on the staff involved. This is particularly difficult when one considers that the vast majority of staff involved in such maintenance systems are likely to be perfectly trustworthy and most cases of expenditure fraud come as a shock to others in the workplace.

Theme 4 – contracts and cartels

Typical identifying characteristics:

- Multiple perpetrators, led from the top of third party organizations.
- Risks generally appreciated and poorly addressed by management who may lack the necessary skills in identifying risky situations.
- Internal control is often complex and relatively ineffective, or in some organizations only applied selectively.
- Externally driven fraud, though some cases of internal collusion/abuse of power.

From the previous theme it is natural to move on to this one. An organization does not have to be in a state of corporate malaise to suffer from fraud and corruption in the area of contracts (though such a state often encourages fraud in this area). In the public services there has always been a long tradition of awarding large contracts to private companies: the Ministry of Defence and local authorities, for example.

Cost overruns and unfair/illegal tendering procedures are often at the heart of contract frauds, though these may be complicated by poor budgets and estimated, unneeded works, poor quality, payments that are (often mysteriously) miscalculated and con icts of interest. At the risk of repeating a theme it is worth noting that in 2001 a Belgian report stated the contract for renovating the EU headquarters in Brussels was likely to cost 700m euros compared to the original 100m. In this country the Treasury publish an annual Fraud Survey (see the Bibliography) which details the types and causes of frauds reported by central government departments and it is interesting to note the details of contract frauds which cover a wide range of contracts, not just major capital works.

There is a wide range of possible fraudulent activities connected with contracts, and although those connected with widespread corporate corruption are often for very large amounts as indicated in the last theme, most are for relatively small amounts and relate to a limited number of contracts. The two examples below are from many others summarized in *Audit Viewpoint*.

> A highways inspector and a contractor colluded to defraud a council of £86 000 over 18 months. The contractor created invoices for fictitious work, the inspector passed these through the payments system. False authorization and coding slips were attached to the false invoices and an authorizing officer's initials were forged.

A street lighting contractor invoiced and was paid by a council approximately £500 000 for changing lamps. Although the payments were passed and the contract was genuine, subsequent review of lamp failure statistics and work invoiced, by internal audit and the council's engineers, revealed the work had not taken place.

Cartels are often more serious than individual frauds relating to a single contract but they are usually very difficult to spot. The presence of a cartel may perhaps be indicated by all quotes being higher than expected, relatively small select lists of contractors or regular winners from among a small group. The summary recommended below, also from *Audit Viewpoint*, indicates how difficult this can be to detect.

Suggested references: regular summaries (in more detail than given above) are available in *Audit Viewpoint*, published quarterly by the Audit Commission.

LESSONS

Public services contracts inevitably attract some level of fraud risk. The salaried public servant is often placed under pressure and some people will always be tempted to act improperly when very large sums are at stake. On the contractor side the entire future of a firm may hang on the winning of a large government contract. This is a volatile mixture of temptation and pressure. Key controls along the lines suggested in Chapter 4 are vital, as are clear lines of financial and public accountability.

Theme 5 – corporate wide deception

Typical identifying characteristics:

- Multiple perpetrators and/or 'ruling clique' of perpetrators.
- Risks generally known but ignored or underestimated by management, development-type risks related to financial expansion and accounting.
- Internal control is often ineffective as top people override corporate governance and internal regulations.
- Externally and internally driven, cases of collusion/abuse of power between directors and external auditors.

This category is similar to and often overlaps that of corporate malaise. But now there is a more active attempt to hide the widespread fraud and corruption from outside parties. It is as if the body corporate, at least among its senior managers and directors, acts in unison to perpetuate a wide ranging cover-up. In the corporate malaise situation senior officials may attempt to deny or cover up particular events but the organization will keep on going at least for the foreseeable future – it is not faced with direct threat of bankruptcy as a result of disclosure. Usually some measure of monopoly protection characterizes ongoing malaise whereas in this category the whole fraud is hidden from the start, otherwise financial confidence would collapse. This means that corporate-wide deception is more of a problem in the competitive, private sector whereas ongoing malaise is more common in the public or near monopoly situations. Though exceptions to both trends can occur.

ENRON

The collapse of the Enron corporation is perhaps one of the most devastating examples. Though the dust has yet to settle on this case, there can be no doubt that senior directors and even the external auditors were involved in hiding the true extent of Enron's off-balance sheet liabilities from the public view and perpetuating a false picture of financial soundness when the reverse was true. This case is complex and not yet fully open to public scrutiny. However various reports are emerging and it is remarkable that internal auditing was out-sourced to the external auditors, Andersens, whose staff and former staff took on key roles and in uence inside Enron.

THE QUEENS MOAT HOUSE HOTELS

This case, though much earlier and smaller, is similar in many respects to the way the much larger case of Enron is unfolding. The directors adopted aggressive accounting policies that hid the true financial position. The auditors colluded with the directors and were involved in in uencing decisions. Eventually the true financial situation became so far removed from the deception perpetrated that it was impossible to hide. When the accounting situation was eventually cleared up the results, going back to 1991, had to be restated. QMH had shown a profit of £90.4 million for that year which had to be restated as a loss of £56.3 million!

The market went into a state of shock when the shares were suspended – QMH had been the darling of the stock exchange. Then came the inevitable question – although unusually, it was who, not where, were the auditors?

Julia Irvine, *Accountancy*, June 2001

The auditors turned out to be a small virtually unheard of firm, Bird Luckin, who had acted for QMH for 24 years since its creation. BL supplied a wide range of audit and non-audit services, even having their senior partner sit in on routine board meetings! They worked on the personal affairs of QMH directors and ex-BL staff often went to work for QMH. Such standards were highly irregular and today would be considered totally unacceptable. This incestuous professional relationship had inevitably sucked both parties more and more deeply into the mire of corporate-wide deception.

The article in *Accountancy* sums up the case.

Suggested references: archived articles and updates available from the IIA, *Accountancy*, June 2001.

LESSONS

Perhaps such cases as these should be classified as 'audit failure' as this is one of the features they have in common. Surely one of the most important lessons to emerge from these and other cases is the vital position of the auditors and their independence. This is indeed emerging as important in the way corporate governance requirements are being reconsidered, particularly measures to increase the independence and impartiality of auditors. Another lesson is the way corporate-wide arrogance seems to accompany corporate-wide deception, a common failing of the powerful and insular.

Theme 6 – housing benefit and related frauds

Typical identifying characteristics:

Multiple perpetrators.
Risks generally appreciated and addressed by management, but size of problem is huge.
Internal control is more effective in some organizations than others but can not (yet?) completely eliminate the problem.
Externally driven fraud though some cases of internal collusion/abuse of power.

Although these two categories can be considered separately, housing benefit fraud is a major part of total benefit fraud and each usually has implications for the other. Many fraudsters abuse both housing and other benefits, grants and transfer payments in general.

Housing benefits

Although the number of cases and the overall size of the problem are huge, far outstripping the losses likely to be incurred from other sources of public services fraud, most individual cases are relatively small beer and escape widespread publicity. When the attention of the press is attracted to this area it is often to surveys, which while they illustrate the growing problem, do less to focus attention on cases or solutions.

Housing benefit frauds have much in common with the risks and controls outlined in Chapter 8. One of the main problems is the inbuilt incentive to falsify claims, forge supporting documents such as rent books, claim a tenant is still lodging after they have left, fail to declare earnings, and so on. In some London boroughs sample checks by internal audit in the 1990s estimated that about one-third of housing benefit cheques were likely to be for fraudulent claims and in Haringey the Council estimated that 10 per cent of all claims were fraudulent. There is little doubt that this area continues to dominate the statistics for public services fraud and the struggle to counter it is a war of attrition. Various reports have suggested countermeasures from the simplification of benefit regulation to widespread data matching. The solution, short of abolition of such benefits (which might itself have crime-enhancing effects in other areas) is likely to be complex and never reach perfection. A 1997 Audit Commission report, *Fraud and Lodging: tackling fraud and error in housing bene t*, proposed six key elements of a strategy to improve benefit administration and anti-fraud measures.

1 Corporate framework – including member support, reliable housing records, internal audit work, sound homelessness and assessment procedures.
2 Managing benefits administration efficiently – no backlogs, clear responsibilities, training, good communication with claimants and landlords.
3 Preventing fraud and error – adequate resources, internal defences, fraud awareness, national verification framework.
4 Managing investigations – terms of reference, clear procedures, targets, code of conduct for investigations, cutting down on cheque abuse.
5 Investigating cases – rent allowance and rent rebate, residency investigations, proactive work, data matching, cutting down on overpayments.

6 Deterrence – recovery, fixed penalties, prosecution.

BENEFIT FRAUD IN GENERAL

In February 2003 a report by the Comptroller and Auditor General to the House of Commons, *Tackling Bene t Fraud,* examined the size and nature of the problem and the role of the Department for Work and Pensions who spend about £100 billion a year on welfare benefits. The report mentions that around £2 billion are lost to fraud mainly via housing benefit, income support and jobseekers allowance. The report ranges over many aspects of this type of fraud and the governments responses. It highlights the operational situation: the complexity of the claims and the administration involved – likely in itself to encourage or hide fraudulent actions – and the complex organizational changes and information technology initiatives being undertaken. It stresses the need for more rigorous vetting of new and high risk claims and is concerned at the regional variations in investigations and the falling number of cases actually investigated. Greater cooperation is sought with other agencies and departments, particularly with local government, to fight housing benefit fraud.

The report is something of a global critique of the administration and as such it is excellent. It is clearly aimed at a strategic view of bureaucratic directions: its recommendations include measures such as '*addressing the decline in* ' and ' *raising regional performances* ' or ' *assessing the effects of initiatives* ' and so on. But, like many top level reports it tends to shy away from the detailed mechanics of what should actually be done or improved, how and by whom. This is perhaps understandable given the strategic orientation of the report. But this type of public services fraud usually involves the bottom of the organization, in this case where the outside world of desperate claimants meets the official world of rules, claim forms and interviews. Indeed, one of the key conclusions of the report is that fraudsters weigh up the situation and cheat the system '*when the gain from cheating outweighs the risk of detection and the likely penalty*'. The solutions presented by the report all sound sensible and difficult to fault, but tend to boil down to long-winded exhortations to lower officials to do more to prevent fraud and to get on top of the problem. More effort will be put into monitoring, comparing, evaluating, and so on. Whether this will actually result in fewer frauds remains to be seen. A summary of the overall conclusions is given below.

It is interesting to compare the current situation regarding benefit fraud with that regarding the centralized yet perhaps more practical approach taken to health fraud (see page 257).

LETTINGS

Social housing has presented a relatively high risk of fraud for many years. It is often difficult to pinpoint the causes, in particular cases from among the many failures in control and evidence of poor management. But at a macro level, breakdown of performance measurement or the link between performance and accountability/reward is, as is so often the case in large-scale bureaucracies, an underlying feature. Social housing has banished slum landlords who could take advantage of the poor, which is a great social benefit. But this has also meant the absence of individual landlords who will lose money if lettings are badly managed. It is now more likely that tenants (often claiming housing benefit), housing officials and others will take advantage of the 'landlord' that is, the public taxpayer and community charge payer. A report in the *Independent* in 1992 told of a housing officer who controlled her own property empire of over 100 council ats to which she sold the keys for a down payment of £1200 and a rent of £100 per week. The lettings and the control of the housing stock are often a complex set of arrangements and procedures involving 'voids' (properties temporarily unavailable for lettings) and 're-let repairs' (where properties are awaiting repairs after one tenant leaves and before another can be allocated). Some councils have inaccurate and outdated records of their housing stock and its condition, and so the true picture of what is available may be hidden from senior managers.

In recent years the position of stock records may have been improved by the need to update these prior to the sale of properties to housing associations but the problems and risks of control and management have not gone away, even if they have been devolved into more manageable chunks.

HOUSING REPAIRS

The cases just mentioned often involve abuse of the system for repairing properties. Sometimes properties that needed little if any repairs were kept off the available list while awaiting so-called repairs, sometimes unneeded repairs were charged to the housing revenue account (whether undertaken or not) and sometimes genuine repairs were overcharged. This area of fraud has links to the area of contract fraud covered in Chapter 4 and links into the theme of corporate malaise considered below.

Suggested reference: Tackling Bene t Fraud, Report by the Comptroller and Auditor General, 13 February 2003, HC 393.

LESSONS

Although much has been done in recent years to improve accountability and transparency in public services, social housing is an area that suffers from inbuilt disadvantages. The breakdown between performance and reward mentioned at the start of this section is difficult to avoid. Individual officials may be encouraged with performance-related schemes, though this is an area that is often short of such incentives. But, in common with much of the public services, such rewards are likely to be relatively minor or spread widely to achieve a common level of reward for normal competence. It is very difficult in public services bodies such as local authority departments or housing associations to mimic the cost consciousness, individual attention to detail, exible duties and knowledge of tenants common among successful, usually small, private landlords. However while many would argue that some level of economic inefficiency is worth paying for to increase social justice and standards of housing for the very poor, few may be as prepared to accept that this has to involve poor standards of probity and abuse of the system. The conclusion seems to point in the following directions.

Smaller and/or localized bodies where individual managers can achieve close supervision and both staff and managers can keep up to date and aware of the profile of tenants and claimants as well as the performance of contractors.

Sound internal controls over lettings, claims and contract performance, along the lines of Chapters 4 and 8 and possibly involving some degree of centralized checks and balances or at least regular audits.

Public campaigns to discourage tolerance of benefit cheats and the attitude of acceptability in eecing the public purse – such campaigns have already had some success in respect of central government-administered benefits.

Theme 7 – health frauds

Typical identifying characteristics:

Multiple perpetrators.

Risks here are generally difficult to assess and easily underestimated, often a source of routine maintenance-type risk.

Internal control is often in place and relatively effective in some organizations but ineffective in others, the effectiveness of control often varies over time.

Externally and internally driven, cases of internal collusion/abuse of power.

In the UK the National Health Service provides the vast bulk of healthcare despite the increasing role of private healthcare. Over the years it has suffered frauds that fall into the categories already mentioned. But like housing, health services generate some specialized concerns in combating fraud and to some extent the NHS has its own way of doing things.

The NHS is above all a political creation; in many ways it has been successful and emulated in other countries. Since the creation of the Ministry of Health in 1919 each new government has sought to put in place its own policy on health. There have been centralizations, decentralizations, increased layers of administration, fewer layers of administration, taking on board of market and commercial practices, shunning of such practices and a continual ow of new political and policy initiatives. Such a background creates uncertainty and sometimes insecurity. Although the NHS has not suffered from any of the large-scale redundancies that have hit traditional industries, 'de-layering' has hit many posts and morale has at times suffered, responsibilities have frequently changed hands, both within the NHS and between the NHS and third party organizations, and this has sometimes led to confusion. Fraudsters can of course take advantage of such a long running saga of change and reorganization. Corporate malaise, due sometimes to lack of clarity about shifting responsibilities or to disgruntled entrenched interests, can sometimes arise.

From a financial viewpoint the NHS may be considered a huge spending machine of great complexity, far more complex than any single government department, on a par in some ways with the totality of local government. As one might expect the service has suffered its share of expenditure, claims and contract-type frauds. The NHS Executive has issued breakdowns on a regular basis and these make interesting reading. But the nature of healthcare, with its undertones of personal vulnerability, gives some types of fraud, which are serious enough in any industry, an added dimension of urgency.

SUBSTITUTION FRAUDS

In any business fraudulent substitution by forging documentation or illegal display of brand names and so on can cause serious loss, but counterfeit medicine has even deeper implications than the financial loss, as reported in *The Times* 6 September 1998.

> *Gangs Target NHS with counterfeit medicine.*
> The NHS is being targeted with millions of pounds worth of counterfeit medicines by international criminal gangs Last week the health department confirmed that the Medicines Control Agency (MCA), which regulates drug supply, was working with Italian authorities after stolen and counterfeit drugs worth more than £7 million were seized . The Italian police secretly filmed the mafia-style gang for eight months before arresting them.
> Experts warn that although fake medicines identified within the NHS to date have proved inert or imperfect rather than toxic the risk of patients being poisoned by a 'bad' batch is growing. The World Health Organization estimates that as much as 10 per cent of the world's supply of branded medicines are counterfeit, rising to 50 per cent in some developing countries.

It was about the time of this article and a little earlier that concerns with NHS fraud were higher than they had been for some time. The Audit Commission reported 282 NHS cases worth £2.6 million, some of which seems to have related to false or in ated claims from health professionals such as doctors. At the same time in 1998 the Healthcare Financial Management Association estimated that the real value of frauds perpetrated over the past year was around £14 million. Of course no one really knew. A major part of the policy response was to set up a specialist NHS Counter Fraud Service (CFS), the first time this had been tried throughout the long years of policy initiatives.

As reported by Rachel Fielding in *Accountancy Age*, February 2003 the CFS seems to have made good progress claiming to have recovered almost £200 million in the first five years or so of its operations since 1999. The NHS CFS uses a fraud detection system that involves neutral networks – artificial systems capable of calculating where fraud is most likely to occur. In recent years the CFS has claimed its proactive approach has led to significant reductions in pharmaceutical patient fraud, dental patient fraud, optical patient fraud, and fraud by NHS professionals. Recent cases include the chief executive of one NHS trust who was prosecuted for £50 000 over mileage claims and a GP prosecuted for £800 000.

Suggested references: apart from the article mentioned above, NHS frauds tend to be well summarized in *Audit Viewpoint*.

LESSONS

The NHS undoubtedly faced a rising threat from fraud of various types and its response was to centre its counter-fraud effort under the direction of a unified CFS. There have been similar attempts of a more limited nature to unify counter-fraud initiatives on a sector or industry-wide basis, for example in local government and the insurance industries. But the NHS CFS seems to have been the most successful so far. Clearly the CFS has worked in conjunction with NHS management and particularly its internal audit services, and one of the great advantages for the CFS has been the relative transferability of situations and working environments across the NHS trusts. Even though no two frauds may be identical, common risks and countermeasures often are. Perhaps it will be more difficult to repeat the NHS CFS model in other areas of the public services, but together with the lessons from many audit and other agencies it offers at least some hope for the future.

Theme 8 – advance fee fraud

Also called 'West African' fraud, or 419 fraud after a section of the Nigerian law.

Typical identifying characteristics:

- Multiple perpetrators.
- Risks not appreciated by victim or addressed by management.
- Internal control ineffective or overridden when victim is acting in a corporate capacity.
- Externally driven fraud.

This fraud operates at both a personal level, where unfortunate individuals are the victims, and at a corporate level when the victims are whole organizations. It has been going on for many years in various guises, like a mutating virus attacking the gullible and greedy.

Individual public servants tend to be located in easily identified offices, be very active in the use of emails, e-government activities and similar, their email and ordinary postal addresses are easily 'collected' and often sold on. So indeed are many other people in financial services, industry and very often as private individuals. We all find that we receive Internet communications that are scams, unwelcome 'spam' messages and the like. After a while such intrusions become tiresome and frustrating, but unfortunately many individuals from all walks of life have suffered more than mere annoyance.

Although there are many variations of this scam, they share the common aim of getting gullible individuals to send cash and/or details of their own or their organization's bank accounts. It is not only West African sources that perpetuate this fraud though currently there does seem to be a preponderance of Nigerian and other African sources. Usually an email arrives in your inbox which explains in formal but awkward English how sizeable sums need to be transferred out of the country but suggest using your name, a UK bank account details, and so on. Of course there is no money. But the gullible respondent is duped by the apparently believable circumstances into sending an (initially modest) sum to the fraudster, often followed by larger amounts and even trips abroad! Further related risks involve gradual identity theft as the respondent releases more details, and even the possibility that the victim will be lined up as the 'fall guy' to take the blame for an actual illegal money transfer or theft.

It is difficult at first to see how anyone would be gullible enough to respond to such scams let alone keep on being duped – a typical example of the initial approach is at Figure A14.1 – and yet, years on from the first reports of such cases, there seems no shortage of victims.

Nigerian fraudsters have a particular reputation of attacking UK public bodies, for example NHS bodies were each being offered a £7.37 million to move monies out of Nigeria. The fraudsters purported to represent the quite legitimate Nigeria National Petroleum Corporation – of course they did not, nor was there any money to be moved. The fraudsters did not even demand the usual advance fee from the NHS bodies to arrange the transaction. They simply wanted to get their hands on various NHS bank account details and signed letters on NHS headed notepaper, easily used in forgeries for fraudulent transfers of funds out of the NHS accounts. Without naming names here, reports mention that several public services bodies have fallen foul of this type of scam.

The advanced fee frauds take on numerous guises. Just to balance any unfair impression that only West African fraudsters are behind advance fee type frauds: at a corporate level around 200 private sector companies were defrauded when a false bank was set up in Torquay, Devon. Coming to light as early as 1995, this fraud involved false bank premises (purchased and renovated from a genuine high street branch) and the use of genuine banking system transfers – a complete veneer of respectability. Once again the basic scam was simple: the offer of very favourable lines of credit to corporate clients for which the bank received a non-refundable arrangement fee in advance. Needless to say the credit was available from complex overseas sources, usually arranged via 'agents' using faxed documents and was never actually forthcoming. The amounts

URGENT AND CONFIDENTIAL
(RE: TRANSFER OF ($ 152 000 000 000 USD
ONE HUNDRED AND FIFTY TWO MILLION
DOLLARS

Dear Sir,

We want to transfer to overseas ($ 152 000 000.00 USD) One hundred and Fifty two million United States Dollars from a prime Bank in Africa, I want to ask you to quietly look for a reliable and honest person who will be capable and fit to provide either an existing bank account or to set up a new Bank a/c immediately to receive this money, even an empty a/c can serve to receive this money, as long as you will remain honest to me till the end for this important business trusting in you and believing in God that you will never let me down either now or in future.

I am MR. BANABAS MARTIN, the Auditor General of prime banks in Africa, during the course of our auditing I discovered a oating fund in an account opened in the bank in 1990 and since 1993 nobody has operated on this account again, after going through some old files in the records I discovered that the owner of the account died without a [heir] hence the money is oating and if I do not remit this money out urgently it will be forfeited for nothing. The owner of this account is Mr. Allan P. Seaman, a foreigner, and an industrialist, and hedied, since 1993, and no other person knows about this account or any thing concerning it, the account has no other beneficiary and my investigation proved to me as well that Allan P. Seaman until his death was the manager of Diamond Safari [pty]. SA.

We will start the first transfer with fifty two million ($52 000 000) upon successful transaction without any disappoint from your side, we shall re-apply for the payment of the remaining rest . . .

. . . the message continues on for 3 sheets of A4 and is too long (and tedious) to reproduce in full.

Figure A14.1 Typical initial email for an advanced fee fraud

lost were reported to be around the £100 million level.

Suggested reference: article by Seamus Ward in *Public Finance*, 23 August 1996.

LESSONS

It is difficult to set in place specific arrangements and procedures that will definitely prevent this type of fraud as the victim must be tempted to respond to an offer that sounds dubious or improper but still seems plausible (at least to the victim), and quite often it is the individual rather than the organization that suffers. Rules can be promulgated forbidding officials to enter into unauthorized transactions originating via the Internet or postal system, the emails and ordinary post can be vetted, and everyone can be warned – but still the greedy and gullible seem ready to put themselves or their employers at risk. Perhaps the best countermeasure is publicity and awareness at least among officials with access to corporate bank accounts, combined with a warning that anything that sounds too good to be true almost certainly is.

Bibliography

This bibliography is intended for the practitioner to gain access to conventional works, reports and other sources of information the author has found useful in providing practical help or expanding the knowledge and skills base that is bound to be limited in any one book such as this. It is not intended as a comprehensive listing that might be suitable for an academic treatise. For this reason the bibliography has been divided into themes related to chapters, intended to help you more easily follow up a topic or reference with related titles. At the end is a short listing of useful web sites.

Fraud and corruption in general, standards and guidance

Audit Commission, *Audit Viewpoint*, a journal published by the Audit Commission which includes useful summaries of fraud cases, London.

Audit Commission, *Protecting the Public Purse: Ensuring Probity in Local Government*, 1995, (with various updates since) London: Audit Commission. ISBN 0118864289.

Audit Commission, *Fraud and Corruption: Audit Manual*, 1997, London: Audit Commission. ISBN 1862400261.

Audit Commission, *What to do if you Suspect Fraud or Corruption*, 1999. London: Audit Commission.

Audit Commission (for Local and Health Authorities in England and Wales), *Surveys*

of Computer Fraud, these are done on a regular basis approximately every three years and are becoming wider in scope, for example, *Ghost in the Machine*, 1998, and *yourbuinsess@risk*, 2001, London: Audit Commission.

Auditing Practices Board, *SAS 418 The auditor s responsibility in relation to fraud, other irregularities and errors*. London: Auditing Practices Board.

Bologna, J.G., Lindquist, R.J., *Fraud Auditing and Forensic Accounting: new tools and techniques*, 1995, New York: Wiley. ISBN 0471106461.

Bologna, J.G., Lindquist, R.J. and Wells J.T., *The Accountants Handbook of Fraud and Commercial Crime*, 1993, New York: Wiley. ISBN 0471526428.

Chartered Institute of Public Finance and Accountancy (CIPFA), Statement of Professional Practice (SoPP) on *Suspected Fraud and Corruption*, 2002, London: CIPFA.

Chartered Institute of Public Finance and Accountancy (CIPFA), *The Investigation of Fraud in the Public Sector*, 1994, London: CIPFA. ISBN 0852996071.

Coderre, D.G., *Fraud Detection: using data analysis techniques to detect fraud*, 1999, Global Audit Publications. ISBN 0968440088 (available from their web site www.komtas.com).

Comer, M.J., *Corporate Fraud*, (6th edn.), 1998, Aldershot: Gower. ISBN 0556078104.

Doig, A., *Corruption and Misconduct in Contemporary British Politics*, 1984, London: Penguin, ISBN 0140223460.

HM Treasury, *Annual Fraud Report,* a survey published annually of analysis of frauds affecting government departments, London: HMSO (also available online via the website www.hm-treasury.gov.uk).

Home Office, *Evidence from the UK in cases of serious or complex fraud ...some questions and answers*, 2001, via www.homeoffice.gov.uk

Institute of Internal Auditors (IIA), *Fraud and the Internal Auditor,* Professional Briefing Note 12, 1998, Altamonte Springs, Florida: IIA.

Jacobson, A., *How to Detect Fraud through Auditing,* 1990, Altamonte Springs, Florida: IIA. ISBN 0894132199.

Levi, M., *The Prevention of Fraud* (and various briefing and research papers for the Home Office), via www.homeoffice.gov.uk

National Audit Office (NAO), *MoD - The Risk of Fraud in Property Management,* 2000, London: NAO. ISBN 0105567701.

Reuvid, J. (Ed), *The Regulation and Prevention of Economic Crime Internationally*, 1995, London: Kogan Page. ISBN 0749415398.

Ruimschotel, D., *The EC budget: ten per cent fraud?*, 1994, Italy: European University Institute, EUI/EPU 93/8.

Van Buitenen, P., *Blowing the Whistle: one man s ght against fraud in the European Commission,* 2000, London: Politico Publishing. ISBN 1902301463.

Williams, R. and Doig, A., *Controlling Corruption,* 2000, Camberley: Edward Elgar. ISBN 1840641150.

Health Service fraud

Audit Commission, *NHS Fraud and Corruption Manual,* 1997, London: Audit Commission. ISBN 1862400180.

Audit Commission, *Protecting the Public Purse: Ensuring Probity in the NHS,* 1998, Audit Commission. ISBN 186240061X.

Department of Health, *Countering Fraud in the NHS,* 1999, London: Department of Health (available from the department or via its web site www.doh.gov.uk).

The Public Sector

Baird, A.M., 'Wagner's Law of Expanding State Activity', *Public Finance,* 1971, No. 26.

Chartered Institute of Public Finance and Accountancy (CIPFA), *Approaches to Corporate Governance in the Public Sector,* 2000, London: CIPFA.

Financial Reporting Council (FRC), *The Combined Code on Corporate Governance,* 2003, London: FRC.

Keynes, J.M., *The General Theory of Employment, Interest and Money,* 1936, Basingstoke: Macmillan.

Keynes, J.M., *How to Pay for the War,* 1940, Basingstoke: Macmillan.

Mumford, L., *The City in History: its origins, its transformations and prospects,* 1961, London: Seeker and Warburg.

Peacock, A.T. and Wiseman, J., *The Growth of Public Expenditure in the UK,* 1961, Princeton, NJ: Princeton University Press.

Pigou, A.C., *A Study in Public Finance*, 1928, Basingstoke: Macmillan.
Rostow, W.W., *Politics and the Stages of Growth*, 1971, Cambridge University Press.
The Beveridge Report of 1942, (Cmnd. 6404 – *Report on Social Insurance and Allied Services*).

Risk and SBA

Buttery, R., Simpson R.K. and Hurford C., *Audit in the Public Sector*, 1993, London: ICSA.
Chartered Institute of Public Finance and Accountancy (CIPFA), *Guide to Systems Based Audit*, 1996, London: CIPFA.
Chartered Institute of Public Finance and Accountancy (CIPFA), *It s a Risky Business ...The Auditor s Role in Risk Assessment and Risk Control*, 1996, London: CIPFA.
Chartered Institute of Public Finance and Accountancy (CIPFA), *Code of Practice for Internal Audit in Local Government in the U.K.*, 2003, London: CIPFA.
Institute of Internal Auditors (IIA), *The Role of Internal Audit in Risk Management: Draft Position Statement*, 2002, Altamonte Springs, Florida: IIA.
Jones, P., 'A review of risk and the practical use of risk models by auditors', 2002, *Corporate Governance*, ISSN 0219-1040.
Jones, P., *Statistical Sampling and Risk Analysis in Auditing*, 1999, Aldershot: Gower.
Williams, P. and Richer, G., *Use of Risk Analysis as an Audit Planning Technique*, 1994, research report No. 42, London: IIA.

Contracts

Office of Fair Trading, *Cartels and the Competition Act 1998*, London: Office of Fair Trading (also via website www.oft.gov.uk).
Chartered Institute of Public Finance and Accountancy (CIPFA), *Contract Audit ...JCT Guidance Notes*, 1992, London: CIPFA.
Chartered Institute of Public Finance and Accountancy (CIPFA), *Financial Management and Audit of Construction Contracts: a practical guide*, 1999, London: CIPFA.

Information Technology

Audit Commission, *Code of Data Matching Practice*. London: Audit Commission.
Chartered Institute of Public Finance and Accountancy (CIPFA), *Computer Audit Guidelines* (6th edn.), 2002, London: CIPFA.
Chartered Institute of Public Finance and Accountancy (CIPFA), *Computer Survival Guide: fraud*, 1991, London: CIPFA.
Lindup, K. and Reeve L., *The Computer Security and Fraud Prevention Audit*, 1999, London: Financial Times/Prentice Hall.
Stern, D.L., *Preventing Computer Fraud: you may already be a victim and not know it*, 1993, London: McGraw- Hill.

Benefit fraud

Audit Commission, *Audit Commission has uncovered £50m in fraud in largest ever data matching exercise,* Press release on the Report of the 2000 National Fraud Initiative.

National Audit Office, *DSS ..Measures to Combat Housing Bene t Fraud,* 1997, London: NAO.

Public sector accounting and auditing

Chartered Institute of Public Finance and Accountancy (CIPFA), *Councillor s Guide to Local Government Finance,* 2002, London: CIPFA.

HM Treasury, *Government Accounting 2000,* available in a CD-Rom from the Stationery Office, www.hmso.gov.uk (also on line via www.government-accounting.gov.uk).

Jones, P. and Bates, J., *Public Sector Auditing,* (2nd edn.), 1994, London: Chapman & Hall.

Jones, R. and Pendlebury, M., *Public Sector Accounting,* (5th edn.), 2000, London and Harlow: Financial Times/Prentice Hall/Pearson Education. ISBN 0273646265.

Web sites

The following sites have proved useful, though the contents of any site will of course be changing all the time. Other useful sites exist that have not been included and many useful sites come and go. So apologies to readers who feel that other sites should have been included or some of the following should have been left out.

Anti corruption site www.transparency.org
Anti-fraud practitioners www.fraudweb.co.uk
Association of Certified Fraud Examiners www.cfenet.com
Association of Payment Clearing Services www.apacs.org.uk
Audit Commission www.audit-commission.gov.uk
Australian National Audit Office www.anao.gov.au
Chartered Institute of Public Finance Accountants www.cipfa.org.uk
Enron case www.enronfraud.com
Home Office fraud site www.crimereduction.gov.uk
ICAEW fraud advice site www.fraudadvisorypanel.org
Institute of Chartered Accountants www.Icaew.co.uk
Institute of Internal Auditors www.iia.org.uk
Institute of Public Finance www.ipf.co.uk
IT audit site www.itaudit.org
London team against fraud www.ltaf.fsnet.co.uk
Public sector audit in the UK www.public-audit-forum.gov.uk
Site against advance fee fraud www.419fraud.com
UK Auditing Practices Board – Accountancy Foundation www.apb.org.uk
UK Benefit Fraud Inspectorate www.bfi.gov.uk
UK fraud information site www.fraud.org.uk
UK Govt departments and other public services qqq.open.gov.uk
UK Home Office www.homeoffice.gov.uk

UK Metropolitan Police Fraud Squad www.met.police.uk/fraudalert
UK National Audit Office www.nao.gov.uk
UK National Criminal Investigation www.ncis.gov.uk
UK Serious Fraud Office www.sfo.gov.uk
UK Treasury www.hm-treasury.gov.uk
US Department of Justice www.usdoj.gov
US national fraud information www.Service fraud.org

Index